COLDER THAN HELL

A MARINE RIFLE COMPANY
AT CHOSIN RESERVOIR

Colder than Hell

JOSEPH R. OWEN

FOREWORD BY GEN. RAYMOND G. DAVIS, USMC (RET.)

NAVAL INSTITUTE PRESS • ANNAPOLIS, MARYLAND

To Kelly, who rated a medal but never got it.

And Chew Een Lee, who rated more.

And Dorothy, the finest ever seen.

CONTENTS

FOREWORD

Twice in 1950, during the first months of the Korean War, the United States faced military catastrophe. Both situations occurred because of American errors of diplomacy and faulty intelligence, and because our military was not prepared to meet a determined enemy on the battlefield.

North Korea and China were the enemies that exploited our failings. On two occasions that year they caught us by surprise, launching massive attacks first against our ally, South Korea, and then against our own inadequate forces. Both times the consequences were devastating. There were tragic numbers of casualties in the ranks of our soldiers and Marines, and American prestige, worldwide, was severely impaired.

The surprise invasion of South Korea by North Korea—with the support of Communist China and the Soviet Union—was virtually invited by the United States and the South Koreans.

South Korea was vulnerable; its soldiers were ill equipped, poorly trained, and improperly deployed. The American forces at that time, victims of Washington politics and false economies, were nearly as bad off. Following the end of the World War II drawdown, they were in skeletonized formations, sadly undertrained and inadequately equipped.

Moreover, our Secretary of State had proclaimed to the world that the Korean peninsula was outside the area of American vital interest. North Korea, China, and the Soviet Union read that message to mean that the United States would not defend South Korea against outside aggression. South Korea would be theirs for the taking.

We now know of messages exchanged between Josef Stalin and the North Korean president, Kim Il Sung, that explored our weakness and concluded that South Korea could be captured in five days. Subsequently, the North Koreans launched a sudden and massive invasion. Seoul, the South Korean capital, was quickly taken, and soon all of that country was overrun, except for one small pocket around the port of Pusan.

That pocket was formed by American troops—unready as they were—that President Harry Truman hurried into Korea in response to the crisis. At great sacrifice, these American soldiers, with a follow-on brigade of Marines, held the Pusan perimeter long enough to allow forces to assemble for an amphibious assault on Inchon, behind the North Korean lines. We recaptured Seoul and the North Koreans were put on the run. Fearing entrapment, they fled back across their border to the north. American and South Korean troops were joined by soldiers from other United Nations countries, and they pursued the aggressors deep into North Korea.

Our mission was twofold: to punish the North Koreans and to block the Chinese Peoples' Liberation Army if it threatened to enter the war. Because of a failure of intelligence, however, we were far too late to deter the Chinese. They had already positioned vast numbers of their well-trained soldiers in the mountains of North Korea. We were soon under heavy attack, fighting a numerically superior enemy in unfavorable terrain and brutally cold weather. The UN forces, predominantly American, were chased out of North Korea. At the Chosin Reservoir, where we were outnumbered ten to one, the Chinese generals prematurely boasted of the destruction of the 1st Marine Division.

Yet, the opposite happened there. Although the Marines were forced to withdraw, we destroyed several Chinese divisions as we fought our way to the sea and escape. Our withdrawal was a successful one, but we paid a terrible price: casualties reduced the division to nearly half of its strength. The three rifle companies of 1st Battalion, 7th Marine Regiment, which I was privileged to command, endured losses of even greater proportion. "B" Company—the Baker-One-Seven of Joe Owen's narrative, *Colder than Hell*—came off the Chosin Reservoir, and out of North Korea, with only twenty-seven men, the survivors of more than three hundred of its original Marines and their replacements.

Baker-One-Seven, like the rest of my battalion, had been hastily activated in response to President Truman's urgent call to action. It was a thrown-together rifle company, a collection of regulars, gathered from Marine Corps posts and stations all over the world, and reservists, mostly untrained, who were suddenly called from their homes, jobs, and schools. With only a few days of training they were embarked aboard a ship heading across the Pacific, and thrown into combat. They had to learn to fight while under enemy fire. Their saving grace was that they were led by disciplined officers and NCOs who showed them, by up-front example, how to fight like Marines. Although they suffered casualties that proper preparation would have avoided, they learned well and they hardened into a fine rifle company. No North Korean or Chinese force ever stopped them from taking an objective or overcame their position. Baker-One-Seven was as tough and gallant an outfit of Marines as I have ever led in three wars.

The men we read about in *Colder than Hell* exemplify the Marines, soldiers, sailors, and airmen who went to a war, sacrificed, and fought well because their country needed them. Because of them, the United States averted a total, ignominious defeat, and it was able to resume its role as leader of the free world.

Let us do all we can to assure that no future generation of young Americans need go to war unprepared, as were those heroes who went to Korea in 1950.

Gen. Raymond G. Davis, USMC (Retired)
Medal of Honor

PREFACE

Colder than Hell pays tribute to the men of one Marine rifle company—Baker-One-Seven—who fought during the early days of the Korean War in 1950. To have served with them is the proudest achievement of my life.

Rarely have Americans been sent into battle as ill prepared as were these men. More than half of them were young reservists called abruptly from their homes; they had neither active service nor combat training. The regulars in the company, although well trained for combat, had never served together. Only a few weeks after we first formed the ranks of Baker-One-Seven, we were under enemy fire. At first our performance was ragged, and tragic mistakes were made. But these were young men of great courage, and they quickly learned the deadly business of fighting a war.

Baker-One-Seven was one of twenty-seven rifle companies that were part of the 1st Marine Division in 1950. Each of those companies performed magnificently, up to the highest standards of our Corps. Still, by the time we fought our way up to the Chosin Reservoir—and back again—we knew that Baker-One-Seven was the best rifle company of them all.

That's the way Marines thought of themselves during this period: we were the best of the best. I hope that Marines still think that way.

The sources for this narrative are my own memories, as well as those of the Marines who were my comrades from the time we formed up at Camp Pendleton in August 1950 until we came off the Chosin Reservoir in December of that year.

At times these memories differ from each other, but after forty-five years, that is to be expected. Nevertheless, our remembrances vary only in the details, not in the principal elements of the accounts.

All the men portrayed here are real, and the substance of their stories is faithful to the actual events depicted.

The archives of the Marine Corps Historical Division in Washington, D.C., contain no documents or reports specifically dedicated to the activities of our company and battalion—1st Battalion, 7th Marine Regiment—during 1950. I have used as general references *U.S. Marine Operations in Korea*, Volumes I, II, and III (Historical Branch, G-3, Headquarters, U.S. Marine Corps, Washington, D.C., 1954, 1955, and 1957) and *7th Marines Special Action Reports for the Periods 17 August, 1950–15 December, 1950*.

In certain instances these sources diverge somewhat from this narrative; however, it is worth noting that these "official accounts" also differ from each other in some particulars of dates, locations, and situations.

The names of some of the men have been changed in this narrative to protect their anonymity. There are very few such alterations.

ACKNOWLEDGMENTS

Thanks to these Marines who helped me write this narrative: Dick Bahr, Charley Baldwin, Allan Bevilacqua, Pat Burris, Jerry Couture, Bill Cartledge, Corpsman Bill Davis, Gen. Ray Davis, Harold Elder, Bob Fisher, Rev. Glenn Galtere, Gilberto Garcia, Joe Glasgow, Joe Hedrick, Jack Hinderscheid, Ted Hudson, Joe Jane, James Jones, Harold Kane, Dave Koegel, Floyd Kogel, Ben Kowalski, Chew Een Lee, Ray Leffler, Tom Lineberry, George Lipponer, Johnny Lopez, Ron Moloy, Red McDonough, Gene Morrisroe, Arthur Ochoa, Raul Rendon, Ray Richard, Lee Rux, Woody Taylor, Tony Tinelli, John Wade, Bob Wilson, Mark Winget.

And Vi Graeber, Dorothy Owen, and Kay Wilcox, who also remembered.

And Denise (Dinny) Owen Harrigan and Therese Litz, who showed me how to write a book.

And Pete Greene, Don Nealon, and Bill Topp, who listened.

PROLOGUE

8 December 1950, in the first year of the Korean War

In the ice-bound mountain country that encloses the Chosin Reservoir in North Korea, Baker-One-Seven—a rifle company of the 1st Marine Division—fought for survival. We were surrounded by overwhelming numbers of the Chinese Peoples' Liberation Army. Our ranks were sorely reduced; only a few dozen of us remained from the 215 men who had mounted out for this campaign, and another 75 replacements who had come to us during weeks of bitter fighting. I was a second lieutenant, the most junior of seven officers who had formed up the company. I was the only one of the seven still standing.

On that December morning the temperature was twenty-five degrees below zero and fierce, biting winds swirled around us. The snow was deep and difficult to wade through.

We formed up to attack in the dark, before the light of a dim, frozen dawn. We moved along a narrow, steeply flanked valley toward the Chinese positions, which were concealed by the blowing snow. Their mortars exploded as we approached, and we took our first casualties. The screams of the wounded men mingled with the shrill winds and the coarse shouts of squad leaders and officers who called their Marines forward.

"Move up, you people. Keep your intervals. Keep it moving!"

"I'm hit! Oh, God!"

"Corpsman! Corpsman! Man down. Over there, Doc."

"Oh, God! Oh, God! Oh, God. . . ."

"Move up! Move up!"

We crawled through blood-splotched snow toward our objective, the crest of an icy hill that was studded with granite boulders and the black scars of bomb craters. The Chinese—quilted white shadows, armed with spitting burp guns and grenades—hid among the boulders. The ground before them was laced with lethal bands of mortar and automatic fire. A heavy machine gun pounded at us from a log bunker below the crest.

In the gray murk we couldn't see to call in support from our airplanes; there was no help from artillery or mortars, either. We had only our rifles, grenades, and bayonets.

We stretched our thin line along the base of the slope. Our men lay prone, bodies burrowed into the snow. As they waited for the order to rise against the Chinese fire, they pointed their Browning Automatic Rifles—BARs—and M-1 rifles tipped with bayonets. None of our machine guns still functioned; they had been destroyed by enemy fire or had seized up from the paralyzing cold.

Already that morning two of our officers had fallen. Joe Kurcaba, the company commander, was one of them. As our worn-out men struggled through the blizzard and the enemy fire, Joe called me to him. We stood together, holding his map, as he traced a move for my platoon, an attempt to go around the Chinese flank.

We were face to face, inches apart. Suddenly a black dot appeared in the middle of his brow, beneath the rim of his steel helmet. A Chinese bullet had pierced his forehead. His eyes continued to look at me, but life was gone. He crumbled toward me slowly. I caught him in my arms and lowered him carefully into the snow. I did not want to let him go. I wanted to stay with him, kneel beside him, and say a prayer. And cry, too. I loved Joe Kurcaba like a brother.

Our attack moved forward, though, as Chinese bullets whined overhead and their mortars exploded along our line. I took Joe Kurcaba's map and went through the snow to find Lieutenant Chew Een Lee, our next senior officer. I handed him the map and told him that he had command of Baker-One-Seven. Minutes later a burst of automatic fire took Lee down, the second time within a month that he had been wounded.

Woody Taylor and I were now the only officers who remained. Woody was a replacement first lieutenant who had been with us through the toughest fighting, and he was a fine combat leader. He was senior to me, and he became our third company commander that day.

A pair of Marine tanks had crept to the front along an ice-coated logging road, and they set up to support our attack. They were big, lumbering Pershings armed with 90–millimeter cannons and .30–caliber machine guns.

"Tell the tanks to zero in on that machine gun up there," Woody shouted to me against the wind. His deep Alabama drawl was hoarse from shouting.

We could not see the Chinese gun; we could locate it only by the clattering noise it made.

"Aye, aye," I shouted back. I had to turn into the wind to hear. In a few seconds my face was numb with the cold.

"We'll jump off when you get that gook gun shut down," Woody yelled.

"Aye, aye, Woody," I yelled back.

"On this signal." Woody waved his arm forward, the command I would watch for. "Have the tanks fire the cannon, and we'll move out."

I waved and called back again, "Aye, aye."

Chinese fire scathed the open field, and I scurried, low to the drift-covered ground, toward the tanks. They waited at the right flank of the company, just off the road. I checked the line of our men as I ran.

These Marines had fought through frigid weeks with no shelter except the holes they scooped into the snow at night. They functioned at the primal level: they ate, slept, and fought, and they tried to get warm. The hooded green parkas that covered the lengths of their bodies were streaked with the blood of the wounded men they had carried and the stains of half-frozen food spooned from ration cans. Their faces, the only flesh exposed to the cold, were crusted with dirt that went deep into blackened pores. Lips were puffed and split. Stubbled beards held smears of food and rivulets of frozen mucus and saliva.

They had fought the Chinese on many hills like this one. While they waited, they jabbed into cans of fruit with their fighting knives and sucked at the sweet slush. Those who had filched sick bay alcohol gulped at their canteens. The others, whose water had turned to ice, scooped up snow to slake their thirst.

The snow drifted against the side of the lead tank. Its engine idled easily, and the exhaust stank of burning diesel fuel. The exhaust was warm, and I leaned over the rear grille to let the warmth penetrate into my parka and layers of clothing. I wanted to stay there, luxuriate in it.

The tank was buttoned up against the Chinese bullets that banged its hull. Spurts of snow popped up where they ricocheted to the ground. I spoke into the telephone at the rear of the tank. "Put your thirties across the ridge. Gook machine gun at ten o'clock. Then I'll tell you to open up with the cannons. On my command. We'll jump off on that."

A tinny voice came from the tank. "Hear you loud and clear. Stand by!" Immediately the twin machine guns of both tanks began their jack-hammer pounding. I watched the red tracers slice through the blowing snow, up the hill toward the dug-in Chinese gun.

Ignoring the tank's recoil vibrations that shook my body, and the Chinese bullets that rattled its hull, I leaned over the warm grille and watched for Woody. His dark shape was barely visible through the ghostly snow clouds, and I strained to see his signal. When it came, we would attack up the hill, into the Chinese fire. But for the moment, we waited.

CHAPTER ONE

The Korean War came as a sudden and harsh surprise to both the United States and the Peoples' Republic of China, which became its principal combatants. The United States was pledged to protect South Korea; the Communist Chinese were committed to North Korea. Neither power was prepared to fight, but each misread the other's intentions. By mutual error, America and Red China were drawn into a war that would last more than three years and cost millions of lives.

The war began on 25 June 1950 when the Peoples' Republic of Korea (North Korea) sent a massive armored force across the border they held in common with the Republic of Korea (South Korea). At four o'clock on that steamy June morning, fast-moving columns from the north overwhelmed the thin defenses of the South Koreans. Their way paved by intense artillery bombardments and Russian-made T-34 battle tanks, the columns sped on to take control of key roads and communications centers. Several hours after they first opened fire, the North Koreans transmitted their declaration of war on the South Koreans.

• • •

When we first heard that a war had erupted in Korea, we were on the officers' beach at Camp Lejeune, the Marine base on the North Carolina seacoast. It was Sunday, an off-duty day, and my wife, Dorothy, and our two babies were there, soaking up sunshine. We played with the children in the gentle waves and stretched lazily on the warm sand. Nobody at Camp Lejeune had expected a shooting war. Nor were we ready for one.

Above the beach, on the shaded veranda of the Officers' Club, there was a grille where we could get steak sandwiches for a quarter and paper cups of draft beer that cost a nickel.

The grille was manned by a Negro Marine, Sergeant Dale. He wore a starched white chef's hat, and his khaki shirt was bleached by the sun, the mark of a Marine with long service in the Corps. There was talk coming from the Washington politicians that Negroes would soon be integrated into the ranks with white Marines. With the exception of some die-hard southerners, most of us thought that was a good idea. The politicians had slashed military budgets so deep that many units were less than half strength; we could use all the men we could get. The overriding thought was that, white or Negro, a Marine was a Marine.

That Sunday several of us clustered around the grille, waiting for Sergeant Dale to catch up on the sandwich orders. We were the junior officers of the 2d Marine Division, young lieutenants and a few captains, all of us regulars. The work we did during the week—training troops in the field and practicing amphibious operations—demanded that we be in top physical condition. We were well muscled, flat bellied, and generally tall in stature. At six feet five inches and 220 pounds, I did not stand out as a particularly large man.

While we waited for the sandwiches that sizzled on the grill, we listened to Sergeant Dale's tinny radio, which was playing country music, the music of the South.

Someone mentioned having seen a brief report about fighting in Korea in Sunday's *Greenville Record*, but that paper had gone to press before many of the details were known. So we bought each other nickel beers and listened closely to the radio for bulletins. And we speculated about the situation, wondering whether it was serious enough to involve American combat forces.

A captain who had been to Korea as a military advisor, working with the fledgling South Korean Marine Corps, commented, "Nothing to get excited about. Those people are always making raids across the border on each other."

"What's it like over there?" one of the lieutenants asked.

"Korea? One lousy place to fight a war," the captain answered. "Too hot in summer, too cold in winter, and straight up and down mountain terrain all year around. Except for those stinking rice paddies down in the valleys. Human manure they use. Worst stink in the world."

"I've heard *that* song before," said another captain, who had fought the Japanese across fetid rice paddies on Okinawa. "No place for gentlemen to fight a war."

We laughed at the captain's judgment, and the conversation turned to the baseball season. Joe DiMaggio had belted out his 2,000th hit the past week; Ted Williams, who had been a Marine fighter pilot in World War II, was hitting at .315 for the Red Sox. The Brooklyn Dodgers led the National League.

Suddenly the country music stopped and a local announcer came on the air. His Carolina drawl seemed out of sync with the gravity of the bulletin he read. "According to information reaching Washington, massive North Korean forces have penetrated deep into South Korean territory. A state of war now exists between Communist North Korea and the Republic of South Korea. The South Korean government is supported by the United States and the United Nations."

"That's more serious than a border raid," said the captain who had served in Korea.

We were silent now. The radio had our full attention as the announcer drawled on. "South Korean troops are in retreat, offering little resistance in the face of North Korean armor. The South Korean capital of Seoul is feared lost."

"Where's Seoul?" asked one of the lieutenants. "How far has our side retreated already?"

"Pipe down!" the captain snapped.

The announcer continued. "More than two thousand Americans, military advisors and civilian workers and their families, are said to be in the path of North Korea's surprise aggression. Their fate is unknown at this time. American involvement in the new war is not clear."

"War! Yeah!" The possibility of American Marines in a combat role excited us. We crowded around the radio, leaning closer to catch the announcer's words. The bulletin ended with a pronouncement that Gen. Douglas MacArthur's headquarters in Tokyo was on full alert.

The country music resumed. We watched our children playing happily in the water and our wives tanning themselves on the sand. The scene was the same, but we knew that our lives were about to change.

• • •

It was a difficult drive home from the beach that evening. I tried to conceal my excitement from Dorothy. The news about Korea had inflamed my hope for an opportunity to lead troops in combat, to put myself to the test. I was a twenty-four-year-old second lieutenant, a professional Marine officer, intensively trained for combat leadership but as yet untried in battle.

During World War II, I had served more than three years as an enlisted Marine. While in the Pacific preparing to go against the Japanese, I had been selected for officer's training and was sent back to the States. However, the war ended before I finished the course and I was discharged. I married Dorothy, my high school sweetheart, and graduated from Colgate University. We had two babies while I was still in school. When I graduated, the Marine Corps offered me a regular commission. Dorothy had misgivings about military life, but she agreed to give it a try. We were young and this seemed to be the time in our lives for adventure and excitement.

I went through the nine months of arduous training that the Marines gave their new lieutenants. We were painstakingly taught how to use men and weapons to destroy an enemy. Our teachers were rugged, hard-eyed fighting men, officers and crusty old NCOs. They had learned their trade on the Pacific islands during World War II, in Haiti and Nicaragua throughout the 1930s, and in China's civil wars. They were fierce warriors who inspired us with their dedication to the Corps, and they demanded that we maintain their standards.

After that training I had learned by experience to train and discipline my own rifle platoon. I had forty Marine infantrymen, all of them salty and wily regulars, many with World War II combat experience. We trained ceaselessly, practicing the difficult art of fire and movement across surf-swept beaches, into rank swamps, and through miles of thick pine forest and thorny brush.

On Saturday mornings we would form up for parade—dress uniforms sharply pressed, brass polished, and weapons gleaming. Scarlet and gold pennants snapped in the breeze, and the 2d Marine Division band stirred us with "shipping over" music. Dorothy would bring the babies—Mike and Dinny—to watch the parades. She, too, had been infected with the spirit of the Corps.

When the Korean War started, my battalion had just returned from a six-month "show the flag" cruise through the Mediterranean with the Navy's Sixth Fleet. It had been an exciting time, filled with amphibious landings and rubber-boat mock raids on European and North African beaches. We had maneuvered the ancient, battle-worn mountains of Sicily, Greece, and Crete, and we had traced the ground of such great generals as Hannibal and Patton. Sometimes we had been called upon to celebrate the American presence at the grand embassies and admiralties of the Mediterranean, clad in our starched dress whites bedecked with boldly colored campaign ribbons. There were the ports of call, too—the casbahs, the bazaars, and the raunchy waterfronts. It was easy for young men of spirit to love the peacetime Marine Corps of 1950.

It was not an easy life for Dorothy, though. Married second lieutenants had little choice in housing. The places we could afford were off the base, cramped, scruffy, and depressing for a young family. Often I had to leave Dorothy alone with the babies for weeks at a time when we mounted out for field maneuvers and amphibious operations.

Now, on my return from the Mediterranean cruise, Dorothy was anticipating a "husband-at-home" kind of life, at least for the immediate future. A few days earlier, we had found a tiny cottage on a dirt lane in Jacksonville, the shabby little town that serviced Camp Lejeune. It had two bedrooms, one for us and one for the babies. Dorothy was excited about buying furniture and the other things that she needed to make a home for us.

On the drive back from the beach, the babies—Mike was two years old and Dinny was one—squabbled and squalled in the heat of the back seat of our decrepit '39 Pontiac. Dorothy quieted them, and we opened all the windows to cool them off. The wind blew Dorothy's hair in golden tangles. My buddies said that she looked just like Doris Day, but I thought she was more beautiful than that.

We were both silent for most of the ride. Dorothy, too, was thinking about the Korean situation. Finally, she spoke. "Will you have to go to Korea if America gets into this war?"

"Probably not," I answered. "First Marine Division is on the West Coast. They'll get the call if the situation gets that serious."

The Pacific area, which included the Korean peninsula at its far western extremity, was 1st Marine Division territory. The 1st was stationed at Camp Pendleton in Southern California. If the Marines were called, they would mount out for Korea long before we did.

That explanation made sense to Dorothy; it was what she wanted to hear. She changed the subject to a furniture sale that had been advertised by one of the pirate merchants who preyed on the young Marine families of Camp Lejeune. We owned a bed, two cribs, a kitchen table and three chairs, and two highchairs, and she had a list of essentials she thought we could afford. It was a short list. Second lieutenants brought home very little money in 1950.

It was difficult for me to focus on furniture and budgets. I could think only about Korea. I wondered how I would stand up to combat. If I could get there.

• • •

The next day, back on duty, we stayed near the radio in the first sergeant's office. One of the enlisted clerks had tuned in the NBC Radio Network station from Raleigh. Bulletins were relayed in quick succession. The North Koreans were sweeping the South Korean Army out of their way, and they were doing so with ease. South Korean soldiers were said to be fleeing in panic; those who stood to fight were ineffective. The heavily armored North Korean juggernaut was unstoppable. The fate of American military advisors and civilian workers and their families remained unknown. It was all bad news, unless you wanted to go to war.

Confusion flowed from Washington. President Truman demanded that the United Nations condemn the North Koreans, and he ordered American warplanes to support the South Koreans. Still, in a nationwide radio broadcast, the president declared that commitment of American force would not put the United States at war. Instead, he said that we might be involved in a "police action."

The rumors came, as they come in all wars. Marines call rumors "scuttlebutt," a term derived from their seagoing duty. Aboard ship the scuttlebutt is a sand-filled metal box used to extinguish cigarettes. Like the drinking fountain in the halls of business, the scuttlebutt at sea is a place where gossip and unofficial information are exchanged. Scuttlebutt was seldom accurate in detail, but it flowed deep and fast in the first days of the Korean War.

The more believable scuttlebutt had it that the 1st Marine Division was on alert and awaiting orders to load ship and embark out of San Diego. The 2d Division would be broken up to provide replacements for casualties.

One story alleged that a "commando force" of volunteers was forming up for immediate commitment to battle. That one tied up phone lines on the base as we tried to track down "commando headquarters" in order to volunteer.

It wasn't scuttlebutt, though, that division headquarters was working overtime. Lights burned late every night in the big brick building where our commanding general had his office. All other offices remained lit, as well. Down at the lower ranks, we knew that plans were proceeding on the highest level. We just didn't know what those plans were.

With news of the war we doubled up on field training, and the troops responded energetically. Although budget cuts had left us short of both people and ammunition for training purposes, we took to the swamps and woods and beaches with half platoons and shrunken rifle companies. We didn't realize its value then, but we were learning how to make skeleton formations cover large pieces of terrain. It proved to be good experience for the fighting we would do when we were spread perilously thin at the Chosin Reservoir.

Forward observers—the FOs—from the artillery battalions came into the field with us and gave us refresher training in range estimation and the procedures for calling in close support. Although the artillery usually sent their FOs to work with the rifle companies in combat, it was useful for us infantry lieutenants and the NCOs to be practiced in calling fire orders. In combat, the FOs frequently suffer a high rate of casualties.

We polished our close air support techniques. We talked on the radio to the fighter pilots who flew above us, then directed them to targets as they streaked low across our front. Close air support was a system developed by Marines in the Pacific during World War II. By 1950 every infantry leader knew how to summon and direct our flying artillery against enemy positions, often bringing it in only a few hundred yards to our front.

• • •

The North Koreans continued to overpower the meager resistance offered by the South Korean soldiers—the ROKs as they were called, derived from Republic of Korea. Seoul, the South Korean capital, fell with hardly a fight, and the Red blitzkrieg rolled southward. In response, President Truman escalated American involvement in the war. He ordered General MacArthur, America's supreme commander in the Far East, to use U.S. Army troops stationed in Japan to stem the invaders.

The first American soldiers that were available to General MacArthur were occupation troops, soldiers who had become softened by easy garrison duty. An inadequate budget had limited their field training. They were woefully out of condition and unprepared for the strenuous work of fighting on the steep hills and in the sweltering heat of the Korean peninsula. When they went into combat, these soldiers were no match for the superbly trained North Koreans.

Americans at home were stunned by reports that their Army, the conqueror of mighty Germany and Japan only five years before, was outnumbered, outgunned, and outfought by the upstart North Koreans. Although their effort was courageous, the best that our first soldiers in Korea could do was to delay the Communist juggernaut. It appeared that the enemy would overrun the entire Korean peninsula and send the once-proud American soldiers reeling into the sea.

General MacArthur called for a full division of Marines to help him turn back the North Koreans. The Marine Corps welcomed the call, but we did not have a full division to put in the field. Like all of the services, the Corps had been stripped of men and weapons and ordered to reduce itself to the level of the 1930s. Both the 1st and 2d Marine Divisions were less than half strength. The Corps would need to draw men from guard detachments, ships' companies, and posts and stations throughout the world, but it still wouldn't find enough troops to fill a division.

President Truman thus authorized the commandant of the Marine Corps to call up the reserves.

• • •

The 1st Marine Division quickly put together a skeleton regiment, the 5th Marines, composed solely of regulars. Although the regiment was understrength, these Marines were well trained for combat. Along with supporting aircraft and artillery units, the 5th Marines shipped out of San Diego. The rest of us would follow as soon as enough men, weapons, and shipping could be assembled.

More than seven thousand of us at Camp Lejeune received orders to proceed by rail to Camp Pendleton. There we would form into companies and battalions and embark for Korea. All hands—the riflemen, the gunners, the drivers, the bandsmen—went on full alert. Stand by to ship out!

On the Saturday evening before we left Camp Lejeune, Dorothy hired a baby-sitter and we went to the Officers' Club for dinner. There were candles at our table, which was covered in white linen and set with heavy silverware. The food was delicious and plentiful, and I would think about it often in Korea when my men and I were hungry and cold.

That night Dorothy's hair glistened like gold in the candlelight, and her eyes smiled, bright and blue and warm. We danced and laughed with the other lieutenants and their wives. For some of the couples, our closest friends, it was to be the last night they would ever have together.

The next morning our chaplain said Mass and blessed the families. Then we settled the babies into our old car along with those belongings that Dorothy thought were worth keeping. She would drive back to Syracuse, our home town, to stay with her Mom and Dad until I returned from Korea.

Seeing the packed car and their Mommy getting ready to drive, Mike and Dinny knew that this goodbye was special. Their little arms clung tightly around my neck, and I felt their squeeze long after the old Pontiac had disappeared down that dirt lane in Jacksonville, North Carolina.

CHAPTER TWO

All through the month of August, under a broiling sun that seared the Camp Pendleton hills, the 1st Marine Division pieced itself together. Baker-One-Seven became one of three rifle companies of the 1st Battalion, 7th Marine Regiment; the other two were Able and Charlie Companies.

We were activated without ceremony; our scarlet and gold battle guidon was posted before the Quonset hut that was the company command post, or CP, and the muster role was opened. The guidon was the same one carried by an earlier Baker-One-Seven, a reminder of battles fought on Guadalcanal, New Britain, Pelilieu, and Okinawa.

Our ranks were filled by 215 men and 7 officers who had never before served together. Half of our enlisted men were infantry-trained regulars. The other half were reservists, most of whom were youngsters who knew little of Marine infantry and its methods.

Five weeks after we first formed up at Camp Pendleton we went into the attack against North Korean soldiers who were dug into a hill north of Seoul. We had spent half of that time aboard ship, on the way to the war.

• • •

I was not immediately assigned to Baker-One-Seven when I reached Camp Pendleton. Instead, I had a cadre of regulars who met the train-loads of arriving reservists. We counted them, herded them aboard trucks, and sent them to distribution depots. There they were divided arbitrarily and marched off to join the rifle companies.

The reservists were a mixed lot. Most of their officers and sergeants had served in World War II. They knew the ways of the Corps and the rigors of combat. They had kept their fighting trim and they arrived at Camp Pendleton still looking like Marines.

The ranks, though, the privates and pfc's, were a different sort. Many of them were beardless teenagers with little training beyond the basics of shouldering a rifle and marching in step. As they tumbled off the trains—pale of skin and shaggy-haired—they had the bewildered air of raw recruits. Some had just begun their first civilian jobs; others were college boys. A few were on summer vacation from high school. All of them had been called abruptly from their homes, and none had signed on for reserve duty with expectations of a shooting war.

• • •

While the remainder of the division formed up at Camp Pendleton, the 5th Marines were already fighting in Korea. Although shorthanded, the regiment stopped the North Koreans in a series of crucial engagements. Their superb performance inspired glowing press accounts of "Marines to the rescue."

Another of our regiments, the 1st Marines, had embarked from San Diego, en route to battle. Adding to MacArthur's force were well-trained Army troops, regular infantry from Hawaii, Okinawa, and the West Coast. The Americans had slowed, if not stopped, the North Korean juggernaut.

Suddenly it seemed that the war might end before I had a chance to get into it. Billets in the front-line units were going fast, and a surplus of lieutenants were scrambling for those that were left.

Col. Homer Litzenberg had been my regimental commander at Camp Lejeune, and I had received a good fitness report from him. He now had come to Pendleton to command the newly formed 7th Marines. I wangled an audience with him to request assignment to one of his rifle companies. With his endorsement I captured the regiment's last available billet for a lieutenant—mortar officer for Baker-One-Seven.

• • •

The first person I met in Baker-One-Seven was the first sergeant. In my five years in the Corps I had never met a first sergeant like this one.

First sergeants are the most senior NCOs in a rifle company. Informally called "Top," for "top sergeant," these men usually have vast field experience and are the repositories of barracks wisdom. To them, paperwork and record-keeping are necessary evils that are foisted off on the company clerks, the "office pinkies." First sergeants are ham-handed disciplinarians, for it is their purpose to maintain order among the troops. With a good "Top," the company commander need take disciplinary action only against the most flagrant miscreants. There are few Marines in the lower ranks who do not fear their first sergeant.

First Sergeant Caney was an entirely different breed. He was a runtish fellow, narrow from the shoulders all the way down. His face was pale and the skin of his hands was soft. He wore wide, black-rimmed glasses that were better suited to a bookkeeper than to a field Marine. I assumed that he was a professional office pinkie, misplaced in a rifle company by the Corps' scramble for bodies. That turned out to be true. Caney had earned his six stripes by doing superb administrative work for rear echelon headquarters outfits. At first he was an asset to Baker-One-Seven; there is much paperwork to be done when an outfit forms up.

"Good morning, Top," I said when I entered the company office. Caney was dwarfed behind a desk stacked with neat piles of paperwork. I towered over the little fellow and gave my biggest, friendliest smile. It is prudent for a second lieutenant to be on the good side of the first sergeant. "I'm Lieutenant Owen. Reporting for duty. Is the skipper aboard?"

First Sergeant Caney had to tilt his head back to look up at me, and his scowl told me that I had stirred the animosity that some small men have for big men.

"I know who you are," he said. "Battalion called. Said you were coming." After a pause, he added, "Sir." Peevishly he continued, "Captain Wilcox is not here and I don't know where he is." He moved a stack of papers to the side of his neatly ordered desk. "He was supposed to sign these forms first thing. Regiment and battalion are screaming for them."

"Well, First Sergeant," I said, "I'm taking the mortars. I'll meet the skipper when he comes back. Tell me where to stow my gear, and then I'll go look at my men."

"Officers' hut is next door. You'll see the mortar section in the training area at the end of the company street." Another measured pause, then, "Sir."

I said, "Please have my gear taken to the officers' hut. I'll be with the mortars. Carry on, First Sergeant."

The first sergeant and I would not come to like each other very much.

There were twenty men, including NCOs, in the mortar section. They had three 60–millimeter mortars that fired at a high angle, their shells coming down on targets a thousand or more yards out. The "sixties" were the rifle company's miniature artillery, providing close-in support for attack and defense. They were set up close behind the rifles, and they were useful in hitting enemy who were dug in or emplaced behind hills and other obstacles.

The sixties fired two-inch-diameter high explosive, white phosphorous, and illumination shells. The high explosive rounds—HE— would demolish enemy soldiers, their weapons, and light earthworks within a twenty-yard diameter of impact. White phosphorous shells— WP—sent up a plume of white smoke where they hit, and we used them for smoke screens and for marking targets. The WPs were especially useful for signaling our low-flying air support. Illumination rounds, fired at night, lit a diameter of one hundred yards with high-intensity light for twenty seconds.

Each gun weighed forty pounds and broke down into three parts for carrying—tube, base plate, and bipod. These were assembled for the fire mission, and a bubble sight was attached to the bipod. By means of a traversing crank on the bipod, the sight was lined up for direction on an aiming stake or a landmark; an elevating crank, along with propellant charges on the fins of the shells, determined range. A first-rate mortar team could assemble the components, sight in, and be ready for a fire mission in less than thirty seconds.

My first look at Baker-One-Seven's mortar section was disheartening. I stood at a distance and watched a sergeant read aloud from a training manual to a circle of Marines seated around him. One of the men held up the parts of a mortar as the sergeant read its description. The youngsters seated around him wore puzzled expressions.

I approached the group and called to the sergeant—I hadn't yet learned his name. "As you were, Sergeant. Fall in the section."

Sgt. Harold Wright, the section sergeant, was a tall, slender man, in his early thirties, and he was still pale from civilian life. He was a communicator by specialty and a reservist who had no experience with infantry weapons beyond the rifle. He may not have known mortars, but he knew the Marine Corps. His field uniform was squared away. Leggings and cartridge belt were scrubbed. His dungarees were spotless, their herringbone pattern faded to a pale green from many launderings. Except for the pallor of his face, he had the appearance of a field Marine. He had made his stripes on rear echelon duty in the Pacific war, and he had stayed in the reserves for the money. Sergeant Wright had left four children at home with his wife when he was called up for Korea.

"Aye, aye, Sir," my sergeant snapped, and he threw a smart salute at me. Then, to the men, he barked, "All right, you people. You heard the lieutenant. Fall in!"

I was further discouraged. They seemed like twenty kids, uncomfortable in their steel helmets and brand new, ill-fitting dungarees, some with leggings on backwards and all milling about to find their places in the ranks. Ruefully, I remembered the quickly ordered regulars I had commanded at Camp Lejeune. By contrast, the disheveled people before me looked like recruits in the first hours of boot camp. The DIs, the fabled drill instructors of Parris Island and San Diego, had twelve weeks to teach boys like these how to march and handle a rifle. I was expected to have them combat-ready and on their way to a shooting war within only a few weeks.

After Sergeant Wright formed the section into ragged ranks, I inspected them. I stopped before each man and asked for name and home town. Minneapolis and St. Paul. Chicago and Rockford, Illinois. Dallas. Most were nervous; I was the first regular Marine officer they had met. They stammered their answers, not certain whether to call me "Sir" or "Lieutenant" or nothing at all.

"No, Lieutenant, Sir, I didn't expect to be going to war."

"No, I never saw a mortar before in my life. I mean, Sir. I mean, no, Sir."

Some tried friendly smiles. "I always wanted to be a Marine, Sir. My uncle was one during the war."

Pfc. Robert F. Fisher, a sunny-faced, gangly teenager, looked up at my height and said, "I'll bet you played basketball, Sir."

Sergeant Wright was at my side. "Just answer the questions the lieutenant asks," he barked.

Pfc. Merwin Perkins had his leggings laced on backward, the light, khaki-colored canvas leggings that wrap over the field shoes and up the calf to shield the legs from brush and keep out sand and pebbles. With a sheepish grin, he said, "Nobody showed us how to put these things on, Lieutenant, Sir."

Next was Pfc. Frank M. Bifulk, a short nineteen-year-old with shaggy hair and thick-lensed glasses. The husky Bifulk was built like a fireplug and already his stiff dungarees were in disarray. "Hey, I got to call my wife," he said. How're chances of getting to a phone? I told her . . ."

"Knock it off, Marine!" Sergeant Wright snapped.

There were some bright spots. Sgt. Mark Winget, a husky fellow with a lantern jaw, had been in the Navy in World War II and had sailed with the Atlantic Fleet as a gunner.

There was Sergeant Lunney, a tall, rangy redhead from Texas who looked like an athlete. He was a senior in college and could have posed for a recruiting poster. He had been a rifle squad leader in the reserves, so he knew something about how troops moved in the field.

Cpl. Alphonzo Burris came from the reserves in Honolulu. He was tanned from the perpetual Hawaiian sun and had quick, dark eyes. Slender and of medium height, he presented himself with assurance. Like Winget, he had served aboard ship in the Navy during World War II. They were the only two in the section who had been under enemy fire. I marked Burris for a squad leader.

Cpl. Hugo Johnson was another good one. He had done a hitch as a peace-time regular and had stayed in the reserves. He had seen no action but had spent much time in the field with the old 5th Marines. He was a strapping six-footer with big hands that had been toughened by working in the oil fields of Texas and Oklahoma.

With these exceptions, my inspection of Baker-One-Seven's mortar section was a disappointment. To the men, I said, "At ease," and then I took Sergeant Wright aside.

"Sergeant, we will have to work these people into the deck. Sixteen-hour training days. Starting now. What kind of physical condition are they in?"

"Not great, Sir. All of us need plenty of work. Including me," said Wright.

"Let's see how bad off we are," I said.

The sun-scorched hills of Camp Pendleton had, over the years, toughened the legs and tested the spirits of thousands of America's best fighting men. One of those towering hills loomed across the road from our training site.

"Fall in the section and follow me," I ordered. I took off at a slow trot up the hill. Several minutes later I was five hundred yards up the mountain, and only Burris and Johnson were with me. Most of the others had dropped to the ground, gasping for air. A few were still making an attempt, but they were nearly crawling. Perkins and Bifulk, I noted, were coming on. And Sergeant Winget. Sergeant Wright was on his feet at the end of the file of exhausted men. From where I stood, though, I couldn't tell whether he was urging them upward or could go no farther himself.

"On your feet! On your feet!" I yelled at my fallen mortarmen as I jogged back down the hill. "Leave those canteens alone. Water discipline, you people. Save your water. It'll save your life!"

A few of the men didn't rise. They just lay there, groaning and looking up helplessly at me. I reached down and grabbed the closest one by the collar and pulled him to his feet. It was Grauman, a skinny teenager.

I put my face close to his and shouted, "Don't you ever fall out on me again. You understand that, Marine?"

The kid was terrified. "Y-yes-yes, Sir. Yessir!"

I released Grauman's collar and he staggered back into the line of exhausted mortarmen. They all looked frightened, but they were all on their feet.

On the road at the bottom of the hill I had Sergeant Wright form up the men once more. "Take them up the hill again. Walk them this time and give them arm and hand signal drill on the way up," I told him. Arm and hand signals are the means used in combat to direct movement and indicate enemy disposition. "Let them know that we'll be running up this hill every day from now on until we go aboard ship. And nobody falls out!"

"Aye, aye, Sir!" answered Sergeant Wright. I turned my back on the mortar section, but I could hear the men muttering as I walked away.

• • •

Captain Wilcox had returned from the field when I got back to the headquarters hut.

"Skipper is in. He's looking for you," said First Sergeant Caney, who hardly glanced up from his paperwork as he indicated the open door to the company commander's office.

I tapped lightly on the door frame.

"Yeah. Come on in," said Capt. Myron E. Wilcox, who was hunched over his desk, frowning deeply. There were piles of papers before him, and he uttered a loud "Damn!" with each one he signed. The papers were orders, requisitions, and receipts, the tedious details that keep line officers beholden to the clerks and supply people.

"Second Lieutenant Owen reporting for duty, Captain. As ordered!" My dungarees were wet with the sweat of my uphill trot, but I was at parade-ground attention.

"Be right with you, Owen. At ease." He nodded toward a canvas chair before the desk. "Sit down, Lieutenant. Got to get these damned things signed or those paper pushers at battalion will run me up to the colonel."

From the look of his desk, Captain Wilcox had several hours of work ahead of him to satisfy the paper pushers. "Damn! Damn! Damn!" he kept exclaiming.

After a few moments he slammed down the pen, declaring, "The hell with it!" He rose from behind the paper-strewn desk, then came around and offered his hand. I stood and we shook. The handshake was strong. He was a big man, almost as tall as me, but a bit flabby around the edges. His last command had been a guard detachment at a Navy ammunition depot, which was not physically demanding duty for an officer. He was a combat Marine, though; when he was a lieutenant he had taken command of a shattered rifle company on Iwo Jima.

"Welcome aboard, Lieutenant," said Captain Wilcox. He wore horn-rimmed glasses that gave him a professorial look. He got right to business. "Regiment said you have mortar experience."

"Yes, Sir, Captain. I had the eighty-one mortars in the Mediterranean for 1st Battalion, 6th. Colonel Litzenberg was my regimental commander."

"I guess that's how you got this billet, then. One of Old Homer's people."

Out of his presence we all called Colonel Litzenberg "Old Homer." He was nearly fifty years old.

Captain Wilcox said, "You know, don't you, that every damn lieutenant in the Marine Corps is trying to sign on with the rifle companies? Most of them have plenty of experience. You're the only second lieutenant in the battalion."

"Second Lieutenant Stemple is in Able Company," I said. Jim Stemple and I had done duty together since officer training at Quantico.

"Oh, yeah. Another one of Old Homer's protégés." Captain Wilcox was not happy about having a second lieutenant forced on him. There were scores of more experienced first lieutenants looking for billets.

I said to the skipper, "Captain, I'll give you the best mortar section in the regiment. You can count on it."

"I'll hold you to that. Now we'd both better get back to work." Captain Wilcox returned to his paperwork. No social talk, no names of folks who might be mutual acquaintances, no duty stations we might have in common. Captain Wilcox was mired in his paperwork, and he was an angry skipper.

However, there was a situation I had to face. "Captain," I began, "I've got some problems with the people in the mortar section."

He shot me a look that said he didn't want to know about my problems.

"They're all reserves," I went on. "I don't have a single regular in the section. I'm hoping you can give me a few regular NCOs to help break these people in."

"Get this straight, Lieutenant." Captain Wilcox leaned across the desk and gave me his "captain's-word-is-law" glare. "I don't have enough experienced NCOs to cover the rifle platoons and the machine guns. That's where the up-front fighting is, and that's where the experience in my company goes. Up front. If you don't like that, you can get Colonel Litzenberg to put you in another outfit where you can pick and choose your own people."

"Aye, aye, Sir!" I stood to attention again, turned about smartly, and got out of there. I was not having a good first day with Baker-One-Seven.

• • •

I was in the officers' hut, stowing my gear, when the rifle platoons of Baker-One-Seven clattered into the company area. They came at double-time, with hoarse platoon sergeants goading them to maintain the pace. Their files were ragged, and several men straggled behind the column, barely keeping their feet. The stragglers were a sorry sight; they looked as bad as my mortarmen had on our earlier hill climb.

There were more than a dozen Negro faces interspersed throughout the column, something I had never seen before. Even more surprisingly, one of the Negroes was at the head of his squad. A Negro squad leader in a rifle platoon! That possibility had been talked about for the past several months, but it hadn't been considered likely. I had heard men—some officers, too—say that they would never serve with "niggers."

The company officers, all first lieutenants, came into the hut to clean up for noon chow. They crowded around me, offering handshakes in welcome. On seeing my gold second lieutenant bars, they joked that they expected due subservience from my humble rank.

"Now we don't have to worry about who gets the crap details in Baker-One-Seven," they laughed. "We got our own personal second lieutenant. Welcome aboard, Second Lieutenant Owen!" I joined the laughter.

The lieutenants were all trim and well muscled, with close-cropped hair and clear, intelligent faces. They could be taken for a group of college athletes. All of them had rifle company experience.

John Weaver was tall with the bearing of an aristocrat. He was the son of a retired Marine general and had been brought up in the Old Corps when all of its officers were gentlemen.

Bill Graeber was a rough-and-ready type, heavyset with energetic movements. The son of a New York cop, he had, himself, been with the military police detachment for occupation duty in Japan and North China.

Hank Kiser, an easy-going Texan, was tall and slender with the wiry muscles of a distance runner. Blond with a baby face, he had a slow drawl that gave him the time to size up a man. He smiled frequently, but his look could grow serious in an instant.

Weaver, Graeber, and Kiser had the company's three rifle platoons. The company executive officer, 1st Lt. Joe Kurcaba, the skipper's second-in-command, wasn't around. He was at the docks in San Diego, already loading gear aboard ship. I wouldn't meet him until we embarked for Korea.

Our machine gun platoon commander was 1st Lt. Chew Een Lee, a second-generation American of Chinese ancestry. Lee, the smallest of us, was slight of build but in excellent physical shape. He seemed charged with explosive energy.

"Lieutenant Owen," he acknowledged me, "my machine guns and your mortars will work together to give support for the rifle platoons. I expect the highest level of performance from my men, and you must demand no less from yours."

I hadn't heard that kind of lecture since graduating from officer's training school. "Thank you for that bit of wisdom, Sir," I mocked.

The lieutenants laughed, except for Lee. He directed a stern glare my way. "We are in a serious business here," he said.

• • •

My mortarmen were formed up for training after noon chow. Sergeants Lunney and Winget were made squad leaders, along with Corporal Burris. Burris, I discovered, had some mortar experience with his reserve unit. I took these three aside and gave them individual training on the workings of the mortars. Sergeant Wright spent the time dividing the remainder of the section into three squads. Afterwards, the section gathered in a circle and we began hands-on familiarization.

Evening chow formation was 1730. By the time we marched the men into the mess hall, each of them had taken apart and put together a mortar and recited the names of its components and its capabilities to his new squad leader.

They were dismayed when I called them into formation again at 1830. We repeated the afternoon training until dark, when they were marched back to their Quonset huts.

Ten minutes after they were dismissed I had Sergeant Wright call them out again. There was much cursing as they stumbled into their squad positions in the dark. Sergeant Wright quickly silenced them. We took apart and set up the guns in the black of night. Blindfold drill without the blindfolds. Three hours of this and we double-timed back to the huts.

I gave final orders. "Squad leaders will instruct their men on making up full transport packs." The full transport pack was fifty pounds of every piece of clothing and gear that a Marine carried into a campaign; weapons and ammo added ten or fifteen pounds more. Mortarmen were burdened with another twenty pounds of gun components and ammunition.

"Tomorrow at 0600 you will be in formation with field transport packs," I ordered them. "Conditioning hike." Squad leaders, check your men's feet before falling in. Smooth, clean socks. Dismissed!"

A voice came from the darkness of the ranks. "Will this be the last time you make us come out tonight?"

I recognized the voice, the young kid Perkins. I bellowed at the section, "You people will learn that you do not speak in the ranks unless you are ordered to speak in the ranks. Sergeant Wright, run them twice around the company area. Then dismiss the section for field transport pack instruction."

I followed at a trot behind the mortarmen as they lumbered around the company area. They didn't see me in the dark, and they swore mighty oaths of retribution against their lieutenant.

• • •

The next morning the conditioning hike of eight miles with full packs and weapons was pathetic. The end of the first hour—a pace of four miles per hour, with a ten-minute break—found half of the men staggering. I gave the section an extra ten minutes to let the stragglers catch up. All hands were sweating and gasping for air when we finally got back to the company area. Sergeant Wright was far in the rear this time, weaving on his feet. But he didn't give up. None of my mortarmen gave up, and all had water remaining in their canteens.

• • •

I met our battalion commander, Lt. Col. Raymond G. Davis, one morning as my mortarmen came off the hill from our early run. The men were bent over and breathing hard, but all were on their feet. A jeep stopped and the colonel leaped out.

I snapped to, but he called, "At ease," before I could command the men to attention.

"Lieutenant Owen, Colonel," I introduced myself, noting the silver leaves of rank on his dungarees.

Lieutenant Colonel Davis returned the salute, then put out his hand. "Ray Davis," he replied as we shook hands. The colonel, trim and of medium height, exuded boundless energy and had eyes that bored into you. He had a youthful appearance, although he had been a much-decorated battalion commander in the Pacific war.

"Came out to see how these mortarmen of yours are coming along," he said.

"Sergeant Wright," I called. "Prepare the men for gun drill."

It was a ragged performance, but there were no major blunders. The squad leaders led their men in a run across the training field. They threw themselves to the ground, assembled the mortar components, and prepared the sights for fire command. We had spent two full afternoons on this drill, and the squad leaders were taking hold.

"Your men are looking good so far. You keep after them," the colonel said in a soft Georgia drawl. Then he climbed back into his jeep and drove away.

I called the troops together and gave them their first "Well done!"

• • •

We went into the Pendleton hills for field exercises, and the mortarmen ate C-rations out of tin cans. Sergeant Wright allowed them to make small fires to heat the rations, and they were like schoolkids on a picnic.

I gave them instruction on mortar tactics, demonstrating how we would use the guns to support the rifle platoons when we got to Korea. I showed them how to estimate range. Every man had practice cranking the sights in response to fire orders. We filled empty ammunition boxes with boulders, then crawled on our bellies, pulling the weighted boxes to simulate ammo supply across open terrain under enemy fire.

The men continued to look ragged in formation, and they still had great difficulty with the proper forms of military address. Bifulk stammered over "Lieutenant" and asked if it would be OK to use "Owen" or "Joe." That was the way he talked to his boss at home, he said, and he saw little difference. "As long as we all know that you're the boss here, what difference does it make what we call you?" was the way Bifulk put it.

Perkins and Fisher babbled out "Sir" with almost every word. "Sir, can I go to the bathroom, Sir? Sir, I have to go real bad, Sir." Sergeant Wright would shake his head and tell me that these people needed to go to boot camp.

Grauman became nervous whenever I came close to him.

But my "boots" were learning their weapons. They were smart kids, eager and willing, and their stamina grew every day. They were now doing fifteen miles on the march. On the breaks they did gun drill. They performed well in live fire exercises. When I took them for a night shoot, they were like kids allowed to stay out and play after dark. I wasted no time with them on parade-ground drill.

They showed well against the battalion's other mortar sections when Colonel Davis ordered us to the range for a battalion shoot. Along with the sixties of Able and Charlie Companies, we were timed putting live ammo on targets from one thousand yards to two hundred yards in. Baker's three guns were first to set up, first to have rounds in the air, and first on their targets. After the colonel's "Well done!" we double-timed all the way back to the company area. When we were close enough that the rest of the company would hear them, my mortarmen sang a bawdy marching song as they ran.

• • •

I barely saw the other officers of the company. At first light each morning we marched off separately to the firing ranges and the tactical training areas, and we stayed out until late in the day. After dark, when we didn't have them out for night training, we put the troops through the administrative details—immunization shots, dog tags, next of kin and insurance matters—the paperwork that documented our existence.

Twice First Sergeant Caney encountered me as I dismissed my men for the night. He complained that I had neglected to turn in the papers that he required to keep the company records in order. Both times he reported my negligence to Captain Wilcox. The skipper voiced displeasure when I told him that I felt my time was better spent training the troops than filling in forms. My mistake. First Sergeant Caney, master of paperwork, had the skipper's ear.

I was alone in the officers' hut one day when Lee came in. He asked me what I was doing inside when my troops were out in the field.

"Catching up on this paperwork," I told him. "Captain's orders, Lee."

"It's Lieutenant Lee to you," he snapped. Rarely did first lieutenants require formal deference from second lieutenants, but it was their privilege.

"OK, Lieutenant Lee, if that's the way you want it," I said. "If I may ask, Lieutenant, why are you inside this morning?"

As I would come to learn, Lee's face was always impassive. His voice, though, was tight with anger. "They are fools at battalion! They called me up there and wanted to put me in the intelligence section. Make me a damned interpreter! What do they think I am, a foreigner?"

Lieutenant Lee's voice dropped to a low, angry growl. "I found it necessary to inform the colonel's staff that I have become an officer in the Marine Corps for one purpose only—to lead troops in battle. I do not intend to sit in a rear echelon headquarters and write intelligence reports. I believe they understand that now."

The words were precise, perfectly pronounced, but they carried traces of Lt. Chew Een Lee's Chinese heritage. He strapped on his gear, aligned it neatly, and stomped out to join his machine gunners in the field.

• • •

Dorothy took seventy-five dollars of our scant resources and bought an airline ticket from Syracuse to San Diego. I met her at the airport at eleven o'clock at night. Hank Kiser, exhausted from the long training days and the bachelor life of Southern California, had decided to rest for a night, and he lent me his car. Dorothy and I drove to an old, wooden hotel near the beach in San Clemente, a few miles north of Camp Pendleton. I was asleep with weariness soon after we locked the door. Dorothy awakened me at four o'clock in the morning, and I drove back to the base. Sergeant Wright already had the section formed up, and I went to morning chow with the troops at 0500.

Bill Graeber's wife, Vi, was staying at the same hotel, along with several other regimental officers' wives. Each night after we had dismissed the troops, Bill and I cadged a ride to the hotel. Restaurants in the little village of San Clemente were closed that late, but Dorothy would have a cold supper waiting for me. Then we would stroll to the beach and listen to the waves crash across the sand. During those walks, we talked about the babies and made plans for my return from Korea. My next assignment, I assured her, would give us at least two years together at a good duty station. Maybe I would be senior enough for us to rate decent quarters.

In the mornings, early and still dark, Bill Graeber and I would ride back to camp with the other officers. Everyone except the driver slept all the way, crowded against each other in the tight seats of the car. We were very tired, but we were young men and we did dearly love our beautiful wives.

CHAPTER THREE

Baker-One-Seven held to the doubled-up training schedule until we shipped out. We ran the troops up Camp Pendleton's punishing hills, and when we stopped running them, we did weapons drill. We ran them through tactics—fire and movement, skirmish lines, sectors of fire, supporting fire, digging in. We ran them into the night to get the feel of the dark. Then came gear issue, physicals, immunization shots, and administrative details in triplicate. At night we gave them five hours' sleep.

For the young reservists the change in lifestyle was profound. The kids I had—Nichols and Grauman, Fisher and Perkins, and the others—were boys who had just come from the shelter of home, family, and Mom's cooking. But they were strong and intelligent, and they went at the work with purpose. They may not have been good at staying in step, but they took to their weapons readily and they hardened quickly.

Baker-One-Seven was blessed with good senior NCOs. They knew combat and they had earned their stripes in bitterly fought Pacific battles.

Gunnery Sgt. Henry Foster, of Lee's machine gun platoon, and Platoon Sgt. Joseph King, of Weaver's 1st Platoon, were regulars stamped from the Old Corps mold. They were expert in the use of all of the company's weapons. Both were lean and bronzed, and they moved easily among their men. They spoke sparingly, but their voices were deep with authority.

Gene O'Brien and Archie Van Winkle, platoon sergeants for the 2d and 3d Platoons, were reservists with as much combat experience as the regulars. In civilian life, O'Brien worked as a carpenter in Philadelphia; Van Winkle was a college student in his home state of Washington.

Gunny Buckley, the company gunnery sergeant, was another old salt. He had been to wars dating back to the jungles of Nicaragua and Haiti in the 1930s. The gunny, though, was nearing retirement, and he had become soft with easy duty since the end of the war against the Japanese. He still made a fine appearance—tall, with military bearing and a thick walrus mustache—but he found the going difficult in the field.

S. Sgt. Ray Richard was an old-line regular, too, a Marine since 1938. Before World War II he had served in China and the Philippines. In the Pacific he had fought in a Raider battalion, from Guadalcanal on to the war's end. In August of 1950 he was dispatched to the vast supply depot the Marine Corps maintained at Barstow, on the edge of the Mojave Desert. As a weapons expert, it was Richard's job to repair and recondition the weapons stored at the depot. Much of the inventory was decrepit stuff left over from World War II, but an experienced armorer could salvage the good components and assemble them into serviceable weapons.

Sergeant Richard didn't know that he had been assigned to Baker-One-Seven. He went about his duty at Barstow, grumbling that he had not joined the Corps to be a rear echelon technician. Like all the regulars, he feared being left behind when a shooting war started. He was cheered, though, when a detail of four Pfcs. showed up at the Barstow armory.

"First Sergeant Caney told us to report to you," said one of the men.

"Who the hell is First Sergeant Caney?" demanded Sergeant Richard. He knew none of these men.

"He's first sergeant for Baker Company, 1st Battalion, 7th Marines. He told us that you're the company armorer. We're supposed to help you get the company's weapons squared away for shipping out."

The man handed Sergeant Richard a typewritten requisition list. It was an inventory of the weapons that Baker-One-Seven would take into combat.

"You people come with me," ordered Richard. He led the men to a corner of a large warehouse where long rows of .30–caliber light machine guns were stored. All were mounted on their tripods. A few of the guns were nearly new; most had been rebuilt. Sergeant Richard knew the condition of each of them. He selected the best of the lot and instructed the men to mark them for Baker-One-Seven. We would have the best conditioned weapons in the battalion.

• • •

The lower-ranking regulars in Baker-One-Seven, the corporals and privates, were hardly older than our reservists. They had joined the Corps following World War II, on the prowl for the excitement and travel promised to them by the recruiting sergeants. Not a few of them had signed on to avoid jail time in their home towns.

They were high-spirited young men, usually aggressive in nature. They had endured the harsh training that the Marine Corps imposed on them, and they thrived in the world of weapons and strenuous field exercises. The strictures of barracks life, though, and the boredom of sentry duty often led them astray. Few of the regulars in the ranks of Baker-One-Seven were strangers to brig time; boozing and brawling and the consequent absences from duty were their principal misdeeds.

On the positive side, almost every one of the regulars had entered in his record an expert rating in the use of the basic infantry weapons—the M-1 rifle, the bayonet, and the hand grenade.

Pfc. Gilberto Garcia had served in Guam and China and was at Camp Pendelton waiting for discharge when the Korean War broke out. He immediately reenlisted and was one of the first men sent to Baker-One-Seven. He was assigned to the headquarters section where he would become Captain Wilcox's radio man and runner.

Garcia first met Captain Wilcox when, with another regular, Pfc. Raul Rendon, from the machine gun platoon, he hitchhiked off the base to the nearby town of Oceanside. Liberty, as Marines call permission to leave the base, had not been granted to Baker-One-Seven. But Gilberto Garcia, artful in the ways of the Corps, had acquired a pair of illicit liberty cards.

To the dismay of Garcia and Rendon, Captain Wilcox came along in his jeep and stopped to give the two Marines a lift. Since all three were new to the outfit, the captain didn't recognize Garcia and Rendon. Garcia explained that they were assistants to the division chaplain, on an errand of mercy for the padre. The captain dropped off his two over-the-hill Marines at the post gate and wished them well on their mission.

While out in the field a few days later, Captain Wilcox encountered Garcia, now serving as a runner. The captain scrutinized Garcia. "Have we done duty together before, son?" he asked. "You look familiar."

"Yes, Sir!" responded the wily Garcia. "I've been working the serving line at the battalion mess hall. I've seen the captain having chow there many times."

"That's it," said the captain. "I never forget a face."

When the troops returned from the field, Garcia sought out his buddy, Rendon. "Never let the skipper see us together, Raul. He might remember where he really met us."

. . .

Glenn Galtere, a blond, rangy nineteen-year-old, had joined the Corps, underage, in 1947. Twice he had made the rank of private first class, and twice was busted back to private. Both busts were for disorderly conduct and absent-over-leave charges. A few months after his last stretch in the brig, he joined Baker-One-Seven from duty on Guam. Although he was expert in the use of infantry weapons, Galtere had begun to think of himself as a "professional private." He became a BAR-man in Hank Kiser's 3d Platoon.

. . .

Cpl. James Kovar had been a Marine guard at the Navy ammunition depot in Hastings, Nebraska. He had recently signed on for another four-year hitch in order to receive the shipping-over bonus that became his down payment on a new Pontiac convertible. The night he acquired the hot, shiny wheels, he proudly drove to a roadhouse on the edge of town. A discussion with another car buff, a civilian, led first to a heated disagreement and then to an exchange of fists. Damage was done, some of it to the civilian, most of it to the front window of the roadhouse.

Now Pvt. Jim Kovar was released from the brig the week after the Korean War started. He was one of the first men to join Baker-One-Seven, and he persuaded First Sergeant Caney to sign him into the company's rocket section. It was Jim Kovar's dream to stand against an enemy tank and destroy it. Especially a Russian T-34 tank, the big monsters that the North Koreans were using to tear through the U.S. Army.

. . .

Pfc. Attilio Lupacchini was happy to become a BAR-man in Bill Graeber's 2d Platoon. Any billet that would get him away from stateside duty would have satisfied Lupacchini. He had recently been promoted to Pfc.—again—and he was finding it difficult to keep his record clean. A clean record meant a great deal to Lupacchini.

No one knew for certain, but the most prevalent story about Attilio Lupacchini was that he had joined the Corps in order to attain U.S. citizenship. He was Italian by birth and a seaman by trade until he had missed his freighter when it sailed out of Hoboken. He had been detained by four waterfront cops who subdued him in a free-swinging brawl—Lupacchini against a crew of drunken Swedish sailors, plus the four cops. The local magistrate put him away for thirty days. When he was released, with no ship, little English, and very few dollars, he met a Marine recruiting sergeant. The recruiter was impressed by Lupacchini's demonstrated fighting spirit. With the understanding that an honorable hitch in the Marines might be rewarded with American citizenship, Lupacchini signed aboard.

When he came to Baker-One-Seven, Lupacchini was finding it difficult to put together an honorable hitch. He was a natural fighting machine, volatile and combative. He was ideally built for brawling, with a squat, thickly muscled body and long gorilla-like arms, from which swung clublike fists.

On duty Lupacchini was a good Marine, industrious on work details, conscientious about learning the language of his sergeants and the weapons of his trade. It was when he went on liberty that trouble ran into him. Lupacchini enjoyed booze, and in the dives where he drank, booze led frequently to brawls. The resulting charges brought against him were most often "drunk and disorderly conduct" and "destruction of property." Although he had spent much time in the brig, and had more than once torn off his Pfc. stripe, Lupacchini was persuasively defended by sergeants and officers who saw his value as a field Marine. They saved him from a bad conduct discharge and kept alive his hope of becoming an American citizen.

• • •

Combat Marines have great affection for their corpsmen, the rough-and-ready "docs" who tend our sickness and our pains when we train in the field. When the shooting starts, they become the bravest people in the Marine Corps. The corpsman is a Navy enlisted man, trained to give rudimentary medical care, and one of them is assigned to each platoon. It is his job to keep the wounded alive until they are carried off the field of battle. Much of this work is performed under enemy fire; he is a visible and defenseless target. In the Corps, tales are told of our corpsmen and the astonishing acts of courage they perform to save the lives of their Marines.

Corpsman Bill Davis came from the diet kitchen of the U.S. Naval Academy. He was trained in the principles of medicine and patient care, but he was thoroughly ignorant of life as a rifle company Marine. He was a scrawny guy, not more than one hundred twenty-five pounds, and soft-handed from duty in the diet kitchen. Although he did not look as though he could stand the rigors of field duty, Bill Davis was signed on as corpsman for Graeber's 2d Platoon.

During our time at Camp Pendleton, Davis had little opportunity to get out with the troops. Like Captain Wilcox and the headquarters people, his time was mostly allotted to administrative work. The "kid corpsman," as the old salts called him, was swamped with fore-and-aft physicals, a bewildering array of shots, medical records, dog tags to punch out, and twenty-hour days. On his first time out with the platoon Bill Davis was barely able to struggle into his sixty pounds of pack and medical kit. He came close to dropping out from the punishing forced march, but instead found himself taking care of cases of heat exhaustion, dehydration, and bloody feet. The kid corpsman kept going.

It was the same for our other rifle platoon corpsmen. Toppel and Mickens—"boots" like Davis—were shifted from hospital duty where they had given shots, emptied bedpans, and fed Jell-O to sick sailors. Neither had knowledge of the Marine Corps except for encounters in barroom brawls. Toppel, a Brooklyn-brash cigar chewer, went to Hank Kiser's 3d Platoon. Mickens was sent to the 1st Platoon, which was Weaver's.

The aptly named Doktorski, a big, tall guy, had a hitch in the regular Navy and had served aboard a destroyer in the Pacific Fleet. He took to field duty right away. Lieutenant Lee grabbed Doktorski for the machine gun platoon.

The senior corpsman was MacIntosh, who had the billet for the headquarters section, which included my sixties. MacIntosh would be corpsman for the mortarmen—when we could find him.

Nobody in the 1st Platoon had ever seen a Negro corpsman before Doc Mickens came to them. But, by the time he got there, the 1st Platoon didn't give much thought to their doc. They had already absorbed into their ranks two Negro sergeants and a sprinkling of BAR-men and riflemen. In peacetime conditions there may have been time for racial distinction and upheaval. In August of 1950, though, Platoon Sergeant King was pushing the platoon hard, and that left his people little time to care about the color line.

One of the Negro sergeants in the 1st Platoon was the platoon's guide. He proved to be Sergeant Dale, whom I remembered from the beach at Camp Lejeune where he had manned the sandwich stand at the Officers' Club. As I walked down the company street one day, I came across the sergeant and we saluted in passing. I recognized him, so I stopped and addressed him as Sergeant Dale. He didn't recognize me. To hashmark NCOs, all second lieutenants look alike.

Sergeant Dale told me that he and Sergeant King were "whacking" the troops into shape, even though he thought that half of them should go to boot camp. He added that he was sorry he didn't have his old squad from Montford Point—the Negro training area in the segregated Marine Corps—to demonstrate the way Marines should move in the field.

He also said that a few of the regulars were still a little too "cracker." "Cracker" was the euphemism that Sergeant Dale applied to Marines who resisted the new color code. Those few hard-core segregationists who remained in our ranks could create serious morale problems, and we kept tight rein on them.

Two of Sergeant Dale's "crackers" approached me early one morning outside of the company office. They had the look of regulars, much-laundered dungarees and naptha-scrubbed web gear. They were rangy lads with the drawl of the Deep South. I knew about them from their involvement in a barracks disturbance that the sergeants had handled.

"Request permission to speak to the Lieutenant, Sir," said the first of them. Both men popped salty salutes at me in a style that they had picked up while on North China duty, the fingers half-curled and the hand thrown straight ahead, in front of the eyes.

I kept them at attention while we talked. Troublemakers like these usually try to test authority. "Sir, we'd like to come over with ya'll in the mortar section," said one of them. "We got plenty of good time on them mortar tubes of yours, Sir. Do some real good shooting for you."

"Yes, Sir," put in the other one. "And we both can set up the guns for registration fire. Done the forward observing, too. Done all of that with the old 5th Marines."

With their experience, they would have been the answer to my prayers, what I had asked Captain Wilcox to give me.

"Why do you want to leave the 1st Platoon," I asked. "Sergeant King too tough on you?"

"No, Sir! That Sergeant King, he's tough enough, I reckon, but we can take it from him all right."

"But we ain't gonna take it from no nigger," broke in the other one. "We got us a nigger sergeant giving orders, telling us what to do!"

"And now we got us a nigger corpsman, too." Indignation rose in their voices. "We ain't letting them niggers run us. Ain't going to let

that happen. How's about ya'll bringing a couple of real good mortarmen over to your outfit, Lieutenant?"

I had no Negroes in the mortars, but I wanted no troublemakers
like these two "crackers."

"Knock it off," I broke in.

"Yes, Sir!" These Marines knew the order of things; they shut up
instantly.

"You men are going to stay with the 1st Platoon until they carry
you off a hill in your ponchos. And you will follow orders that are
given to you by a Marine NCO, no matter what color he is."

They stood stiffly at attention, eyes stony, the proper stance for a
pair of Marines being chewed out.

"If I hear you bad-mouthing any NCO in this company, black,
white, or polka dot, I'll get you run up for serious brig time. Now get
back to your platoon. Dismissed!"

They gave a regulation salute, stiff and formal. "Aye, aye, Sir!" said
the two in unison. Then in perfect step they marched away down the
company street. I sure could have used them, though.

• • •

We could see that the skipper would be a good company commander
whenever he was able to join Baker-One-Seven in the field. When
possible, he would sit with us lieutenants at chow and relate his own
combat experiences. He had been in some tough fighting against the
Japanese, and all of his war stories had a "lessons learned" point to
them. Captain Wilcox knew how a rifle company moved, and he had
an aggressive spirit.

After noon chow one day the captain informed me that he would
inspect the mortar section the following morning. He had come
from a guard detachment where the troops were always spit-and-
polish. Here, mired in administrative work, the skipper had not seen
for himself how ill prepared and undertrained we were. I had little
confidence that my youngsters would stand up to the skipper's
scrutiny when he gave them a parade-ground inspection.

Hank Kiser and I had planned an exercise that afternoon, the mortars working in support of the rifle platoon's attack. Reluctantly, I
canceled the exercise and spent the time preparing the men for the
next morning.

Sergeant Wright lined up the section for my preliminary inspection. To my consternation, there was little improvement in their
disheveled appearance. Bifulk stood at attention like a sack of potatoes, bulges in his pockets, pack straps unbuckled. Perkins's face

was streaked with nervous perspiration, and he mumbled incoherently when I demanded his serial number. Nichols fumbled his carbine and nearly dropped it as he thrust it forward for inspection. Fisher couldn't get the perpetual grin off his face, and he turned several shades of red when I asked him what was funny. The lanky Veeder's dungaree jacket was too short for him, and his wrists stuck out six inches below the sleeves. Grauman gulped and stammered that he couldn't remember how far the mortars fired.

Sergeant Wright saw my discouragement. He said, "Lieutenant, you officers should realize that a week ago these people didn't know a mortar from a bayonet. They all need to go to boot camp. All of us NCOs know that."

"They're not going to boot camp. They're going aboard ship. And then they're going to fight."

"Lambs to the slaughter," said Sergeant Wright.

We had the men break out their scrubbing brushes and laundry soap to wash a uniform for the inspection, a set of dungarees and web gear, which would dry in the afternoon sun. Then Sergeant Wright and I inspected them again, and yet again. One by one we instructed the mortarmen on how to stand at rigid attention and how to present their weapons for the skipper's inspection. I taught them how to respond when they were addressed in the ranks. But I regretted the field training we were losing and had little hope that we would satisfy Captain Wilcox.

The next morning at first light I returned from San Clemente. As I started down the company street someone yelled, "Mortars, fall in!"

My men, carrying their weapons, clattered out of their two huts. They quickly formed into their three squad ranks. Sergeant Wright had them at attention, and they stood stern and still.

"Mortar section ready for inspection, Sir!" Wright reported when I stood before him. He made a brisk about-face and followed me to the first rank. Each man stood rigid at my approach. Weapons were presented, almost to precision. Movements were by the manual; uniforms were without blemish and neatly tucked. Packs were square and aligned. Answers to my request for name and duty were loud and clear, barked out, eyes to front.

"Pfc. Westberg, Sir! Assistant gunner, 1st Squad."

"Pfc. Bifulk, Sir! Ammo carrier, 2nd Squad."

"Pfc. Perkins, Sir! Ammo carrier, 2nd Squad."

Grauman knew the range of the mortars. Nichols's carbine came before me without a fumble. Veeder had acquired a dungaree jacket with sleeves long enough to conceal most of his wrists.

Not a mote of dust or a speck of cleaning rag in the bore or chamber of any weapon. Bayonets free of dust. Every strap and button secured. Leggings scrubbed and properly laced. Bring on the skipper!

The skipper's inspection was no more rigorous than mine had been. Although they were not yet the regulars of Captain Wilcox's experience, the men were straight in line, and they presented their weapons to him smartly and in proper fashion.

There was some nervousness. Perkins stammered over his serial number. "One-oh-four-seven—I mean one-oh—uh, one-oh-four-seven-two-nine-one. Yessir, that's it. I mean, Captain, Sir!"

Nichols's carbine did tremble a bit before the captain grasped it from him.

But when we had finished with the last squad, First Sergeant Caney's notebook was empty. There were no transgressions to record. I accompanied the captain to the front of the section.

The captain addressed the mortar section. "You're beginning to look like United States Marines. You keep working at it."

Then, to me, he said, "Carry on with the training routine, Lieutenant. Well done."

I ordered the section right-face and up the hill. On the double. They stayed with me, whooping out gung-ho war yells. They were beginning to sound like Marines, too.

The men were breathing heavily when we reached the top, but they were all on their feet. I allowed them to take a break, and Sergeant Wright sat down beside me.

"Maybe you could give the men an extra five minutes on the break, Lieutenant. They stayed up all night, and we held practice inspections. They went to work for you."

"I appreciate that, Sergeant," I said. "You NCOs did a fine job."

"It was the men, Lieutenant. They wanted to make you look good." Sergeant Wright's voice took on the NCO-to-lieutenant tone. "The men are afraid of you. But they were afraid they might lose you, too. They think that you'll take care of them."

"Thank you, Sergeant," I said. "It's too bad that we have to be so rough on them. But we don't have much time to bring them along."

"With respect, Lieutenant, you have them coming along about as good as they're going to come along. They don't need to be afraid of you anymore."

I went down the line of the mortarmen as they reclined on the dry brown grass. To each I gave a "well done." They responded with "Thank you, Sir," and "Thank you, Lieutenant." All except for Bifulk. He said, "Hey, Joe, we done good for you today, huh?"

• • •

Gunny Buckley, in the manner of Marine gunnery sergeants, had connections in the division's ammunition depot. In the last days before we loaded ship, he bootlegged a trailer-load of mortar ammunition for our practice. He did better than that; he had us cleared on the mortar range for both an afternoon and a night shoot.

The mortarmen double-timed the three miles to the range, where the gunny met us with the ammo. We had a grand time firing at rusted-out tanks and old artillery pieces that were studded about the range as targets. Every man had a chance at calling range and direction, and calling fire orders.

We stayed on the range, ate chow out of ration cans, and waited for dark so that we could fire illumination. While the men ate, Hugo Johnson and I went over the range and blew up our duds, rounds that had not exploded on impact. We used little balls of plastic explosive that we set off near the duds. Most of the regulars had been trained in explosives, but this was my first use of them outside of training. Hugo, though, had plenty of "boom time," as he called it, from his work in the oil fields.

When darkness came, we set up the guns to fire illumination. We fired at three hundred yards and listened to the popping sounds made by the shells as they released the small parachutes that carried twenty seconds of glaring, blue light. The terrain in front of us turned ghostly, the pale ground contrasting sharply with the black and gray shapes of targets to our front. By timing the rounds, we were able to keep the range lit for several minutes at a time. To the kids who were my mortarmen, our night shoot had the air of a fireworks display.

• • •

The night before we shipped out, I hitched an early ride to San Clemente with an officer from headquarters. It was still daylight when I arrived at the hotel. Dorothy and I went for a dive into the surf, then had dinner at a little Italian restaurant on San Clemente's main street, Route 101. We had plenty of wine with our meal; the owner opened a full bottle of red—on the house—after we had finished the two glasses we ordered.

Over the wine, Dorothy expressed the worries that troubled her. "It isn't fair. Sending men like yours into combat," she said. "Untrained, I mean."

"We have to go with what we've got," I answered. I had tried not to worry Dorothy with my assessment of the backward state of our men, but it was a common topic of conversation among the wives who stayed at the hotel with her.

"It isn't fair to those poor boys," she continued. "And not to their families." Her eyes misted.

"We're working on the men. They're coming along," I said to relieve her anxiety. "Our officers are good. And we have some of the best NCOs I've seen, and that includes our reservists."

"It would be better if you had all regulars."

"Sure it would. But it's the regulars' job to teach these kids to fight. That's how we won the last war."

"In the last war they had time to get ready," Dorothy answered. "Look at all the training you had before you went overseas."

I said, "Don't worry. We'll all fight like Marines when we get there."

She looked deep into the red wine, then took my hand and squeezed it. "I'm afraid. And I'm worried about you. I worry about the babies, too, what will happen if you don't come back."

"I'll come back."

• • •

On 1 September Baker-One-Seven formed up as a complete rifle company for the first time. The men were in full combat gear, field transport packs strapped and weapons slung. The ranks were not perfectly straight, but the men stood at attention as the NCOs and officers reported, "All present or accounted for, Sir!"

Captain Wilcox stood before the fully assembled rifle company, the men he would lead into battle. Then we loaded on trucks and within two hours we were filing aboard ship, the Navy transport USS *Okanogan*. Ready or not, we were on the way to war.

Our wives were at the docks, bathed in the bright sunlight, more beautiful than they had ever been. We tried to fix the sight of them in our minds, images that would stay with us and lend us courage in battle.

Those of us with families at the pier were allowed to break ranks for a final goodbye. With my clumsy pack strapped to me, I held Dorothy tight and tried to smile at her tears. Damned if I was going to cry! Behind me, from the ranks, I heard Bifulk. "Give her a big one for us, Joe!"

Dorothy had a farewell present for me, an envelope of black-and-white snapshots. There were pictures of her and Mike and Dinny on the beach at Lejeune. And the babies and Dorothy dressed up, going to Mass at St. Cecilia's, back home. I tucked the envelope inside the webbing of my helmet, and we held on to each other until it was time for me to go up the ladder to the ship.

The wives remained on the dock long after we had gone aboard. The skirl of bagpipes sounded as we waved to them. Pfc. Timmy Killeen, Able Company, stood on the fantail of the *Okanogan*, and his bagpipes filled the fading afternoon with the "Marines' Hymn." Handkerchiefs fluttered from the dock, and the ship's horn blasted. We were under way. There were tears, but Marines and Marine wives aren't ashamed of tears when their hymn plays.

CHAPTER FOUR

Our sea voyage to the war in Korea took three weeks. Twelve hundred combat-loaded Marines packed the USS *Okanogan* to the gunwales, and it was a dreary time of cramped quarters, terrible chow, and rough seas. After sundown we sailed "darken ship": hatches dogged shut, no lights showing, and the smoking lamp out, meaning no smoking on deck. The Navy was wary of Russian submarines; at this stage in the Cold War no one could predict Russian behavior.

Shipping out was a familiar routine to our regulars, and they were well experienced at life aboard the transports. Down in the troop compartments the old salts knew which of the sleeping racks were least uncomfortable, and they put immediate claim to the top tiers. The racks were sheets of heavy canvas laced by rope to metal frames. Stacked five and six high, with sixteen inches of vertical space between them, they afforded little breathing room. The top tier, however, offered a few more inches of space, and another body didn't sag down from above. The men in the bottom racks, the new men, were kept awake by the old salts who climbed up and down past their heads.

On our first day out of San Diego we hit the chopping seas of the offshore shallows. The ship pitched and wallowed, and seasickness quickly claimed its first victims, mostly the young reservists who were not accustomed to the sea's motion. They were banished from the troop holds so that their vomit would not foul the area. The only comfort offered to the seasick youngsters was advice from the regulars to stay by the lee rail and eat no greasy pork chops.

Seasick or hale, the troops spent as little time as possible in the cramped compartments. Below deck the air was close and sour with the stench of bodies, sweaty clothing, and the toilets in the adjacent heads. The few showers dispensed only cold salt water. But on the decks, crowded as they were, a man could breathe fresh air. He might even find a quiet place where he could think about life and death at a young age, and write letters home.

Deep in the cargo holds the ship's crew—"swabbies" we called them—made space for high-stakes poker, blackjack, and crap games; men on their way to battle have little regard for money. Navy regulations forbade gambling, but the officers seemed unaware of its presence.

Much of the troops' time was spent waiting in the long chow lines that ran along the outer decks. At the end of the wait the food was, at best, edible: grayish stews, grayish potatoes, grayish canned vegetables. A man could have as much as he wanted, and there was always applesauce to spread over everything. Navy coffee that was strong enough to corrode a canteen cup was available in unlimited quantity. Everyone on board—troops, crew, and officers—shared the same mediocre chow.

We maintained the training schedule all the way to Korea. The mortar section laid claim to a cargo hatch cover, an unencumbered open space that we used as a classroom. During most of the daylight hours we drilled on setting up, aiming, and tearing down the mortars. We practiced preparing ammunition for fire missions. We went through misfire drills, the emergency procedure of clearing faulty rounds from the tube, and hoped it would never need to be done with live ammo.

• • •

It was aboard ship that I first met Joe Kurcaba, the company's executive officer. While we were putting the company together at Camp Pendleton, Joe had been at the San Diego docks preparing for our embarkation.

First Lt. Joseph R. Kurcaba was a Pole from Brooklyn, tough-looking and tough-spoken. He was of medium height but wide-bodied, and his hard-callused hand grasped mine firmly when we shook. High cheekbones in his broad face and blondish hair reflected his Slavic ancestry. He was thirty-three, old for a lieutenant. He had been in the Corps since 1935, recruited out of the Great Depression of the thirties when the military was the only place to find a job. Joe's adult life had been spent in Marine rifle companies, and he had been promoted from sergeant to second lieutenant while fighting the Japanese in the violent battle for Saipan.

Joe Kurcaba's first words to me were, "They give you the sixties, huh? Damn good weapons if you know how to use them." He said "day" and "dem" for "they" and "them."

I said, "They also gave me twenty people who never saw a mortar before a few weeks ago." We were watching my men tear down and reassemble the guns while the squad leaders timed them. "But they're learning," I added.

"It takes a lot of shooting to make a good mortarman," Joe said. "I had the sixties when I was a sergeant on Tarawa."

"I agree with that," I said. "But battalion didn't have the ammo to spare for enough shooting time."

Joe Kurcaba winked at me. "You got to know the right people. Let's see what we can do."

The next morning Joe Kurcaba and Gunny Buckley produced sandbags and had them layered across the fantail, the rear deck of the ship. The gunny told Sergeant Wright to send a detail of mortarmen down into the cargo hatches, and they returned with a load of high explosive shells.

We set up the guns on the sandbags and held live fire exercise, much to the astonishment of the sailors, who had never seen a mortar. The sandbags were thick and sturdy, and they absorbed the recoil shock. Tin cans and refuse from the galley, thrown into the ship's wake, served as our crude targets. As each round hit the surface, it sent up a ten-foot high geyser of white water. The sailors "oohed" and "ahhed," and my mortarmen put a swagger to their work.

When we had fired off all of the HEs, Chew Een Lee's machine guns were set up, and they stitched patterns of tiny white plumes across the wake. This, too, greatly entertained the swabbies.

Corporal Burris—Pat, the mortarmen called him—was one to take advantage of the sailors' curiosity. When I was called away from the sandbag drill, Burris offered a boatswain's mate the opportunity to fire off a few rounds with the mortar. I found out later that Burris had traded with the bos'n for a berth in the crew's quarters. I saw no reason to discourage Burris's initiative, but I told him to be careful that our first sergeant didn't learn of his chicanery.

When we weren't holding school on the hatch covers, we used them for physical exercise. Running in place, squat jumps, physical-drill-under-arms, and push-ups. There were few complaints from the troops about the intensity of these workouts. Word had come from the 5th Marines that the fighting on Korea's bare, steep hills in steaming heat had quickly exhausted even those superbly conditioned troops.

Staff Sergeant Richard revealed himself to be an all-purpose NCO and an "acquisition specialist." One day he produced a set of boxing gloves, and the men of Baker-One-Seven immediately became avid pugilists.

We had a few experienced boxers. Pfc. Ron Moloy had fought as a middleweight out of Camp Pendleton for the fleet championships. Moloy enjoyed displaying his prowess against the larger men like Tony Swandollar. Swandollar, a sergeant squad leader from the 1st Platoon, was a six-foot, two hundred-pound bruiser. Moloy would dance around Swandollar, flicking jabs into his face, and then would fancy-step out of reach. The big sergeant was a durable fighter, though, and patient; he would plod after Moloy, fists slung low and poised for a chance to throw a powerhouse punch. When it came, Moloy would be bounced halfway across the makeshift ring, which was bordered with raucously cheering Marines. Swandollar would grin and bow to the crowd, then raise his gloved hands in the victor's pose until Moloy came at him again.

Other than Moloy's exhibitions, the fights were down-and-dirty slugfests. There was an abundance of roughhouse brawlers among the troops, regulars and reservists alike, and they swung the gloves with gusto.

Pvt. Attilio Lupacchini was one who fought with little skill but great enthusiasm. He had the build of a small gorilla and, when it landed, the punch of a large cannon. Sherman Richter, a burly machine-gun sergeant, would take on all comers. Jim Kovar and Jose Jane, a BAR-man from the 2d Platoon, were an energetic match. Then Glenn Galtere, boyish looking but tough as leather, would go at the hefty machine gunner, Raul Rendon, and both would slug until their gloves were wet with blood.

The majestic Gunny Buckley served as referee in these brawls, but he showed little interest in enforcing collegiate boxing rules. Sergeant Richard was timekeeper. Both the gunny and the sergeant were said to have wagers on these slugfests, as did most of the troops.

I was gratified to see my own Pfc. Frank Bifulk in the ring with Lupacchini. Bifulk was short-sighted without his thick spectacles, which he removed for the fight. He was also short-statured, like Lupacchini, and built like a bull. His fighting style, necessitated by his limited vision, was to get close to the victim and pound, hammer, and attempt to destroy. Lupacchini, on the other hand, utilized a windmill style. For three exuberant rounds, to the delight of the company, the little bull, Bifulk, and the little gorilla, Lupacchini, engaged in mutual annihilation. When Sergeant Richard clanged his mess gear to end the brawl, the troops and much of the ship's crew were in a cheering frenzy. It had been a grand fight. Both men were covered with blood and bruises, but at the final clang they wrapped arms and leaned against each other, exhausted.

My mortarmen swarmed into the square, pummeling Bifulk with congratulations. Perkins, who had been holding Bifulk's glasses, placed them carefully over his swollen eyes. I saw Burris then gently guide Bifulk out of the ring. Gene O'Brien, Lupacchini's platoon sergeant, followed with his man, and Baker-One-Seven was still whistling and cheering when the two fighters and their handlers went through the hatch and down the ladder to the sick bay.

Joe Kurcaba stood next to me. "This outfit is coming together," he said. Joe rarely smiled, but there was a big grin on his face after that fight.

• • •

In the transit officers' quarters the bunks were stacked only four high, and we enjoyed the privileges of the ship's wardroom, a combination dining room, conference room, and lounge. Although we ate the same grayish food endured by the troops, it was served to us on china plates and white linen tablecloths, and we didn't wait in the chow lines.

When we weren't on deck with the troops, the officers spent the waking hours around the wardroom tables. Captain Wilcox led us in review of the principles and lessons of rifle company combat. He and Joe Kurcaba used their own battle experiences as illustration. They focused on the chaos of combat and how the "best laid plans" always disintegrated under enemy fire.

"War is hell," Captain Wilcox, who had much experience at it, would tell us, "but you never know what particular kind of hell it's going to be."

We studied the after-action reports that had come from the 5th Marines. The North Koreans they had faced were tough, skilled fighters, every bit as tenacious in battle as the Japanese had been in the bitter Pacific island fighting of the last war. The Red soldiers—the 5th Marines called them "gooks"—were well trained in the Russian style of combat, with effective use of supporting armor, mortars, and artillery. They were also adept at night fighting. Fighting at night was a combat skill that we had yet to learn. We would do so under fire, and at terrible cost.

The 5th Marines' reports made much of the battle terrain, difficult tangles of high, sharp hills that were interwoven with twisting valleys and wet rice paddies. It was ground that was easy to defend but difficult to attack, and the well-led North Korean soldiers used it to their advantage.

The heat was a major problem encountered by the American troops. In Korea, late summer temperatures were commonly over one hundred degrees, saturated with steam-bath humidity. Even though they had been conditioned on the sunbaked hills of Camp Pendleton, the 5th Marines had not been prepared to climb and fight in the debilitating temperatures that hit them when they went into battle. Up with the rifle companies, where movement was rapid and water scarce, more men had dropped from heat exhaustion than from enemy fire. Availability of water on the fighting hills had become as critical as supplies of ammunition.

Now that he was spending time with us, Captain Wilcox gained the full respect of the lieutenants of Baker-One-Seven. We appreciated that he was a thoroughly professional combat officer. He had firsthand knowledge of conditions under enemy fire, a great benefit, especially since all of us, except Joe Kurcaba, were untested.

We realized, too, the enormity of the job our skipper had done at Camp Pendelton. He had gathered under him a hodgepodge of 215 men, most of them untrained for the job, and had formed them into a Marine rifle company. He had worked through stacks of forms and records and affidavits. He had assumed accountability for each of our hundreds of weapons. He had chronicled and signed off on medical examinations and immunization shots, and had seen to it that dog tags were stamped out and issued. It was good that he had a first sergeant such as Caney, because Captain Wilcox was no more a paperwork Marine than were his lieutenants.

After Captain Wilcox's "lessons" were over, the lieutenants would linger over cups of the potent Navy coffee and talk of our time in the Corps, about home, about women, about sports and cars, and about the great liberty ports of the world. All of us, except Weaver, had served enlisted time during World War II, and we had learned the art of telling sea stories.

Bill Graeber spun lurid tales of MP duty that had taken him into the back allies and bordellos of occupied Japan and North China. Hank Kiser's outside interests went to hot cars and tall blondes, and he described in loving detail the acquisitions he had made in both hobbies.

Weaver, the general's son, had grown up in the Corps and could tell stories about legendary names, the Marine generals we lieutenants knew only from afar. As a boy growing up on Marine Corps bases he had been patted on the head, had gone horseback riding, and had hunted with the likes of General Cates, our commandant, and General Shepherd, who commanded all of the Marines in the Pacific theater.

Although he knew little about life outside of the Corps, Weaver had no enthusiasm for being a career Marine. He had failed to qualify for the Naval Academy, or didn't try sufficiently to make it. Instead, he had attended a small California college and had acquired a taste for civilian life. He had taken his commission after college only to please his father, the retired general. Weaver had intended to resign at the end of June, when his current contract expired, but Korea had changed that plan.

"As soon as we get back to the States. . . ," Weaver would muse, ". . . as soon as we get back, I'm getting out. Then I'm going to find out what it's like to live a real life in the real world."

We tolerated Weaver's lack of dedication to the Corps. His experience in the field was similar to ours; he knew tactics and weapons. He was an amiable guy, and the firsthand stories he told about our generals gave us amusing glimpses into a world that was far over our heads.

Chew Een Lee seldom participated in our conversation when it drifted from serious business. He would talk only of tactics and weapons capabilities, and when we tired of those subjects, he would withdraw to another table and study a training manual or read a book on tactics. He was hardly a congenial companion, but on duty he had our full respect as an unequivocal professional.

One night I found myself standing next to Lieutenant Lee at the ship's rail. We were both breathing in the fresh air, relief from the stuffy troop officers' compartment, which afforded little more space and ventilation than the enlisted men's hold. We stood in silence for a few moments, watching the phosphorescence that gilded the black waves rolling below us.

"You are satisfied with your men?" Lee asked. His words were, as always, abrupt.

"I'd like to put them all through boot camp and then give them six months more training," I answered. "But they're hard-working kids. They've come a long way."

"You are too soft on them," said Lee.

"I can only get a sixteen-hour day out of them," I replied.

Lee straightened from the rail. In the dark I could feel his eyes boring into me. "They have no discipline. They fail to stand at attention properly. They fail to salute. I have heard them address you by your first name."

"Well, Lieutenant Lee," I retorted, "I can teach them how to use their weapons, or I can teach them military courtesy. If we're going to fight, it's more important for them to know how to shoot than to salute."

"They are disgraceful," Lieutenant Lee said. He spun from the railing and walked away from me.

To hell with you, I thought. I didn't say it, though. He might have run me up for insubordination—second lieutenant to first lieutenant insubordination. First Lieutenant Lee went by the book.

• • •

Joe Kurcaba never had much to say. He was amiable enough, but since he was in his thirties, we thought of him as an older man. He was friendly with me because I could use some of the Polish words and expressions I had learned from my wife's family. Joe and I talked about Polish holiday customs, especially Easter and Christmas when the priest would come to bless the home. Then everyone would share the special bobka bread and drink vodka; that was the tradition at Dorothy's house.

• • •

Pfc. Perkins approached me on deck one evening. "Sir," he said, "I mean, Lieutenant." The apple-cheeked kid had an air of innocence about him, and his mild manner made me wonder what had motivated him to join the Marines, even as a reservist. He was strong, though; I had seen him lug heavy loads of ammo up the Pendelton hills without tiring.

"Good evening, Perkins. At ease."

"Thank you, Lieutenant, Sir." Perkins fidgeted with his hands. He didn't know whether to leave them at his side or clasp them at the parade-rest position, behind his back.

"Relax, Perkins," I said.

"I never talked to an officer alone before," he said. "I mean, Sir." He jerked the utility cap off his head and held it at his side.

"Relax," I repeated. "How was your chow tonight?" Perkins was gaining a reputation as a chow hound; he ate more than anybody else in the mortar section. When I had inspected the chow line earlier, I had seen him going back for seconds. Or maybe it was thirds.

Troop compartment aboard the *USS Okanogan,* where there was space only for reading, writing, and sack time. Racks were stacked five and six high. Space on deck was limited, too, but the air was fresh. The voyage from San Diego to Inchon, Korea, took twenty days. PHOTO COURTESY RICHARD BAHR

On deck aboard the *USS Okanogan,* Tom Lineberry, left, with Frank Bifulk and Attilio Lupacchini, who put on a morale-building "boxing" match. Most of our on-deck time during the daylight was devoted to training. PHOTO COURTESY TOM LINEBERRY

Second Lt. Joe Owen takes a helmet bath after we had mopped up the last enemy position above Uijongbu. Five days of "combat training under fire" had made Baker-One-Seven a good Marine rifle company.

Platoon Sgt. King, left, and Gunny Foster were two NCOs of the "Old Corps" Marines who set high standards for the troops of Baker-One-Seven.
PHOTO COURTESY RAY LEFFLER.

Richard Lisota was a BAR-man with the 1st Platoon. Each fire team had a Browning Automatic Rifle (BAR), and there were nine fire teams per platoon. The BARs gave us fast-moving, heavy-hitting fire power. PHOTO COURTESY RAY LEFFLER

Ron Moloy, left, and Tony Swandollar make themselves pretty after the battle for Uijongbu. When we went back to Seoul, Captain Wilcox gave the company liberty and many of our troops ran afoul of rear echelon military police. PHOTO COURTESY RAY LEFFLER

Corporal Alphonzo "Pat" Burris was the only man in the sixty-mortar section who had experience on the gun before we formed up at Camp Pendelton. In combat he had a cool head and a sharp eye, and was an outstanding squad leader and forward observer. PHOTO COURTESY ALPHONZO BURRIS

In a surprise night attack, the Chinese hit us hard on this hill that looks down on the Sudong valley. It was our first encounter with the Peoples' Liberation Army. Our casualties were heavy, but theirs were horrendous and we held the hill. PHOTO COURTESY RAY LEFFLER

A squad of the 1st Platoon after the fight for Sudong-ni. Baker-One-Seven was among the first units to integrate. There were some "snapping in" problems initially, but none after we shipped out. Standing, Corpsman Mickens, Sergeant Allen, Pfc. Keister, Pfc. Wade, and Pfc. Littrel. Kneeling, Corporal Allen, Pfc. Godwin, Pfc. Lisota, and Pfc. Bardon. PHOTO COURTESY RAY LEFFLER

Getting a ride on the trucks usually meant that a firefight waited at the end of the trip. Unless we were needed in a hurry to repel or pursue the enemy, the rifle companies walked. PHOTO COURTESY RAY LEFFLER

Pfc. Tom Lineberry shows off his new winter gear. The parka and shoe-pacs and several layers of clothing gave protection from the cold, but they added weight to the weapons, ammunition, rations, sleeping bags, and ponchos that we carried up the mountains. When we climbed the mountains, we perspired; when we stopped, the sweat froze. Sweat-damp socks in the airtight shoe-pacs was the major cause of frostbite. PHOTO COURTESY TOM LINEBERRY

Machine gunners John Conlon, Sherman Richter, and Raul Rendon with an enemy soldier who came too close to their gun at Sudong-ni. Platoon Sgt. King stands behind Richter. Two Marines at right are unidentified. PHOTO COURTESY RAY LEFFLER

A rifle company prepares to attack the high ground. When we could get it, air support or artillery scathed the hill with preparatory fire for the assault. The Chinese knew our tactics well and, after Yudam-ni, never gave us a hill without a stiff fight. PHOTO COURTESY FRANK KERR

At the battalion aid station at Yudam-ni only the seriously wounded men were kept inside. The walking wounded who could handle a weapon were sent back to the line to fight. Blankets cover dead Marines in foreground.
PHOTO COURTESY FRANK KERR

Marines killed in action—KIAs—are loaded aboard trucks before the breakout from Yudam-ni. We never left our wounded behind and, when possible, we carried out our dead. In the rifle companies it was an article of faith that no wounded man would be abandoned to the enemy. PHOTO COURTESY FRANK KERR

"My Mom cooks a lot better than what they give you here," he answered. "But they give you plenty."

He reached into the breast pocket of his dungaree jacket and brought out a small Bible, its cover containing an engraved metal plate. "My Mom and Dad gave this to me before I left home," he said.

He handed me the Bible. Its engraving said, "To our beloved Merwin. May the Lord protect you."

"Do you think it will work, Lieutenant?" Perkins asked. "I mean, do you think it will stop a bullet?"

"It's as good a guarantee as you're going to get," I said. "As long as you do a good job with your mortar, and keep the enemy pinned down, you're going to make it OK." I put the Bible back in his pocket. "You keep right on carrying it."

"My Mom told me not to forget to say my prayers every night, too."

"That's going to help. Say some for me. For all of us."

"I do, Lieutenant. I say prayers for all the men and all you officers, too."

"We're going to need all the help we can get."

"Can I ask you something, Sir?"

"Go ahead."

"I'm trying hard to learn my job, but First Sergeant Caney says we'll never make good Marines."

"That's the way first sergeants are," I said. "That's his way of getting you to try harder. You'll be a good Marine if you keep working at it. When I was in boot camp, my drill instructor told me I would never make a good Marine, either. You just keep working hard at it. I'll keep an eye on you."

A big smile lit Perkins's baby face. He put on his cap, stiffened to attention, and gave me a parade-ground salute. He had been practicing that salute.

I stood at the rail for a long time, thinking about my men. Then I took out the snapshots that Dorothy had given me on the dock at San Diego. I had placed them in an order that I could remember when I fingered through them in the dark, one by one. The first picture was of Dorothy, trim and blonde in her glistening white bathing suit on the beach at Lejeune. Then, with the babies, Mike and Din, on the beach, splashing in the waves. Dorothy, dressed for Mass, with a wide-brimmed hat, standing on the steps of St. Cecilia's. Mike in a cowboy suit, two six-shooters dragging to the deck. Dinny, the baby ballerina. Dorothy and the babies together, waving at the camera. *Dear God, I did miss them.* In the dark Pacific night I saw

Dorothy laughing and I felt the plump arms of the babies squeezing around my neck.

• • •

NCOs are the heart and guts of an outfit.

Sergeant Winget, the former gunner's mate of the World War II Atlantic Fleet, took over small arms weapons instruction for the section. One of his methods was to take apart a BAR, an M-1 rifle, a carbine, and a pistol, then mix the pieces into a pile and have a man reassemble the parts. Blindfolded. It was a training trick he had learned from the company armorer, Staff Sergeant Richard.

Corporal Burris was a good instructor, and I let him give most of our hands-on mortar training. Like Winget, he had been a sailor in World War II and had seen combat in the Pacific. During the Okinawa campaign, while on a shore detail delivering gear to the Marines, Burris had hitched a ride on an amphibious tractor taking supplies up to the line and had spent some days humping ammo for a rifle company. Burris was the only one of us in the mortar section, including me, who had been under fire in ground combat.

Sergeant Lunney always looked like a recruiting poster Marine; his dungarees appeared freshly laundered and without wrinkles. He understood mortar section tactics, and I often turned the lessons over to him when we covered how the squads would move in support of the rifles.

Lunney was fortunate to have Cpl. Hugo Johnson in his squad. Johnson, the big, rock-hard ex-regular, had plenty of rifle company training, and he was filled with practical knowledge. With the possible exception of Burris, Johnson was our best gunner.

The men had begun to take pride in their outfit. They knew their weapons, and they stood well at the full-gear inspections we held on deck every day. The skipper remained as stern as before, but he could find little fault with their appearance. First Sergeant Caney's notepad went unmarked when he accompanied the captain on the inspections.

Each morning the company officers visited the troop compartments; often Colonel Davis would come along with Captain Wilcox. The sixties' area was always squared away: decks clean, racks clear, and weapons and packs properly stowed.

Morale was good. The men grumbled about the lousy chow, the cramped quarters, and the long hours of repetitive training. Sergeant Wright recognized the complaining for the good sign that it was. "As long as they keep bitching," he would repeat the old Corps bromide to me, "the troops are doing fine."

Another good sign: my young troops were getting salty. One early morning, with the sun still off the fantail and flying fish skipping out of the waves that ran the flanks of the ship, I gave the men instruction on the international rules of warfare—chiefly what a man is required to do if captured and interrogated by the enemy. The essential part of the lesson was that he would reveal only his name, rank, and serial number. "Name, rank and serial number, you people. Nothing more than that!"

Pfc. Robert Fisher, one of my gangly teenagers, had lost interest in the subject; his attention was fixed on the flying fish that skimmed the waves.

"Fisher!" I snapped. "Stand to!"

Fisher was jolted out of his reverie. He whipped into a rigid parade-ground stance, his eyes blinking into focus and a blush showing under the tan of his face. Only a few weeks ago this kid might have been receiving admonishment from one of his high school teachers.

"Y-y-yes, Sir! Uh, aye, aye, Sir!"

"What do you tell the enemy if you surrender to them and you are interrogated?"

Fisher's answer was immediate. "Sir, I won't surrender. I'm a Marine, Sir!"

Fisher's gung-ho response drew guffaws from the men of the mortar section. "Wrong answer, Fisher," I came back at him. "But you've got the right spirit."

Fisher smiled broadly. He began to sit down.

"Not so fast, Fisher," I stopped him. "You are at attention." I turned to Sergeant Wright. "Sergeant, see to it that Pfc. Fisher puts that gung-ho spirit to work cleaning out the heads for the remainder of the cruise."

"Aye, aye, Sir," responded Sergeant Wright, pencil to the notepad that sergeants carry. The men guffawed louder. Fisher's eyes stayed riveted on me for the remainder of that morning's school.

• • •

While Baker-One-Seven was still on the way to the war, the 1st and 5th Marines forced a landing across the tidal flats at Inchon harbor. The radio in the ship's wardroom was tuned to the tactical net, and we listened to commanders on the beach as they reported the action to their senior echelons, and made calls for air and artillery support and ammunition resupply.

Over the static and the crackling transmissions we could hear shells exploding, small arms fire, battlefield curses, and the screams of wounded men. The transmissions were piped out to the deck where the troops also listened to the grim sounds. I left the wardroom and went out to be with my mortarmen. They sat in a tight cluster, staring intently at a loudspeaker, and they heard the war that was about to swallow us.

CHAPTER FIVE

Baker-One-Seven didn't go ashore until six days after the 1st and 5th Marines stormed Inchon harbor. By then the fighting had spread across the Han River and into the city of Seoul. We were making bets that the war would be over before we got into it.

At first, we had the ignoble work of unloading supplies in the hot, stinking harbor. Shells from the Navy's big guns thundered overhead, and the crooked-wing Corsair planes catapulted from the carriers, headed for the battle lines. Distant artillery rumbled and machine guns and rifles crackled faintly. Landing craft and amphibious tractors marked by large red crosses carried casualties toward the USS *Hope*, the hospital ship.

Our troops, stripped to their skivvies, sweated, labored, and bitched. I overheard Sergeant Dale complain to a working party. Dale was a veteran of a Negro supply company during the Pacific war. "Hell, I was ten times closer to the action when we brought in the gear on Iwo Jima. I thought this time I'd see some real fighting, being in a gung-ho rifle company with you white boys."

I resolved to request a transfer up to the line before the fighting ended. Casualties were high among the lieutenants in the forward regiments; there had to be a need for replacements.

I found Captain Wilcox on the docks near a huge pile of crates marked for forward deployment. First Sergeant Caney was with him, checking off the numbers that were stenciled on the crates.

"Skipper," I approached him, "any word when we're going up on line?"

Captain Wilcox looked up from his clipboard, annoyed. "Last word I had, Colonel Davis said we are doing a good job unloading ship."

I should have backed off; I plowed on. "Sir, the word is that the 1st and 5th Marines are running short on lieutenants. I'd like to request transfer as a replacement . . ."

The captain turned to Caney. "First Sergeant, if you will excuse us, I'd like a word alone with Lieutenant Owen."

"Yessir!" responded Caney. He knew I was about to get reamed, and he smirked at me as he disappeared behind the piles of crates.

Captain Wilcox gave me that glare once again. "You want to transfer out of Baker-One-Seven?"

"Sir, it's only that I want to put my training to some use before the fighting ends."

"And to hell with your men. To hell with the company. Is that right, Lieutenant?"

"No, Sir, Captain, it's just that . . ."

"It's just that you want to jump ship on us." The skipper's face glistened with perspiration, and he had turned a steaming red. He had been angry with me before, but never like this.

"Sir, I . . . "

"OK, Lieutenant, here's what you do. You put your request for transfer in writing and I'll forward it. Approved. No sense holding back a gung-ho, hotshot second lieutenant."

"Sir, it's not that I want to leave the outfit. I just . . . I thought. . ."

"Put your request in writing. That's all, Lieutenant. Dismissed."

"Sir, I . . ."

"Dismissed!"

I went back aboard the *Okanogan* and sat in the wardroom, pondering the mess I had created for myself. I was dismayed at Captain Wilcox's reaction. After the fact, though, I understood it. He didn't relish our rear echelon status either; it was a greater stigma for him than for me. My request to "jump ship" was a slap in his face. Now I no longer wanted to transfer, but my skipper had ordered me to put forward the request. I struggled to write it.

Joe Kurcaba came in for a mug of coffee. Joe drank more coffee than anyone I had ever known. He pulled up a chair beside me.

"You screwed up with the skipper, huh?" he said.

"He told you about it? Yeah, I screwed up. Wish I could figure a way to take it back."

Joe took a deep drought of the steaming coffee. "You boot lieutenants got to learn to take off your pack and stand at ease," he said. "There'll be plenty of action. More than you want."

"Yeah, I know you're right," I said. "Except the skipper ordered me to write this request for transfer. I hate to think what he'll say in his endorsement letter."

Another gulp of coffee. "Don't write it," Joe said.

"But, the skipper told me . . ."

"Forget it. I'll talk to the skipper." Joe finished the coffee and stood up. "Remember, Captain Wilcox was a second lieutenant once himself."

"Joe, thanks," I said. "Thanks beaucoup."

"I don't want to have to snap in a replacement mortar officer," our exec answered as he left the wardroom.

I wadded up my half-written request for transfer, poured myself a steamer of coffee, and figured I owed Joe Kurcaba a big one. The skipper, too.

The next day, after Joe Kurcaba told me that he had squared away the situation, I apologized to Captain Wilcox for my misguided request for transfer. He told me to keep my mind on the responsibilities I had been given. Aye, aye, Sir!

• • •

Finally, a long line of trucks pulled up to the docks and Baker-One-Seven clambered aboard them, on the way to the front. The 7th Marines, our regiment, had the division's left flank north of Seoul, and the North Koreans were giving them stiff resistance. After several days of slugging it out, Colonel Litzenberg calculated that it was time to commit the regimental reserve, which was Baker-One-Seven.

The trucks meandered over bomb-damaged roads and around shattered buildings. The stench of smoldering fires, rotting corpses, and human excrement was everywhere. Streams of weary Korean civilians headed in all directions. Women carried huge bundles on their heads and pushed carts that overflowed with belongings. Dirty children toddled beside bent grandparents, and the troops tossed candy bars to the kids. The Koreans, old and young, scrambled in the dirt for the candy.

The ride ended on the south bank of the Han River, outside of Seoul, and we went aboard amphibious tractors for the crossing. On the other side stretched a line of ambulance jeeps loaded with casualties from the forward battalions and headed back to the harbor. The sounds of combat were close now, and excitement rippled through the troops. Colonel Davis came by with Captain Wilcox and said that tomorrow morning we would lead the 7th Marines' attack north. "Good hunting!" the colonel wished us.

We set up shelter-half tents and bivouacked next to the howitzers of the 11th Marines, the division's artillery regiment. The big guns pounded all night, sending HE shells into the hills where the North Koreans waited to take us on. We had little sleep because of the din of the guns, and we were excited at the prospect of meeting the enemy face to face. I lay awake all night, wondering how I would measure up in combat.

At first light the battalion field kitchen gave us chow—powdered eggs, scrambled, and stacks of pancakes. We cleaned our weapons, and we each had a full issue of ammo, two grenades, a day's rations, and a canteen of fresh water. The trailer on the company jeep was loaded with extra mortar shells and cases of grenades.

The mortarmen were nervous when I inspected their weapons.

"Think we'll get shot at today, Lieutenant?" asked Pfc. Perkins as I handed his pistol back to him.

"We're taking the point for the regiment," I told him. "If the gooks are there, they'll be shooting at us."

"We heard that the 3d Battalion got hurt bad yesterday. Think it'll be rough today, Lieutenant?" Fisher wanted to know.

"Let's hope the 3d Battalion softened the gooks up for us," I answered.

Gunny Buckley came along the road where we waited to move out and told us to drop off our packs. Battalion would send them up later by truck. Then came the gunny's call, "Saddle up, Baker Company! Saddle up!" We formed two columns, one on each side of the dirt-packed road that headed north. Captain Wilcox was at our head. He shouted, "Baker Company, move out!" and we slung our weapons to our shoulders and marched after him into the war.

The sun came up hot, and we were soon perspiring under its fierce heat. It was a long, thirsty march, and the officers walked the files, reminding the men to go easy on the water. Trucks and jeeps drove between our two columns, spewing swirls of dust that coated our sweaty faces. As we passed by rice paddies we were greeted by the stink of human manure. I remembered the comments the captain had made on the beach at Camp Lejeune: "No place for gentlemen to fight a war."

White-clothed farmers worked barefooted and bent over in the paddies. They paid no attention as we went by. Nor did they heed the gunfire and explosions that grew in volume as we approached the steep hills ahead.

We passed a company of the 3rd Battalion that had been pulled off the line. Its men were sprawled along the road, unshaven and ragged, wearied by days of fighting. They yelled at us, noting our fresh faces and clean uniforms. "Hey, lookit the rear echelon commandos." "Where the hell have you girls been?" We ran a gauntlet of whistles and jeers.

Gunny Buckley came up the column. "You people knock it off," he bellowed at the hecklers. The gunny's big mustache bristled and his eyes glared. The jeers trailed off. Nobody messes with a rifle company gunny.

• • •

"Company halt! Officers forward!" came the order. I ran up the road to where Captain Wilcox stood, his binoculars raised. He told the platoons to form skirmishers across a bean field, on the east side of the road. There was an outburst of firing ahead, from Able Company's direction; Able had begun to attack a hill on the other side of the road. North Korean mortars whistled in and exploded, and Able's people hit the deck.

We quickly moved off the road, and when we were in position, each lieutenant reported to Captain Wilcox on his hand radio, the walkie-talkie. On the company net, "Baker-Six" was the company commander; "One," "Two," and "Three" were the platoon leaders; "Four" was the machine guns; "Five," the mortars; and "Seven" was the exec.

"This is Baker-Six. Move forward. Out!" Captain Wilcox ordered when we all reported ready. As we started across the bean field, we were greeted by a fusillade of "thwacking" sounds—North Korean bullets tearing through the bean plants. Thwack! Thwack! Thwack! all around us. I kept an eye on my men. They crouched low, but they stayed together and moved ahead.

Then the cry, "Corpsman! God, I'm hit!" A few feet from me a Marine from Kiser's platoon writhed on the ground, his hands clutching his belly. Grayish-red intestines pushed through his fingers, and blood stained the ground as he thrashed about, screaming his pain and terror. For the first time I felt the shivers of dread, the awful fear that comes with combat.

I froze—*A second! How many seconds?*—until I once again became aware of the thwacking sounds of the bean plants, and I yelled at the men. "Move it, you people. Keep it moving!" They bent lower to the ground as we went forward.

The North Korean mortars came. Spouts of earth and black smoke leaped about us, laced with flame and screaming shrapnel. The leaves from the bean plants spun in flurries, and the ground shook.

I was suddenly in the midst of a frenzied storm of noise: mortars whistled and crashed, bullets whined and leaves thwacked, men shouted prayers and blasphemies.

At the far end of the bean field was the dike of a rice paddy. We headed for its cover. A string of mortar shells exploded around us, and a man threw himself to the ground, kicking and screaming.

"Can't take this! Can't take this!" screeched the fear-stricken Marine, and he curled himself into a fetal ball.

I ran to him and prodded at him with the butt of my carbine. "On your feet!"

His head was buried in his arms. "Can't take it!" he wailed.

"Get up or I'll shoot you!" The sound of the words, coming from my mouth, was unreal to me.

"Jesus, don't shoot me," the man whined. Tears cut pale streaks through the dust on his cheeks, and he stared in horror at my carbine, which was inches from his face.

I grabbed the man by his collar and pulled him to his feet. "Move!" I yelled.

Sergeant Dale from the 1st Platoon ran toward us. "I got him, Lieutenant," Dale said. "He's from my platoon."

Dale spun his man around and booted him forward. "Don't you fall out on me again. Never!" Sergeant Dale roared, and the two of them ran, crouching against enemy fire, to rejoin their advancing platoon. A few yards from where we had been standing a mortar shell exploded, creating a shallow crater among the bean plants.

I scurried for the dike. Three of our men were still down in the field behind us, and the corpsmen—Mickens, Davis, and Toppel—crouched over them.

The mortarmen huddled in the shelter of the dike. Bullets swarmed overhead, but the enemy mortar shells were hitting behind us. The stench of the rice paddy mixed with the acrid smell of gunpowder and exploding cordite. My body trembled.

Sergeant Wright scurried to me and reported that all of our men had made it this far. "No one hit, Lieutenant. You want the guns up?"

"Yeah. Keep them close to the dike, though. I'll see if I can spot where that gook fire is coming from." I hoped that my voice wasn't shaking.

"Aye, aye, Lieutenant," said Wright, and he ran to the men who waited for orders.

I crawled up the dike to peer over the top. Smoke obscured my view, but far ahead and across the road I detected some movement. The enemy positions were difficult to locate; no flash came from their weapons when they fired.

I raised my binoculars. Before I could focus on the target, however, a flurry of bullets pelted the dike, and spurts of pebbles and dirt stung my face. I jerked my head back down into cover. Beside me a rifleman tumbled away from the dike. He made a choking sound, and his helmet bounced to the ground. Blood gushed from his head, which had suddenly become a wet, crimson pulp. Another wave of fear shuddered through me, a massive, paralyzing force. Again I froze, aware only of that blood-drenched face and head.

Captain Wilcox's voice crackled out of my walkie-talkie. "Baker Five. This is Six. Come in."

The voice snapped me from my paralysis. "Baker-Six, this is Five. Come in, Six." I was already scrambling back up the dike; I knew the skipper wanted the sixties to bear on the North Koreans who had us under fire.

"You getting those guns cranked up, Five? Over."

"Roger that, Six," I said into the radio. "On the double."

Sergeant Winget's gun was a few yards away, behind the dike, and I crawled over to get in front of it. "Stand by for HE fire mission," I called to Winget.

"Number one gun standing by. HE fire mission," the staunch Winget called back.

With all the will I could muster, I forced my head above the dike, binoculars at the ready. The terror of having my head blown to a pulp was diminished by my fear of losing the respect of my men.

The smoke near the dike hid me from the enemy. North Korean bullets flew nearby but over my head. Streams of tracers floated toward us, coming from the enemy hill. I followed them back to their source, a concealed machine gun.

I raised my carbine straight up to serve as an aiming stake, on line with the enemy gun. "Aim on me," I yelled to Winget. "Range five-zero-zero. One round. Fire when ready."

"One round HE. Range five-zero-zero," responded Winget. Veeder, his gunner, set the bipod, while Fisher readied a round, pin pulled and two charges removed from the tail fins.

"Fire!" called Veeder, and Fisher dropped the round into the tube.

A hollow "thunk!" and Winget yelled, "On the way!" My sixties had fired their first round in a shooting war.

I held the glasses on the target. After ten seconds a puff of smoke appeared—off to the right and short. Enemy bullets thudded the dike and buzzed overhead.

"Left five-zero. Up five-zero," I called the correction, which Winget echoed to Veeder.

"Thunk!" went the tube again, and Winget yelled, "On the way!"

I caught the arc of the shell and followed it toward the enemy machine gun. A ball of black smoke puffed up, a close hit. "Fire for effect!" I called. Winget began to pound the enemy machine gun, and its tracers stopped coming at us.

All along the dike our Marines were sprawled, heads below the edge. The corpsmen had moved their wounded alongside the road, waiting for the ambulance jeeps—the meat wagons—to come up. There were two bodies, faces covered by ponchos. They were Baker-One-Seven's first killed-in-action, the KIAs.

My radio crackled again. "This is Baker-Six. Start moving your men across the paddy. On the double. Acknowledge. Out."

The lieutenants acknowledged, and we led the men over the dike into the stinking rice paddy. The water was ankle deep and had the stench of an open latrine. The men splashed through the vile stuff, voicing their disgust.

My temperamental walkie-talkie stopped communicating. Gilberto Garcia, now the captain's runner, ran to me with a message. "Skipper wants you to bring your mortars to the road, Lieutenant. On the double. We're gonna take a hill up ahead."

I told Sergeant Wright to lead the men to the road while I went ahead to meet the skipper. I went at a trot, and the troops cursed at the filthy water that I spattered on them. Enemy fire had all but ceased, and the cold lump of fear was gone from my stomach.

When I reached him, Captain Wilcox was soaking wet, stinking awful, and cursing. A close round had sent him diving full length into the paddy. Hank Kiser and Chew Een Lee were there, along with Jim Stemple from Able Company. We tried to ignore the odor that came from the skipper.

The captain outlined the situation. Able Company, on our left, was held up by heavy flanking fire from the hill that rose immediately in front of us. At its crest was a long, jagged ridge that dominated the way north. Able's skipper had sent Jim Stemple to scout the hill, and he estimated that an enemy platoon was dug in up there, thirty men or more, and reinforced with machine guns. The hill was covered with scrub brush and scored with deep ravines. The North Koreans were well concealed, and they had good cover from our fire.

The skipper showed his stuff; he was all business. "Stemple, you go up the left. Kiser, bear on Stemple and take the right. Owen, put your mortars on anything the gooks have showing on the hill. Artillery will cover while all of you get into position. When the big guns lift, watch me for the signal to go up the hill. Who has questions?"

Lee asked if there would be air support. The skipper said no; there wasn't enough air to go around. The planes were busy supporting the 1st Marines' attack through Seoul.

"That's it, then. Let's do it," said Captain Wilcox. He went to his radio to call preparation fire from the big guns. This was a far different skipper from the paper pusher we had known at Camp Pendleton.

My mortarmen watched with awe as the artillery bombardment began to pound the hill in front of us. Geysers of black smoke marched along the upper heights, throwing flame and shreds of torn steel. The concussions trembled the ground beneath us.

Someone said, "Won't be nothing left up there by the time that artillery lets up."

Staff Sergeant Richard, the company armorer, was crouched near us. "Don't fool yourself," he said. "Artillery never wipes out the gooks. Softens them up and keeps their heads down. But they'll be there waiting when the guns let up." Richard had fought with the Raiders in the Pacific, and now he carried a sniper rifle, the old-style Springfield ought-three with a scope.

Sergeant Wright pulled me aside. "Lunney's squad hasn't made it up here yet. Got tangled in with Lieutenant Weaver's platoon back in the rice paddy. I sent Branek to get them."

I needed Lunney's gun, but there wasn't time to wait. "When they show up, I'll be on the hill," I told Wright. "Bring them up with all the ammo they can carry."

I brought the other two squads up behind the rifle platoons that were forming for the attack. An artillery round landed close by, not fifty yards away; it was one of our own, a short round. It exploded with a terrible, shattering roar, like nearby lightning and thunder, and its concussion sent us diving to the deck.

"Jesus! What was that?" a voice quivered.

I scrambled to my feet. "Keep moving!" The men were all up, and they ran after me, bent under the weight of their guns and ammo.

"Get us the hell out of here!" someone cried.

I dropped Winget's squad off to cover Stemple's advance. While Winget and I talked with Stemple, Timmy Killeen, Stemple's runner, dashed across the field toward us. He had his helmet off, waving it and yelling, "Look what the slant-eyed devils have done!" He pushed the helmet at Stemple and me. "Lookit, Lieutenant! Shot a hole through my helmet. Right here!" He shoved his finger into a hole that went through the camouflage cover and the steel of the front of his helmet. "See? Went right through, ricocheted around, and dropped out! Might have killed me, the savages!"

"Damn it, Killeen," said Jim Stemple, smothering a laugh. "I told you to stick by me. You get killed, it's your own damned fault. Now stay where I can keep an eye on you."

Pfc. Killeen, who had endured combat at Peleliu and Okinawa, rammed the punctured helmet back on his head. "And it would make no difference if I told you the terrible headache it's given me? Sir!"

• • •

Our artillery had slowed by the time I reached Kiser's line with Burris's squad. The North Koreans were still buttoned up and weren't firing. Burris, with his sharp eye, pointed out a brushy area that was likely to conceal an enemy machine gun. I told him to register on it, and we would use that as a reference when I spotted targets up the hill. I took Nichols from his squad to serve as my runner. Nichols had impressed me as being a bright young lad. The two of us went to join Hank Kiser and we all waited for the artillery to lift.

Hank's radio squawked. The skipper's voice said, "This is Six. Final preparation fire on the way. Stand by to move forward." He stood with Lee on the road between the two platoons. There was a final crescendo of explosions. Then Captain Wilcox raised his carbine over his head and waved it forward. Baker-One-Seven went on the attack!

"Let's go, 3d Platoon." Hank Kiser went at a trot up the hill and his men followed, the line of them spread across a hundred yards of front. There were shouts, war whoops, and rebel yells. Lee's machine guns began to clatter, their tracers arcing over the advancing line and blazing into the upper hill. Behind us, Burris had a round out of the mortar within seconds. I walked up behind Kiser, now positioned between his leading squads, and I watched a line of our mortars hit above us. From Stemple's sector I heard Winget's gun going.

Two of Kiser's squads moved up in short bounds, while a third laid a base of fire. The first fifty yards went easily. Then the North Koreans popped out of cover and took us under fire. Suddenly the ground before us was scathed with torrents of bullets. Mortar shells whistled in and exploded along Kiser's line.

"Corpsman! Corpsman!" came a despairing wail. Ed Toppel lurched up from the prone position and ran toward the wounded man as enemy bullets spurted around him. Beside me another man went down with a grunt and did not move. Fear slammed at my gut once more, and I was flat on the deck. Nichols was down there with me.

"What do you want to do, Lieutenant?" Nichols's plump, young face, streaked with dirt and sweat, showed the same fear that had me in its terrible grip.

Jesus! The boy depends on me! I forced my head up.

Near a cluster of boulders, embedded at the upper end of a gully, there was a North Korean machine gun spitting down at us. A squad of rifles fired from there, too. Kiser's return fire was ineffective; the bullets from our machine guns and rifles splattered against sheltering boulders, doing the enemy no harm.

I forced myself to stand, but I was unable to see Burris at the foot of the hill to signal him.

Nichols stood up with me. "Nichols," I instructed, "get down to Burris. Fast as you can. If he can see that clump of boulders up there, tell him to drop some HE on it."

"HE on the clump of boulders," repeated Nichols in the fashion of a good runner.

"Right. And if Lunney's squad has shown up, bring them back here with you."

"And bring Sergeant Lunney's squad back here with me." The lad's voice trembled. "OK, Lieutenant."

Nichols scrambled back down the hill toward Burris, a flurry of bullets kicking up around him as he ran. He tripped but rose again and then disappeared out of the line of fire.

I stayed on my feet and went over to check Hank Kiser's situation. Hank was upright, but the front of his dungarees was dirt-covered. I wondered if he, too, had been forced to ground by the same overpowering fear that I had felt.

Hank yelled to his platoon sergeant, Archie Van Winkle, to put down covering fire on the enemy strong point. Then he told his runner, Jack Gallapo, to get over to the 3d Squad with the word to move up the ravine, under the cover of Van Winkle's base of fire.

The enemy fire had become more intense. There were more cries for the corpsman. Hank turned to me. "Can't you do anything with that machine gun up there?" My easy-going buddy had anger in his eyes; it was directed at me.

"I sent word back. We should be on it real soon," I told him.

"Well, damn it! I'm losing people up here."

"Coming right up, Hank," I said lamely.

Charley Baldwin's machine gun kicked up a cloud of dust every time it went off, and the dust drew enemy fire. Baldwin wanted to move the gun, but he didn't think he should do so without orders from his squad leader who was engaged elsewhere on the hill.

Lieutenant Lee came upon Baldwin's gun.

"Sir, I think we should move this gun," Baldwin said to his lieutenant. "It's kicking up dust."

"You have a good position here, Baldwin," responded Lieutenant Lee. "I'll show you how to handle the dust problem."

Lee opened his canteen and walked around the machine gun, sprinkling precious water as he went.

"Now fire off a burst," ordered Lee.

The machine gun fired but raised no dust. Lieutenant Lee walked on up the hill, ignoring the enemy bullets that hit around him. Charley Baldwin was impressed with his lieutenant's calm.

Cpl. Charles Love's fire team of four men dashed across an open space toward a deep crater where they could get better aim on the enemy firing at them from above. Three of the men made it to the safety of the crater. The fourth man took a hit in the chest and went down before he reached the depression. Love crawled back to the wounded man. Enemy fire enveloped him, but he put himself in front of the man who was gurgling blood and trying to say prayers.

From where they lay sprawled on the ground, Love could see the North Koreans who were firing at them. He called to Galtere, his BAR-man. "Glenn, up there at ten o'clock. That line of bushes. Give 'em a burst."

Glenn Galtere had never known greater fear than this, but realizing that his fire team leader was risking his life, Galtere stood up quickly, spotted the line of bushes, and let loose a string from his automatic rifle. He ducked back down again and the rifleman beside him popped up, emptying the remains of his clip at rapid fire.

Love called, "Little higher, Glenn. Give 'em a long burst. We're coming in!"

The two Marines in the crater arose together and put down covering fire with the BAR and the rifle. Love dragged the wounded Marine into the shelter of the crater, but he was already dead when his three comrades tried to tend to him.

• • •

Nichols was out of breath and exhausted when he reached Burris's position at the bottom of the hill. He blurted out his message, though, and Burris set the gun in the direction I had instructed.

Lunney's squad—minus Sergeant Lunney—had reached the position, and Burris told Nichols to lead them up to me. He sent his ammo carriers with them, loaded with the ammunition that Joe Kurcaba had brought along the road in the company jeep.

Bifulk went with the ammo carriers. Halfway up, he and the rest of the mortarmen dropped to the deck under a barrage of Korean mortars and small arms fire. Bifulk knew he should keep moving, and as he looked for the next safe spot, he saw Lieutenant Lee walking up the hill through the thick enemy fire. Bullets scraped the ground, and a mortar round exploded so close that its concussion staggered him. But Lee kept walking.

"Hey, Lee," yelled Bifulk. "Get down. We're getting shot at."

Bifulk had Lieutenant Lee's attention. The lieutenant dashed to where Bifulk was hugging the ground. "You addressed me as Lee?" he asked, standing over the astonished young Marine.

"Jesus, yeah. Get down, you're drawing fire."

"You! On your feet," demanded Lee. Bullets zipped through the air, punctuating the bizarre scene of a lieutenant bracing a Pfc. to attention in the midst of a firefight. "You call me Lieutenant Lee! Or Sir! You understand that, Marine?"

"Yes, Sir! Y-y-yes, Sir!" stammered Bifulk, wishing that he were in a very deep foxhole.

"And you never forget that. Understand? Now carry on," said the lieutenant, and he proceeded to walk farther up the hill, seemingly oblivious to the enemy fire.

"What the hell," thought Pfc. Bifulk, and he got up to walk behind Lee. The rest of the mortar squad arose and followed Bifulk.

• • •

Although it seemed much longer, it was only minutes before Burris had the mortars firing on the boulders where the Koreans had set up their machine guns and supporting rifles. Not direct hits, but close enough to force the enemy to keep their heads down and raise enough smoke to enable Kiser to move his people up the ravine and into grenade range.

I was standing at the foot of the ravine when Nichols arrived, bringing the mortar squad. Corporal Johnson led them; Sergeant Lunney, Johnson informed me, was "lost in the shuffle" while crossing the rice paddy.

I found a place for Johnson to set up the mortar, sheltered from the Koreans' direct fire. Platoon Sergeant Van Winkle's rifles and BARs were drawing most of the enemy attention so few bullets came our way. Lee had displaced his machine guns forward, and they now scathed the ground below the ridge.

Gallapo came down the ravine to tell me that Kiser wanted the mortars to pound the North Koreans who were up in the boulders before he made an assault on them. Johnson had already set his gun on that target, and I called for him to drop a registration round. Range was only two hundred yards, and his third shot was a direct hit. We fired for effect, and the concentration blackened that part of the hill.

While the mortars obscured the enemy's view, Van Winkle moved his people up. Near the top of the ravine, Hank Kiser positioned his assault squad to follow a barrage of grenades into the enemy position as soon as the mortars lifted. The ammo carriers for the machine guns filled in with the riflemen on the line of assault, ready to charge up the last few yards of ground. Lee was with them, bayonet fixed to the tip of his carbine.

The mortars fired a final barrage. Their explosions were followed by the sharper impact of grenades thrown at the enemy holes. Shouts and war cries swelled from charging Marines who leaped, bayonets pointed, into the enemy positions that were dug along the face of the ridge. Some of the North Koreans stood to fight, their bayonets also fixed, but they were cut down. Others scurried over the hill; many were shot from behind as they tried to escape.

Van Winkle hurriedly put the men in defensive positions, wary of a counterattack. Staff Sergeant Richard had joined the assault. He propped his sniper rifle on a large boulder and scanned the back side of the hill, searching for targets. Hank Kiser walked the ridgeline, where he met Jim Stemple, whose platoon had won the other end of the ridge. I ran to join them.

"Better late than never," Hank said to me, referring to my earlier delay in giving him support fire. "But damn good shooting."

Chew Een Lee walked over to us. "The men performed well," he said. "We may have the makings of a good rifle company."

Captain Wilcox came up. He had followed the attack from a short distance in back of the 3d Platoon. Behind him, staggering up the steep incline, came Gunny Buckley. He was breathing hard and his face was pale from the exertion.

Captain Wilcox studied the position, ensuring that we had set a proper hasty defense against counterattack. Then he turned to the three of us, Hank Kiser, Chew Een Lee, and me. "Well done," he said. "Tell your men that. Well done!"

We knew that it had been a far-from-perfect exercise. Some of the men had been slow to respond to direction. Not all of our orders were clear enough for quick and effective fire and movement. We were fortunate that the enemy had not chosen a "fight-to-the-death" defense of this hill, as they would when we advanced farther north.

CHAPTER SIX

I t took five more days of fighting for the 7th Marines to push north to the shell-ravaged village of Uijongbu. On every hill the North Koreans resisted with all of their remaining strength. Uijongbu commanded both a mountain pass and the junction of roads they needed to secure their retreat from the 1st Marine Division's main effort, out of Seoul. For Baker-One-Seven it was combat training under fire; in those five days we became a good Marine rifle company.

After we had taken that first hill, Colonel Davis summoned us back down to the road. Up ahead, Charlie Company had been badly hurt while taking stubbornly held high ground. We advanced past Charlie and assumed the regiment's lead. When we came within range of enemy machine gun and mortar fire, we went into the attack again.

We went two platoons abreast, Graeber left of Kiser. Weaver's platoon was company reserve, and I had all three of my guns in support. When we had nearly reached the top, Captain Wilcox pushed Weaver's platoon through Kiser's for the final assault. Platoon Sergeant King led the charge, and we could hear his piercing rebel yells all over the hill.

Once again it was a ragged performance—orders confused in the hellish noise, men who bunched close together, and some who hesitated to risk the move against enemy fire. However clumsy we were, though, we had the fundamentals right: the NCOs directed their sectors of fire; the fire teams went forward in bounds, covering each other as they progressed; our machine gun and mortar fire stayed ahead of the advance and kept enemy heads down.

Our casualties were light: no KIAs on the second hill and only a few men carried off on stretchers. Compared to the bitter fighting of the division's main effort through Inchon and into Seoul, we had an easy time of it.

. . .

Sgt. Earl Kinney earned his second Purple Heart in that fight. Kinney, one of Lee's machine gun section leaders, had been wounded the first time in the Pacific war. As he directed fire for Pfc. Raul Rendon's gun, he was picked off by a North Korean rifleman. It was a shot to the belly, but Kinney's cartridge belt deflected most of the impact. It was enough to knock him flat, though, and open his gut. Doc Mickens put a compress on the wound, and when the hill was secured, the stretcher-bearers came for him.

"See you back in the States, Raul," the sergeant called to Rendon as they carried him off. He sounded happy; for Sergeant Kinney, this had been a far easier war than the last one.

. . .

Corpsman Bill Davis was not with the 2d Platoon in its first assault. Back in the bean field he had sprinted to a man hit by shrapnel. It was the first casualty he had tended, a mangled leg and arm and severe blood loss. Lying on his side, hands trembling and murmuring prayers while bullets and shrapnel screamed inches above him, the teenage corpsman patched the wounds and stopped the blood. He knew, however, that his man needed more attention in order to survive. When his platoon disappeared over the dike, Davis judged it best to stay with the casualty.

After a long time, two Marines in a jeep spotted Davis, and they sped toward him across the bean field. The Marines leapt out, one of them carrying the big SCR-300 radio with the long antenna that whipped through the air. Corpsman Davis recognized the other Marine, Colonel Davis, the battalion commander.

"What's happened here, son?" asked the colonel.

"Sir, I need help with this casualty. He's pretty bad." The wounded man lay still now, wrapped and sedated. There had been no enemy fire in some time.

"What's your outfit, Corpsman?" asked the colonel, noting the red cross armband on young Davis.

"Baker-One-Seven, Sir. Second Platoon."

"Well, that's where you belong. Your platoon is a half mile up the road. They need you with them."

"Yes, Sir, but I didn't want to leave this man . . ."

"You meant well, Corpsman, but your job is with your platoon.

You do the best you can with the casualties and mark their position. The stretchers will come along."

"Yes, Sir, Colonel, but . . ."

Colonel Davis took the downed Marine's rifle and jabbed it into the soil by its bayonet. He set the man's helmet on the butt of the standing rifle. "Mark them like this," he said. Then to his radio man, the colonel directed, "Call a stretcher. On the double!" He turned to Corpsman Davis. "What's your name, son?"

"Davis, Sir. Hospital Apprentice 3d Cl. William Davis, Sir."

"My name's Davis, too," the colonel said. "You stay close to your platoon. You'll make a good Marine, Corpsman Davis."

• • •

We dug in night defenses on the last hill we occupied each day. The jumbled, peak-and-valley geography of Korea forced a change from the Pacific island tactics we had learned from our World War II mentors. The steep hills and tight valleys separated us from the other companies and the main body of the battalion. We had to set our own isolated perimeters, and we couldn't tie our flanks to the other companies for mutual support. The same held true for attack; almost always the battalion was channeled into attacking with one company, one hill at a time.

This isolated kind of fighting, pushing up to Uijongbu, made it difficult to communicate with battalion and the other companies. That problem was not solved. Much of the time we company-level officers were on our own initiative.

I learned how to deflect the fear. After the first jolt of it, which came with the initial shock of coming under fire, I would force myself upright and attempt to read the situation before the skipper's voice came crackling out of the walkie-talkie. Once I had rammed myself into action, the fear subsided. It never completely went away, though.

There was no deflecting the confusion that came with every firefight. Bewildering patterns of noise and grotesque scenes exploded all around. Men screamed in rage and pain and fear; swarms of bullets whined and splattered close by; the mortars blasted, hurled flame and slices of steel, and raised clouds of greasy black smoke. Despairing voices yelled, "Corpsman!" and someone would surely call, "What do we do, Lieutenant?"

In the turmoil the officers and sergeants made themselves visible and we shouted orders: "Watch your sector," or "Move up. Bear on me!" or "Gook machine gun. Ten o'clock. Three hundred yards.

Aimed fire." We subdued the fear and showed the men that we were in command.

We could have alleviated some of the confusion if our walkie-talkies had worked as advertised. The hand-held, two-way radios were supposed to transmit and receive up to a mile in distance. We found that they rarely functioned over a hundred yards, never over uneven terrain. We carried them because they were all we had, but we had little faith in them. Instead, just like front-line military leaders throughout history, we relied on line-of-sight communication—arm-and-hand signals—and we sent runners back and forth. In those first days of combat I learned to stay visible, and I learned the value of a good runner.

The North Koreans used whistles and bugles for battlefield command, more effective by far than our walkie-talkies.

• • •

After the first day's fighting, we dug in a defensive perimeter and Captain Wilcox called his officers together. His command post—the CP—was set in a hillside graveyard, a circular area of grass-covered earth mounds. In the waning daylight, the skipper laid the company map against one of the mounds. We were all there—Weaver, Graeber and Kiser, Lee and me, Joe Kurcaba and the skipper. We were in good spirits; in spite of three KIAs and ten WIAs for the day, we had pushed the enemy off two hills. None of the casualties had resulted from our own fire. Friendly fire is a common hazard in inexperienced outfits.

Captain Wilcox munched a big chocolate bar as he reviewed our performance. Beginning with the 1st Platoon, he told Weaver that he should have moved his people more quickly and restored their formation when we came out of the rice paddy. That was the same place where my third mortar, Lunney's squad, had been delayed. Weaver had little to say in response, just kept answering, "Yeah, you're right about that, Skipper." Almost as though he didn't give a damn. I thought the skipper should have jacked him up some more, and I also thought that I could do a better job running the 1st Platoon than Weaver had done.

The captain told Graeber that his platoon had bunched up too closely in their advance up the second hill. Had the North Koreans used more mortar fire on us, Graeber would have had serious losses.

Hank Kiser got chewed out for going up the gully on the first hill with his maneuvering squad; in doing so he had lost visual contact with the main body of his platoon and the company.

"Hell, Skipper," responded Kiser, "if those damned walkie-talkies were working, I wouldn't have needed to go up that gully. I didn't want that squad to get caught in a blind alley up there."

"Just remember, you're leading a platoon, not a squad," Captain Wilcox told Hank. "But your platoon did a good job today. I'll be around to tell them that."

Then he turned to me. "That third mortar squad of yours was damned slow getting on the hill this morning, Owen. We should have had their fire power while Kiser's people were setting up their assault."

"Sir, that squad got mixed up with the 1st Platoon when we came out of the rice paddy. I've instructed the squad leaders to keep a closer eye on Sergeant Wright and me when we displace."

"See to that! I want you in control of your men at all times." Then Captain Wilcox added, "But you tell your men that they did some good shooting today. I'll stop by to tell them myself."

"Aye, aye, Skipper!"

Lieutenant Lee received a "well done" for the machine guns' first performance. I thought that the captain might admonish Lee for making himself too visible during the fire-fights, but nothing was said.

The skipper then told us that we would jump off in the attack at first light next day. He ordered a fifty percent watch, every other man awake in two-hour stretches, and sent us off with another "well done."

• • •

Battalion acquired South Korean laborers who brought rations and water cans up the hill at the end of each day. They were small men, but they possessed extraordinary strength. On A-frames strapped to their backs they bore loads greater than their own weight. As they climbed the steep slopes, they bent forward until their noses seemed to touch the ground. One day, as a line of them climbed to the top of a hill, enemy mortar shells exploded among them, killing two. The others kept on climbing. Our men had great respect for the laborers and rewarded them with gifts of cigarettes and leftover cans of rations.

• • •

It was a terrible fight, the third day, as we attacked another hill on the approaches to Uijongbu. The closer we came to that junction town, the harder the North Koreans fought.

I moved behind Graeber's platoon, bringing Burris's squad onto the hill. I had made Nichols my permanent runner, and he stayed close. Across the road, to our right, there appeared a formation of North Koreans—twenty or more—who maneuvered to get behind Graeber's right flank.

Cpl. Dick Bahr, one of Graeber's fire team leaders, saw the surprise move and yelled for his men to put fire on that sector. The North Koreans disappeared into the deep ditch that ran along the other side of the road. They were moving in our direction, and we dove for our own ditch. Grenades flew toward us but landed wide. There was a machine gun up ahead; however, I couldn't locate it and its fire started to rain down.

I tossed my two grenades at the ditch where the North Koreans were concealed, and told Burris to have his men crawl over to a clump of boulders, twenty paces away. When the squad and its mortar were in cover, I told Nichols to go for it.

We were crouched together, but as Nichols turned to crawl away, a bullet speared his chest and threw him backward, against me. His blood spattered my dungarees. The boy made a terrible rattling sound, and then he was still, his teenage face expressionless. Burris watched, horrified, and I waved him back when he began to crawl toward us. Then I took a deep breath, pressed myself flat to the ground, and crept rapidly away from the ditch. I left Nichols behind me, where he had died.

Above us, Bahr's squad had its hands full as the enemy continued to shoot down at them. Although we didn't have the fire power of a rifle squad, I set my few mortarmen in a defensive line and prepared to repel the North Koreans if they charged across the road at us.

My calls to the skipper on the walkie-talkie were answered by static. Concussion grenades came from the enemy side of the road, feeling us out. They were short by yards. I heard Korean voices as more of them gathered in their ditch. I hurried to Burris, who had set up his mortar behind a fallen tree trunk. There were a dozen rounds of HE stacked within reach.

"Think we can fire in close enough to get at those gooks?" I asked Burris.

"I'll sure try," Burris replied. He was already cranking the bipod to minimum range—straight up.

Judging from the noise they were making, and the direction of their grenades, the North Koreans were preparing to attack, not more than thirty yards away. As soon as they received the signal—a whistle or a bugle—then they would storm across the road at us.

"Come in as close as you can bring it, Pat," I said. "Over that white rock by the road." The white rock was on our side of the road, in line with the gathering enemy attack. At minimum range a mortar shell makes a nearly vertical flight, vulnerable to wind shifts. We both knew that we risked short rounds and casualties from our own fire.

Under his breath Burris hummed "You Are My Sunshine," his way of deflecting the fear. When he had the hairline sight on the rock, he cranked up another half turn of elevation. The volume of enemy fire from above us increased, and spillover machine gun fire landed nearby. Across the road the North Koreans chattered and threw an occasional grenade.

When he was satisfied that the shot would not land on us, Burris rasped, "One round. HE. Zero charge. Fire when ready."

Merwin Perkins had a round prepared, all of the powder-filled glassine envelopes torn from the fins. "One round. HE. Zero charge. Fire!" he responded, a quiver to his voice. He dropped the shell into the tube.

Thunk! went the tube and whoosh! came the shell out of the tube. Burris crouched behind the gun, hand ready on the crank for the next round. I kept my eye fixed on the white rock we had used as the aiming point.

The explosion, fifty yards out, was a sharp, cracking wham! Dense black smoke and flame spurted upward, clouding the enemy side of the road. The blast was followed by screams of pain mixed with orders shouted in Korean.

"Come up a hair, Pat," I observed. "Just a touch and we got 'em."

"Aye, aye," muttered Burris. He nudged the elevation crank gently, keeping his eye to the hairline sight. "Fire when ready, Perk!"

"Keep your heads down," I called to the remainder of the squad. All of us pressed flat to the ground.

Perkins dropped the stripped round and had the next one ready to go as soon as it fired. He had our third round in the air before the second one exploded, close in to the enemy side of the road. Some of its shrapnel pelted the earth a few feet in front of us.

In the instant before our shells exploded, a whistle shrilled, the signal the Koreans had awaited. As they sprang from the ditch to charge, they were thrown flat and torn to pieces by our barrage of HE. Very few of them made it from the ditch to cross the road. Those who did were cut down quickly by the carbines of the mortarmen.

There were many difficult hills on the way to Uijongbu, but the mortarmen named that one "Nichols Hill." As soon as the company had secured the top, Burris took a stretcher party back for Nichols's body. Perkins, Bifulk, Veeder, and Westberg were all reservists who had come to Camp Pendelton with Nichols, and they went with Burris. When they laid him beside the road, they wrapped him carefully in his bloody poncho and waited with him for the meat wagon to come.

• • •

Each night, after the final inspection of the perimeter with Lieutenant Lee, Captain Wilcox, and Gunny Buckley, I put the mortarmen on fifty percent watch. I always took the first watch; Sergeant Wright would put his feet in his sleeping bag and prop himself against a boulder, a tree trunk, or a burial mound and doze for the two hours until it was time to relieve me. He talked to me about his four kids, and he worried about whether his wife had received his Marine Corps paycheck.

One night, in the early darkness, Wright said to me, "I heard that division's fixing to send the reserves home as soon as we take Uijongbu. Think there's anything to that, Lieutenant?"

There was scuttlebutt that the North Koreans were set to surrender to General MacArthur. Seoul had now fallen, and we heard that our Army was pushing a massive column up the peninsula. The North Koreans, unstoppable only weeks before, now retreated on all fronts.

"Word I get is that they're screening for men with dependents," I answered.

"That'll put me way up the list. With four kids."

"You make sure that First Sergeant Caney gets your name in," I told him.

"Don't worry about that. I remind the little S.O.B. every time I see him," Sergeant Wright said.

"You stay nice to the little S.O.B." I replied. "If anyone knows how to get the paperwork through, it's our first sergeant."

We grew silent, thinking of our families. I took the snapshots from the webbing inside my helmet and remembered their images, one by one.

Then I thought about the next day's mission and reviewed the fighting we had done that day. I tried to blank out the blood-screams, men killing each other and dying, the ground exploding, bursts of flame and stabbing tracers, the hot smell of weapons at full automatic, the stench of guts and feces oozing from a dead Marine. And the shuddering fear.

Nichols's blood still stained the front of my dungarees. My hands were soiled with blood and dirt and gun oil. We were now as filthy as the 3d Battalion people we had seen on our way into battle. The packs we had entrusted to the care of rear echelon were never returned to us. We carried only our ammo and chow, and we lived out of our pockets, with a blanket roll and a poncho for sleeping.

• • •

Under enemy fire, Captain Wilcox, Kurcaba, and Lee all walked straight up. It seemed impossible to me that they weren't hit, especially Lee, who was usually far forward. It set a good example for the men, and I tried to do the same. Although six feet five inches seemed a terrible disadvantage when the enemy was shooting at me, I stayed as erect as possible. When fire got too heavy, though, I went down on my hands and knees or crawled on my belly.

Once, under heavy fire, Joe Kurcaba walked over to me. I was flat on the deck, but I had my head up, peering through the binoculars.

"What can you see?" Joe asked, looking down at me. He seemed unaware of the bullets flying around us.

"Jesus, Joe, get down!" I urged, squirming to my side so that I could face up to him.

Joe shook his head. "If I get down, I might not ever get up again."

I couldn't speak to my superior officer who stood while I groveled on the deck. I forced myself to stand up, and I wished that Joe Kurcaba would get the hell away from me.

• • •

During the firefights, Joe Kurcaba ran the ammo supply up the hills to us. He used the company headquarters people for this work, and he told Lee and me that he wanted to see more of our ammo carriers. "Once your guns are set up in the attack, you send those carriers back down to me for more ammo. That way we don't run dry on the hill."

Keeping the forward weapons supplied with ammunition was a dangerous job that required exposure to enemy view. Under lethal small arms and mortar fire the bearers lugged heavy boxes of rifle, BAR, and machine gun ammunition, as well as crates of grenades, up steep, uneven grades. It was hard labor.

Just as difficult and hazardous was the removal of casualties down to the road where the meat wagons retrieved them for transport to the aid station. Because the hills were so steep, it took four Marines to lift a wounded man into his spread poncho and carry him, one man to a corner. To the great suffering of the wounded, the carriers would frequently stumble or dive for cover, dropping their man heavily to the ground. We could hear their screams all over the hill. Often it was impossible for the carriers to raise themselves higher than a crawl, and they were forced to drag the casualties over the rough ground. It was an article of faith with us that we always brought out our wounded, and only rarely was a dead Marine left behind.

• • •

We made mistakes.

The second night Captain Wilcox sent Graeber's platoon to an outpost hill, isolated from the company except for the SCR-300 radio that the skipper had sent along. I went with the detail, bringing Burris's squad.

It was dark when we climbed a steep, winding trail to the top of the outpost hill. The oppressive heat had dissipated with the sunset, but the men were weary from a day of climbing and fighting. Before us, separated by a valley, was a large rise that might hold an enemy force.

Graeber dug in his platoon, placing his rifles and the machine guns on the forward slope. I put Burris's mortar on the rear slope, a few yards from where Graeber had established his command post. Graeber, Platoon Sergeant O'Brien, and I walked the perimeter. I brought up the ammo carriers from the mortar squad to fill gaps in the forward line. Graeber set a fifty percent watch.

Bill and I didn't dig in; we spread our ponchos on the ground and used our blanket rolls for pillows. Then we took turns crawling the line in the dark to check the holes. Few men slept during the first two-hour watch; we were still green at night fighting, and very nervous. The surrounding hills echoed with sporadic rifle fire and artillery explosions.

All along the line there were fidgety challenges.

"Who . . . who . . . are you?" a shaky voice whispered as I approached a hole.

I hissed the password. "Lucky!"

"Who . . . Halt or I shoot! Who's there?"

"It's Lieutenant Owen. Damn it! Lucky Strike! Get it right!"

"Oh, jeez, yeah, it's Joe. Yeah, Lucky Strike. Sorry Joe," responded Frank Bifulk, the youngster who, six weeks ago, had left his home and teenage wife to become a combat Marine.

It was Bill Graeber's turn on watch when I was suddenly awakened by the loud, whooshing noise of a North Korean rocket flying by my head. The brilliant green streak flashed across our line, followed by a red one from the opposite direction. The North Koreans had our flanks measured. A bugle blared on the lower slope of our hill, the signal for an enemy attack.

Our line of foxholes erupted with rifles at rapid fire—BARs and carbines on full automatic, the machine guns pounding. Graeber rushed to his downhill foxholes. I yelled for Burris to put up illumination.

Burris had a round out of the tube within seconds. I was horrified to see it flare through the branches of a tree. In the darkness we had set the gun only a few yards from a broad, spreading tree. It was our good fortune that illumination shells did not explode on contact; a round of HE would have detonated in the branches and demolished everyone nearby.

"Cease fire! Cease fire!" I shouted. *Dear God, what a stupid mistake.*

The flare traveled two hundred yards and lit the area. There was no movement to our front; the North Koreans had gone to ground. The frenzy of our small arms fire slackened as Graeber, Sergeant O'Brien, and the squad leaders steadied their men.

Burris and I moved to the ridgeline in front of the now silent mortar. As we sought a new position, a machine gun opened on us from the opposite hill. Its tracers made lazy, blue-green arcs, followed by a chorus of "zings" past our heads, and enemy bullets pelted the hillside.

Another machine gun opened, winking short stabs of flame, and its tracers arched into the other end of our line. I stood there, fascinated by the pyrotechnic display. Burris, sensibly, had hit the deck. I yelled to him, "Get the mortar up for those machine guns over there."

"Aye, aye, Sir! On the way," responded Burris, who scurried over the ridgeline to gather his gun and crew.

Along the line Bill Graeber's squad leaders now directed tight patterns toward the base of the hill. The North Koreans down there were quiet. Then, from one of our forward holes came the cry, "They're moving up!"

Graeber shouted, "Steady, you people! Grenades ready."

Gene O'Brien echoed him. "Hold your fire. Grenades ready."

Someone threw a grenade. Another followed and another, and there was a cascade of short, sharp booms as they rolled and exploded down the hill. If the North Koreans were coming up, they came no farther.

Across the valley, the enemy hill erupted with a string of mortar shells that came from Burris's repositioned mortar. One enemy machine gun stopped firing, then the other. A long silence followed our barrage. The North Korean soldiers below us were again quiet. The mortar explosions had set small fires in the brush, but their light revealed no movement.

When dawn came Bill Graeber asked me to patrol the area where the North Koreans had mounted their attack. I took Burris, Bifulk, and Perkins with me; Sgt. Jim Bondurant, the 2d Platoon guide, brought along a four-man fire team. We found no dead enemy, no blood to show for our frenzy of fire. The only signs of the North Korean attack were empty .25–caliber cartridges.

Sergeant Bondurant told Graeber and me that our wild firing of the past night was to be expected of green troops. Bondurant was a reservist from Roanoke who had seen much Pacific combat. "Always the same," he said. "You get new people under fire for the first time and they shoot up all the ammo they got. Shoot anything that moves. Good thing we didn't lose anybody in all that fracas."

Bill took me aside. "I won't say anything to the skipper about that round of illumination that went up through the tree."

"Thanks, buddy," I said.

• • •

We were halfway up a difficult hill, an early morning attack, and the North Koreans were giving us a rough time. I had Lunney's squad with me, behind Hank Kiser's platoon. We weren't moving because above us were well dug-in machine guns protected by a platoon of rifles and automatic weapons. Hank had taken casualties and I couldn't get a decent shot with the mortars. As usual, the walkie-talkies weren't communicating. Captain Wilcox came up to see if he could get us moving, but the North Koreans were raking the hill with their machine guns and small arms fire.

The regimental air control officer, 1st Lt. Danny Holland, reached our position under the heavy fire. He had his radioman, Tony Tinelli, with him, as well as an observer to help him spot targets. The fighting for Seoul had ended, and the Corsairs were now available to support our front.

Danny was a fighter pilot, and he and I had worked training operations together back in the States. "Hey, Joe," he called, "we're here to rescue you. Air power wins wars!"

He crawled to where the captain and I were scanning the hill with our glasses.

"About time you started earning your pay, Danny," said the skipper, who also knew the earthbound aviator from way back. "What can you do for us?"

Danny threw a mock salute at the company commander. "I've got a flight coming on station," Danny said. He and his observer both had their glasses trained on the hill. Tinelli set up the radio, and its antenna glistened in the morning sun.

"Can you drop some smoke up there for a marker?" Danny asked me.

I called to Sergeant Lunney, who was near the mortar. Hugo Johnson was on the gun, already elevating the sights in anticipation of the mission.

"Stand by to fire willie peter."

"We don't have any WP up here," Lunney responded.

Damn! I caught Captain Wilcox's sidelong glance of exasperation.

"Dammit, Lunney!" I shouted, "All right, then, give me a man to run a message."

Lunney sent Pfc. Branek crawling over to us. "You want me, Lieutenant?" Branek was a burly farm kid from Kansas. His face streamed with sweat.

"Yeah, Branek. Get to Sergeant Wright, down by the road. Tell him to put a round of smoke on that outcropping of rocks up there." I pointed. "You see it?"

Branek looked up the hill. "Yes, Sir. I got it. Willie peter on them rocks."

"Take off. On the double!"

Without hesitation, the young Marine got up. "On the double!" he repeated and began to run, crawl, and tumble down the hill.

An alert North Korean machine gunner noted Branek's movement and tracers streaked toward him. Branek went down. All of us watching him let out a chorus of curses. The curses turned to cheers when the lad rose to run again, and the tracers were safely over his head.

Branek's movement, plus Tinelli's long, glimmering antenna, had captured the attention of the enemy. Their blue-green tracers probed around us, and a bullet splattered dirt in the captain's face. "Dammit, Owen!" the skipper kept saying, and it seemed an eternity as I prayed for Wright to get a round of smoke in the air.

"That damned antenna of yours!" I yelled over to Danny. "You people are drawing fire on us."

My aviator buddy, flat on the ground with his face in the dirt, turned toward me and raised a middle finger.

Up ahead, Hank Kiser wasn't moving, and we heard cries for Ed Topell, the 3d Platoon's corpsman. The skipper's walkie-talkie was drawing only squawks of static in response to his calls to the other platoons. I saw Danny Holland talking into his radio, as he and Tinelli huddled tightly together.

From the sky came the thundering racket of four Corsairs circling low. The noise of their engines drowned out all other sound.

Almost at the same time a plume of white smoke appeared, far up the hill. Branek must have reached Sergeant Wright because the smoke landed near the target I had designated.

The first of the gull-winged, dark blue Corsairs peeled from the circle and dove at the white smoke. Red tracers from its guns poured from the forward edges of the wings. The plane leveled off only yards above the ridgeline. We could see the pilot in the cockpit and the big, white Marine Corps emblem on the fuselage.

The next two planes followed in, skimming our side of the ridgeline. They threw white-streaming rockets at the North Koreans that tore up the ground when they exploded.

Then the fourth plane came in, this one dropping a pod of napalm. The big, black, coffin-shaped canister hit the ground, skipped a few feet above the surface, and exploded into a wall of flame that extended the length of the North Koreans' position. Two hundred yards below, we felt the shock of its explosion and a wave of searing heat.

"Jesus!" exclaimed Hugo Johnson, now standing beside his mortar.

"Damn," echoed Dean Westberg, Hugo's assistant gunner, who was not given to profanity.

Danny Holland turned to me and the skipper. "Air power wins wars!" he repeated.

Hank Kiser's men rose and advanced up into the North Korean line. We followed. The grass smoldered and the earth was black. At the top the air was filled with the kerosene smell of napalm and the stench of burned flesh. We saw the charred remains of North Korean soldiers scattered among their destroyed weapons.

I gave Branek a "well done" for running the word down to Sergeant Wright. I kept him as my runner to replace Nichols. Although he had a sullen disposition, Branek was a strong kid, and he had demonstrated that he could take care of himself in a firefight. Wright had told me, back at Pendelton, that Branek had wised off to the NCOs. Wright had straightened him out, though, without the need for me to step in.

The lad stuck close by me when we were on the move. He liked to carry my walkie-talkie, although neither of us had success in getting the thing to communicate.

• • •

The day before the regiment secured Uijongbu we came upon a small settlement, a cluster of mud huts with straw roofs. We had topped a small ridge that looked down into the tiny village. I was alone with Branek on the ridge, searching the terrain ahead of Hank Kiser's platoon, which had already passed through the village. The mortarmen were fifty yards behind us, waiting for me to give them the word to move out. No one had shot at us and my mortars had not fired a round in the day's advance.

Through my binoculars I saw a bearded old Korean emerge from one of the huts. "Papa-san," we called these grandpas who wore the traditional garb of high black top hat and flowing white robes. The old fellow stood before his doorway, watching bewildered as weapons-laden Marines passed through his village.

Crack! went Branek's carbine, only inches from me, and the old man fell to the ground. The tall, black hat fell beside him.

"Got the old bastard!" exclaimed Branek. His carbine was still up, searching another target.

"Goddam fool!" I yelled, astonished at the murderous act. Without thought I slammed the butt of my own carbine into Branek's ribs. Branek screamed with the pain and went to the ground, writhing. I stood over him poised to deliver another butt stroke.

"Goddam fool!" I screamed again as Wright came from behind me and held my arms. Winget was with Wright and pulled my carbine away.

"Hold it, Lieutenant," Wright shouted in my ear. "Hold it. What the hell happened?"

"You see what he did," I screamed. "I'll kill the . . ."

Doktorski, the corpsman, was already kneeling beside Branek. He snapped a syrette of morphine and jabbed Branek's arm.

I endeavored to control myself. Deep breaths. "OK Sergeant," I said, and Wright released his hold. The men were in a circle looking from me to Branek. They were silent.

"Goddamnit! He shot that old man for nothing," I yelled.

Through the pain Branek groaned, "Thought he was a goddamn gook. Thought he had a weapon."

"Any of you people see what happened?" Winget asked the men. No one responded.

"No witnesses," Wright said softly, to me. "Whatever happened, nobody saw anything."

The realization hit me. No-one except me had witnessed Branek shooting the old man. But, if anyone had seen me hit Branek I could be subject to a court martial for striking an enlisted man.

"No witnesses," Wright said again. "No one saw anything."

"This stays in the mortars," I heard someone say.

"Yeah," someone else responded. "This stays with us." There was a murmur of assent.

"Shall I move them out, Lieutenant?" Wright asked.

"Yeah, Sergeant," I answered numbly. "Move them out."

The morphine had not yet taken its effect on Branek. He ground his teeth together to hold back the cries of pain, and he was scared. I bent over him and said, "You and I know what happened, Branek. And you're going to have to live with it."

Branek nodded his head. He said nothing, but he blinked his tear-filled eyes and nodded his head.

"Take care of him, Doc," I told Doktorski. Then, I went to catch up with the mortarmen. When I walked past the old man's hut, a circle of women and children surrounded the body, crying their sorrow. An old woman caught my eye.

"I'm sorry," I said, although she wouldn't understand my words. "We're all very sorry."

• • •

On the last day Colonel Litzenberg had the 7th Marines attack as a full regiment. It was the only time we did so. The 2d Battalion took the high ground west of the road, and the 1st took the east side. When we had secured our objectives, the 3d Battalion, now rested and cleaned up from when we had seen them five days before, barreled up the road and swarmed into Uijongbu.

The North Koreans were spent and gave us little fight that day. They were short of people and ammo, and most of their heavy weapons had been destroyed. Captain Wilcox sent Garcia up with word for us to halt and dig in after we had pushed a few disheartened enemy soldiers off the last ridgeline overlooking Uijongbu. The town was a smoldering shambles, and through our glasses we watched the 3d Battalion searching street by street through the ruins.

My men set up the guns and dug their holes with little direction from me or the NCOs. They were combat Marines now, and they knew their business. Their faces and dungarees were blood-splattered and filthy with sweat and grime. We all needed to shave, even the fuzzy-cheeked teenagers.

"Let's get these people squared away," I ordered Sergeant Wright. "We don't want them looking like this when Colonel Litzenberg comes up to see us."

"Aye, aye, Lieutenant," snapped Sergeant Wright. He turned to the men. "All right, Bifulk! Perkins! Fisher! Veeder! Westberg! You people get down to the road and bring back water. The rest of you start squaring away. When the water gets up here, I want all your filthy faces clean. Turn to!"

The water detail trudged down the hill, the five youngsters bitching mightily. I watched with great pride as they went, my salty Marines.

CHAPTER SEVEN

The Army relieved the 7th Marines as columns of their trucks and tanks sped through Uijongbu in pursuit of the North Korean remnants. Clean-shaven, fresh-looking soldiers waved to us from the backs of their trucks. Our grime-covered people jeered at the soldiers and called them dogfaces and rear echelon commandos; it was very much like the insults we had endured from the 3d Battalion on the way to our first combat.

These Army troops weren't new to combat, though. For three months they had fought their way up the peninsula, taking horrendous casualties. Only when they paused at Seoul had they cleaned up and been issued new gear.

Many of the soldiers in the Army column were youthful South Koreans who were replacements for American casualties. They wore American uniforms and shared foxholes with our own soldiers. None of them spoke English, nor were they trained in the use of our Army's weapons and tactics. We shuddered at the thought that General MacArthur might impose the same handicap on the Marines.

• • •

As soon as word came that Uijongbu was secured and we were relieved, Gunny Buckley called the platoon sergeants together to distribute four gallons of sick bay alcohol. He and Corpsman Doktorski had procured the liquid dynamite from the regimental aid station in return for a North Korean bugle that the gunny had taken from a dead enemy soldier.

Sergeant Wright brought back two canteens of the clear lightning. Pat Burris "slicked" four big cans of pineapple juice, and this was blended with the alcohol in steel helmets that served as punch bowls. "Hawaiian Whoopee," Burris called it.

Into the night, Merwin Perkins, only weeks from home and Mom's cooking, his boyish face flushed with the unaccustomed spirits, raised his canteen cup in salute to his foxhole buddies. "Best goddamn fighting outfit in the whole goddamn United States Marine Corps!" he slurred.

"Yer damn well told, Perkins, ol' buddy!" and "Semper Fi, Perk!" responded his mates, as they drank the Hawaiian Whoopee and created their own legend of the battle for Uijongbu.

There were splitting heads and blurry eyes the next morning. Captain Wilcox came over to the section, shook every man's hand, and offered congratulations for a good job of fighting. He told me that my men had shown well, but he didn't add any personal praise for me. I wondered if he had heard about the mortar we had mistakenly set up under the tree. Nothing was ever said about that incident, which shamed me every time I remembered it.

First Sergeant Caney accompanied the skipper that morning, and Wright mentioned that it was the first time anyone had seen Caney on a hill since the fighting had begun.

"You'd better get on the good side of the first sergeant," I cautioned Wright. "And get him going on your family hardship transfer home."

The scuttlebutt came. We heard that Navy transports were in the harbor, waiting to take us to the States. Or, that all reservists were going to be immediately released from active duty. Or, that the 1st Marine Division was getting permanent occupation duty. The least desirable of all the rumors was that we would make an amphibious landing somewhere in North Korea and finish off the enemy soldiers who had escaped above the thirty-eighth parallel. The North Korean army, it was noted, had run away but had not surrendered.

• • •

We returned from Uijongbu filthy dirty and stinking badly. Captain Wilcox marched us to a field sanitation center where outdoor hot showers were set up and we were issued new dungarees and skivvies. We stood in line, naked, waiting our turn for the glorious hot showers. We were allowed to stay under the water as long as we wanted with all the soap we needed. When we came out, steaming pink and clean, we shaved and put on the new clothing. My mortarmen again looked like the fresh-cheeked kids I had been given only weeks before at Camp Pendelton. Except, there was now a hard look to their eyes.

• • •

While I was pinning my bars on the new dungarees, a second lieutenant with whom I had trained at Quantico and Lejeune came over to say hello. He was the officer in charge of the division's bath and laundry platoon.

"How did you end up with this duty?" I asked my friend. For combat-trained Marines, bath and laundry officer was considered an ignominious assignment.

He answered, "I was with regimental weapons and we weren't doing any fighting when we got here. I requested a transfer to a forward company and my skipper got upset. I got the transfer, all right. Bath and laundry platoon officer!"

"I feel for you, buddy," I said to him, and I gave silent thanks to Joe Kurcaba for saving me from the same fate.

• • •

A convoy of trucks carried us back to Inchon harbor. Baker-One-Seven set up shelter-half tents in a brickyard, a sun-broiled, shadeless place with red dust that smothered everything. The skipper complained about it to battalion, but there was nowhere else to put us. Inchon had become a major staging area, congested with thousands of soldiers and Marines, equipment and vehicles.

• • •

I was alone in the company headquarters tent with the inevitable paperwork when Chew Een Lee entered. With him was another Chinese-American, an Army lieutenant. This was Lee's brother, Chew Mon Lee, who had been with the Army's 2d Infantry Division since the beginning of the war. He had been wounded earlier and now had returned to duty.

Lee's brother was a friendly guy. He gave me a big smile and an energetic handshake. He respectfully addressed his brother as "Daigo," which meant, he told me, "elder brother."

"He demands that I call him that," said Chew Mon.

"I have to call him First Lieutenant," I said, and both of us laughed. I caught Chew Een smiling.

Chew Mon had gifts for Chew Een: a new type of Army belt suspenders and a pair of "banana clip" magazines that each held thirty rounds of ammunition for the carbine. These were new issue to the

Army and hadn't yet reached the Marines. Our carbine magazines held fifteen rounds; the Army's banana clips, taped side by side, held sixty rounds. I would like to have had a pair myself.

The three of us exchanged war stories, although Chew Mon and I did most of the talking, and I knew from the conversation that he was an up-front combat leader. Like his "dai-go."

I excused myself after a time. "You guys want to talk family," I said and left with another warm handshake.

As I was leaving, Chew Een Lee said to his brother, "Second Lieutenant Owen's mortars gave us excellent support."

• • •

Colonel Litzenberg called together the officers of the 7th Marines. We sat on the deck of a warehouse that was piled high with gear and supplies. After he praised us for a good job of fighting, our chunky, gray-haired commander pointed to a big map of Korea that was pinned to a wooden crate. He announced with pride that the 7th Marines would spearhead an amphibious assault on North Korea. The North Koreans still had not surrendered to General MacArthur, but our Army, along with several South Korean divisions, was already chasing them over the thirty-eighth parallel. The 1st Marine Division and the Army 7th Division would flank the remaining enemy from the sea.

Embarkation was less than a week away.

• • •

Sergeant Wright submitted his request for hardship transfer home. Captain Wilcox endorsed it and instructed First Sergeant Caney to move it through channels, on the double. When the word came that we were going to make the North Korean landing, all transfers were stopped. The captain called Wright and me to the CP and expressed his regrets that my sergeant's trip home would be delayed until after the next campaign. It was a decent thing for the skipper to do, but that didn't soften Wright's disappointment.

• • •

Replacements came to Baker-One-Seven the day after we went into the brickyard bivouac. There were thirty of them, to take the place of the men we had lost in the fight to Uijongbu. I had put in for two new men, for Nichols and Branek. Doktorski had turned Branek into sick bay with a broken rib "incurred in a fall."

First Sergeant Caney, now back in command of paperwork, learned that Branek would be released from sick bay within a week. He thus determined that the mortars would rate only one replacement, and he sent Corporal Kelly to me.

I was watching Sergeant Wright run the squads through gun drill in the brickyard when Kelly approached. He had his two stripes stenciled on the sleeves of his much-laundered dungarees. He was trim and of medium height, and even though he was loaded down with a field transport pack and full gear, he had a good step to him.

He snapped to, rendered a proper salute, and pronounced, "Corporal Kelly, Sir! Robert F. One-oh-nine-two-one-eight-one. Reporting to Lieutenant Owen for duty. As ordered, Sir!"

Kelly had a face that showed his Irish origins, a fair complexion, and a gravelly voice. He looked me in the eye as he awaited acknowledgment.

"Welcome aboard, Corporal," I returned the salute. "Take off your pack and stand at ease."

"Aye, aye, Sir!"

"What's your last duty station, Corporal?"

"Guam, Sir! Marine Barracks. Military Police Detachment."

"Know anything about mortars?"

"Sir, I was in the 5th Marines before Guam. Trained on every weapon in a rifle company. Expert ratings, Sir!"

"You in good shape, Corporal Kelly?"

"Yessir!"

"I need a runner. Think you can handle the job?"

"Sir, I think I'm better qualified to take over a gun squad," he said, still looking me in the eye.

"I already have good squad leaders," I replied. "I need a good runner."

"I'll do a good job as a runner, Lieutenant."

"You're hired," I told him. I called Sergeant Wright over and told him to get Kelly squared away with the mortar section.

• • •

As junior officer in the company, I caught the dirty job of loading ship with gear and supplies for the amphibious operation. We were assigned an old LST—Landing Ship, Tank—that our Navy had used in World War II but which was now leased to Japan for use as a cargo ship. *Qoro* was its designation and it had a Japanese crew, none of whom spoke English.

In addition to Baker-One-Seven's personnel and gear, we put aboard a dozen amphibious tractors and as many of the battalion's trucks and jeeps as I could secure to the decks. The Japanese captain thought that we were overloading his ship, and he railed at me in an agitated manner. I tried to convey to him that I was following orders, but he became louder and his gestures more agitated.

I heard the metallic snap of a carbine bolt. Beside me stood Corporal Kelly, his weapon at the ready. The Japanese captain stopped yelling and gesticulating, looked at Kelly and his carbine, looked back at me again, bent curtly, and walked away. "Got to know how to talk to these people, Lieutenant," said the gravelly voiced Kelly.

The Japanese skipper was right, though. We were overloading his ship. However, there was a shortage of shipping available for the landing. And, we were informed, we would be afloat for only a few days.

• • •

After we reequipped and reorganized in the brickyard, Colonel Davis authorized all hands liberty and the troops went to discover the attractions of Inchon. What they found were hole-in-the-wall Korean drinking establishments, most of them with available females. The whiskey in these places was close to lethal, but the beer was American black market. The Korean entrepreneurs sold their spirits and comforts at exorbitant prices, well aware that combat troops place little value on money.

Our troops encountered problems in the rear echelon environment. As they did so, they were escorted back to the brickyard by tolerant Army and Marine MPs and the Navy's Shore Patrol.

Glenn Galtere, illustrating a tale of desperate combat in a bar full of noncombatants, fired his BAR through the ceiling.

The good buddies, Garcia and Rendon, found themselves not welcome in another place that was frequented by "rear echelon pogues," as Garcia loudly proclaimed them. In response to the slow service, the two made threatening gestures with their pistols. They were encouraged to return to the brickyard, accompanied by the MPs.

Pat Burris—mistakenly, he claimed—led his squad into a joint that was exclusively Army. The Marines exchanged uncomplimentary remarks with the soldiers. By force of numbers they were ejected and the MPs brought the men back to Captain Wilcox. Burris later boasted to me of his squad's hand-to-hand combat capabilities.

Attilio Lupacchini and Joe Jane were more serious offenders. The two BAR-men were brought back under guard after trying to hijack a landing craft full of beer as it was unloaded on the docks. To the MPs, Captain Wilcox expressed dismay at his troops' behavior and promised severe disciplinary action.

The skipper adopted a "one punishment fits all" policy for the men whose conduct on liberty had disgraced Baker-One-Seven. He sent them to work for me, loading the Japanese LST. By the time we shipped out, I had much of Baker-One-Seven in my charge.

. . .

Compared with Japanese LST *Qoro*, the *Okanogan* was a luxury liner. The men were stashed away for the short cruise wherever they could find space to spread a sleeping bag. A number of them sacked out in the amphibious tractors—amtracs—or in the trucks on deck. Chow was rations stewed up in big vats by cooks designated by First Sergeant Caney. Pfc. Bifulk was one of these.

Officers were crammed into a pair of tiny staterooms, and we had a miniature wardroom for our meals of stewed rations. In there Captain Wilcox spread the map, and we rehearsed for the landing we would make on the port city of Wonsan. Baker-One-Seven was in the assault wave, and we would hit the beach on the amtracs. Intelligence did not expect heavy resistance, but we would go in prepared for the worst. Like all regular Marines, we were well practiced at hitting the beach and, with the "lessons learned" from Uijongbu, we felt we had good reason to be confident.

. . .

The Navy discovered that the waters around Wonsan were heavily mined, and our landing was postponed. It took the Navy almost three weeks to clear the mines. Our three-night boat ride became Operation Yo-Yo, a three-week ordeal of misery and sickness.

We had come aboard combat-loaded, with full field transport packs that carried all we owned for campaigning. But there was little fresh water aboard the *Qoro*, and less soap; after the first week of Operation Yo-Yo the holds stank with unwashed bodies and sweaty clothes.

The rations allotted for the seaborne part of the Wonsan landing were consumed by the end of the first week. No one knew how long the Navy would take to clear the mines, so Colonel Litzenberg passed the word for us to use the operational supplies. We were back on C-rations, the little cans of meat-and-something; many said it was an improvement from Bifulk's cooking. The Hawaiian-born Corporal Burris, adept at pidgin-Japanese, enjoyed fish-head chowder with the ship's crew.

Most of us came down with a low-grade flu, and the corpsmen had nothing to give the men lined up for sick call but APC tablets—

all purpose cure—the Navy's form of aspirin. The toilets in the tiny heads were inadequate for the men afflicted with "the runs." The stench below-decks made the air unbreathable.

There was no deck space where we could exercise the troops and work off their tensions. The uncertainty and inactivity, the cramped spaces, the stink, and the short rations, brought out bad tempers that flared into fist fights. These were quelled by the NCOs without involving the officers. During the three weeks aboard the LST not a man was run up to the skipper for disciplinary action.

• • •

On 26 October we hit Blue Beach on the northern side of Wonsan harbor. It was an administrative landing, no enemy resistance, no shots fired. The men were excited, recovered from the malaise and dreariness of Yo-Yo. They yelled obscene farewells to LST *Q010* and laughed with the fun of the ride as the amtracs slid off the ramp and churned ashore.

I spotted several gun positions that would have riddled the beach, and I was glad that the North Koreans were not there to man them. The amtracs let us out a hundred yards inland. The troops came off running and whooping the war yells they had learned going up to Uijongbu.

Almost to a man they staggered and fell to the ground. Under heavy combat loads and softened by three weeks of inactivity, and accustomed to hard steel decks, their legs wobbled against the soft earth.

Our landing was a spectator event. The 1st Marine Air Wing had already set up an airfield at Wonsan and the "flyboys" lined Blue Beach to witness our assault from the sea. We went through a gauntlet of derision as we regained our feet and staggered into formation. Further insult was added by troops of the 6th ROK Division who had spearheaded the drive up the east coast of the peninsula. They had learned the middle-finger salute, which they rendered to us with great enthusiasm.

It was a terrible, punishing march that we made toward Hamhung, forty miles north of our landing. There were trucks for everything except the rifle companies. Ill conditioned as we were, and with men still weakened by Yo-Yo's afflictions, we wobbled north under a hot sun. First Sergeant Caney cruised our column in the company jeep, picking up the men who fell out. They were driven to an aid station that regiment had set up. That day the corpsmen were the busiest people in the 7th Marines.

The march took us through tidy North Korean villages that were unscarred by the war. In front of every thatched-roof house the villagers cheered us and waved tiny South Korean and American flags; we wondered how they had acquired so quickly the colors of their enemy.

After the trucks had transported everything else to Hamhung, they came back and took us the final miles to our destination. We were bivouacked in a vast, dirty warehouse made of rusting corrugated steel. It was furnace-hot in the daytime and rats prowled over us at night.

Charley Baldwin, the machine gunner, awoke from an uneasy sleep to find a rat on his chest, staring him in the eye. Gunny Foster, who had endured slimy land crabs crawling over him in Pacific island foxholes, told Baldwin to quit bitching and be thankful for the roof over his head.

The roof had many holes rusted through it. Pfc. Merwin Perkins added another. While practicing with his "empty" pistol in the darkness, he fired a round through the overhead. Captain Wilcox, sleeping nearby, jolted awake, thinking he was back in combat. After he calmed down, he gave me an animated chewing out, emphasizing that my men were untrained, undisciplined, and in need of weapons instruction.

Perkins's words of apology, "Gee, I'm awfully sorry, Captain, Sir," did little to soothe the skipper. He ordered Perkins to permanent mess duty.

• • •

Scuttlebutt came that the Chinese Communists—the Peoples' Liberation Army—were in the war. According to *Stars and Stripes*, the Army newspaper that sometimes reached us, the Chinese presence was denied initially by General MacArthur's intelligence staff in far-away Tokyo. Later they conceded that Chinese soldiers, indeed, were fighting alongside the North Koreans, but they were "volunteers" and few in number.

Colonel Davis had the battalion on maximum training—long conditioning hikes, tactical movement, and weapons drill. The 1st and 5th Marines had gone inland from Wonsan and were clearing pockets of North Koreans who were raiding the supply lines that ran up from South Korea. The Army's 7th Division had landed north of us and pushed rapidly toward the Yalu River, bordering on China. The soldiers met little resistance and, although they took a few Chinese prisoners in patrol encounters, these captives were dismissed by Tokyo as observers or volunteers.

Colonel Litzenberg received orders for the 7th Marines to advance parallel to the Army, north to the Yalu.

• • •

We were glad to leave behind the rat-infested warehouse, even though the first day of our march into hill country was a grueling one. We welcomed the test, though, if only to observe the condition of the troops. Gunny Buckley rode in the company jeep with First Sergeant Caney; he hadn't fully recovered from a bad case of fever and the "runs" from LST Q010.

No one shot at us as we marched, and prevailing scuttlebutt now had the 1st Marine Division returning stateside as soon as the Army's 3d Division could come up to relieve us. The troops sang ribald songs, waved happily, and threw candy at the North Korean villagers who applauded us and fluttered their friendly flags.

Baker-One-Seven bivouacked in an apple orchard, a delightful place of cool shade in the autumn sun. The skipper advised that we would stay there a few days "until Division decided what the hell we're going to do." Word was coming down that there were Chinese volunteers spread throughout the mountains that lay north of us.

We enjoyed a day of light duty, our first since we had formed up at Pendelton in August, excluding our days on LST Q010. After I inspected the mortar section and found weapons and gear squared away, we went to an open meadow to play a game of football. The "ball" was a wadded dungaree jacket held together by a web belt, and rules were minimal. Sergeant Wright and I quarterbacked opposing teams, and both of us were piled on every play—whether or not we were near the ball.

Corporal Kelly, my new runner, was not in the game. Bob Fisher said that Kelly had discovered an abandoned locomotive sitting on a nearby railroad siding. Kelly claimed to have locomotive engineer experience, and he had wagered with his new buddy, Hugo Johnson, that he could get this one rolling.

Our roughhouse game was punctuated by the blast of a train whistle. "There goes Kelly!" whooped Fisher.

"Yea, Kelly!" and "That's our Kelly!" cheered my delighted mortarmen as the unseen locomotive tooted a series of notes.

The game of "get the lieutenant" continued until Garcia sped across our football field in the company jeep. "Lieutenant Owen!" Garcia saluted me. "Captain Wilcox wants you on the double. Your new guy, Kelly. He's got the skipper in trouble with General Smith himself." Gen. Oliver P. Smith was commanding general, 1st Marine Division.

Garcia drove me to a squad tent that was the company CP. Outside the tent the skipper was strapping on his gear. Bill Graeber and Weaver were there, their weapons slung and looking serious. Standing out of the way, with worried faces, were Kelly and Johnson.

The skipper saw me. "Those your men?" He indicated my two corporals.

"Yes, Sir!"

"You know they stole a locomotive? A whole goddamn train? Division thought they were a guerrilla raid. They had all hell busting loose."

"Captain, I . . ."

"Never mind! I don't have time now for another of your screwups, Owen."

Garcia was still at the wheel of the jeep. The skipper yelled to him. "That thing all gassed up, Garcia?"

"Yessir, Skipper!" Garcia gunned the engine.

"Load aboard," the captain told Graeber and Weaver. "Let's shove off!"

The three officers jumped into the jeep and it took off toward battalion headquarters. "I'll take care of you when I get back, Owen," Captain Wilcox called out as they sped away.

Joe Kurcaba was there. "What's going on, Joe?" I asked.

"Regiment wants somebody to look at prisoners the ROKs have taken up north. Supposed to be some regular Chinese outfits fighting in the mountains up there," our exec informed me. "Colonel Davis told the skipper to get up to the ROKs on the double. I got an idea we'll be going up there real soon ourselves."

"What about the locomotive?" I asked. Kelly and Johnson were still standing off to the side.

"Division called right after the colonel ordered Captain Wilcox north," Joe said. "They're raising holy hell about the train. They want an investigation, the whole works."

"Do you think the skipper can handle it within the company?" I asked. I didn't want Kelly and Johnson to get court-martialed and I didn't want to lose them. But I was willing to rip off their stripes, personally, for the trouble they had caused.

Joe Kurcaba said, "If they're lucky, they'll be fighting the Chinese before division gets ready to slap them in the brig."

CHAPTER EIGHT

The next morning, before dawn, Garcia came to my shelter-half tent in the orchard. Kelly shared the tiny tent with me. Because of my size, my feet stuck out the flap end, and Garcia prodded them lightly to bring me awake.

"Sir, the captain wants you and Sergeant Wright at the company CP. Meeting with the officers and the platoon sergeants."

Garcia's Texas border accent was charged with excitement. "We got a brand new war! Thirty miles straight north of here. Ten thousand Chinamen up there, and they're pounding the ROK army to pieces. Captain Wilcox and me, we just got back. Lieutenant Graeber was with us. Lieutenant Weaver, too."

Garcia paused, working his message for full effect. Kelly scrambled out of our tiny tent, aroused by the privileged information.

"These Chinks are regular army. Not them volunteers MacArthur's been talking about," the captain's runner informed us.

"You sure, Garcia?"

"Yessir, Lieutenant. Regular Red Chinese army!" he repeated. "We're moving out this morning. One-Seven's got the point for the whole division! That's the word."

Garcia, the salty regular, snapped a fine salute and moved away in the dark to carry word of the officers' meeting to Lieutenant Lee and the machine gun platoon.

Kelly was sparked by the prospect of first combat, and he wanted to go with Sergeant Wright and me to the meeting with the skipper. The night before I had chewed out him and Johnson for the locomotive trouble and told them that was only the beginning. Now I wanted them kept away from the captain until the incident was forgotten. I told Kelly to stay behind and get our gear ready to move out.

It was still dark as Sergeant Wright and I walked to the CP. I thought it was a good thing that Colonel Litzenberg wasn't paying attention to Tokyo's intelligence. For several days our regimental commander had warned his staff that we were likely to tangle with the Chinese Peoples' Liberation Army, the real thing.

Sergeant Wright was silent on the way over, thinking about his four kids at home. With this new situation, he feared more delays for the hardship transfer that would get him back to the States. I said that I would talk to the skipper for him, try to get him on a rear echelon detail. I did not say it to him, but it made little sense to take Sergeant Wright up on the line with us; he might be more concerned about getting his transfer orders than in helping me lead the troops.

At the CP Joe Kurcaba and Gunny Buckley had the headquarters people turned to, making preparations to move out. Sergeant Dale already had a working party there, a squad from the 1st Platoon. They were loading footlockers filled with company records and transport-ready communications gear on a truck from the regimental motor transport pool.

Captain Wilcox gathered his officers and the platoon sergeants around the company jeep. It was a war movie scene, all of us hunched over the white glare of a Coleman lantern, grim faces in stark shadow, rifles and carbines poking above our helmets into the darkness. Weaver, Graeber, and Kiser were there, the rifle platoon lieutenants. They had their platoon sergeants with them, Joe King from the 1st, Gene O'Brien from the 2d, and Archie Van Winkle, 3d Platoon. Sergeant Wright, Mortars. Gunny Foster, Machine Guns. Lee and Joe Kurcaba. First Sergeant Caney and Gunny Buckley. Weeks later, when the remnants of Baker-One-Seven hobbled the last hundred yards into an unknown place named Chinhung-ni, not one of us would be left on his feet.

Under the glare of the lantern Captain Wilcox spread a map on the hood, and we jostled for a view of it. Maps of this part of the world were scarce; this was the first one we had seen of the country beyond Hamhung.

It was a topographic chart made by the Japanese during their occupation of Korea. The characters and the language on the map were Japanese. Place names and legends had no meaning for us, but we could read the physical features and the contour lines. The terrain they showed was a military nightmare—roadblock and ambush territory. It was a country of high, steep hills, deep valleys, and sharp ridgelines. The lower elevations were largely forested. Settlements were sparse and the few roads twisted snakelike through tight passes and along riverbeds. At the northern extremity of the map, at the end of seventy miles of a narrow, corkscrew roadway, was a meandering blue blot. That was the Chosin Reservoir.

"The Chinese have committed themselves to this war," began Captain Wilcox. "They are in force. They're slicing through the ROKs up north like a hot knife through butter. Up here."

He used his bayonet as a pointer to indicate the Chinese advance. "The people we will fight are the 124th Division of the Regular Chinese Army. Definite and confirmed, no matter what Tokyo wants to believe. They're tough, well-trained soldiers, ten thousand of them. And all of their officers are combat experienced, their very best."

The Coleman lantern hissed and we silently absorbed the geography represented before us.

"How the hell did that many Chinamen get this far without MacArthur's intelligence people knowing about it?" asked Hank Kiser.

Captain Wilcox gave Hank the glare. "We know about it. That is what's important. A few hours from now we'll have the Chinese army in our gunsights. We'll be in their gunsights. You damn well better have your people ready for some serious fighting."

"Aye, aye, Sir!" Hank responded, his question answered. We all murmured assent.

The skipper said that Colonel Davis and a reconnaissance patrol were at the railroad and logging village of Sudong-ni, where the ROKs had retreated. Baker-One-Seven would move as battalion reserve, Able and Charlie Companies forward. Trucks would carry us most of the thirty miles to Sudong-ni.

After the briefing, I requested a word alone with Captain Wilcox to ask him if we could leave Sergeant Wright behind when the company moved out. "Sergeant Wright has done a good job for us, but he's a short-timer, just waiting for paperwork," I offered. "Furthermore, Sir, it's not good for the troops to see him with his morale down. I'd like to replace him with Sergeant Winget before we hit anything serious up ahead."

"Good idea," the captain said. "Except it's too late. Battalion says we mount out as we are. I'm not about to snarl them up with transfer details now. You tell Sergeant Wright that I'm sorry we can't do anything for him."

"Aye, aye, Sir!"

As I started back to the mortars, Captain Wilcox called after me. "Don't think I've forgotten about that goddamn locomotive."

"No, Sir!" I answered.

I told Sergeant Wright that my appeal for him had not succeeded. He went off to be by himself.

• • •

We struck bivouac and had the men fed and formed up on the road by first light. Then we waited for the trucks that would carry us to Sudong-ni. There were only enough of them for one company at a time, so they shuttled back and forth on the rough dirt road that was the only route into the mountains.

We waited a long time. The sun rose and promised a bright autumn day, football weather stateside. There was great energy in the ranks: strong, healthy young men on the way to adventure. We cleaned and recleaned weapons and earnestly sharpened bayonets and fighting knives. The old salts retold stories of Japanese ferocity on the Pacific islands. Others remembered pitched battles with Chinese bandits, along with the pleasures of the North China occupation. The newly blooded veterans of last month's fight for Uijongbu boasted to the replacements about their triumphs over the stubborn North Koreans.

All hands speculated about whether the quality of the Chinese army would be equal to that of the North Koreans we had beaten down south. The fear that settles in the gut before combat had not yet surfaced. On that crisp morning, with our clean-shaven faces, clean dungarees, squared-away gear, full canteens, full bellies, and full issue of ammunition, the Marines of Baker-One-Seven feared no one.

• • •

When we had formed up, I asked Sergeant Wright to make a final count of the section and then take the roster to the first sergeant. He got the count wrong by one man; Branek had not returned from sick bay where he was having his ribs retaped. Caney was quick to spot the discrepancy, and he dutifully reported it to the skipper. While we were loading onto the trucks, Captain Wilcox called me aside and chewed me out for that administrative error. These needless mistakes kept coming between my company commander and me.

Our ride to Sudong-ni was dusty and bumpy on the hard wooden-slat seats of the open trucks. It was a ride, though, far better than a thirty-mile hike. It ended when Colonel Davis and a South Korean officer met us a few miles south of the grimy little village of Sudong-ni. From there we went on foot.

The road was worse than it had appeared on the map, little more than a packed earth trail and barely wide enough for the trucks. Hard work would be required of the division's engineers before the road could bear the tanks and the tractors that pulled the artillery pieces. For the rifle companies, inadequate roads meant we would go short on support from the big guns and the tanks.

The road twisted and climbed into steep hills that glowered with dark pine forests. On the west side ran a shallow river and railroad tracks. Next to the road, in a broad grassy meadow, sat a cluster of jeeps and trucks that formed the battalion command post. Staff officers studied their maps and pointed to the jagged terrain that surrounded us. Radios squawked messages from communications jeeps bristling with antennae. Headquarters people raised their tents and strung telephone wire. The Marines of Baker-One-Seven, endowed with the arrogance of front-line troopers, jeered at them and called them rear echelon pogues, and worse.

Colonel Litzenberg was there. He stood beside the road as we passed, nodding and smiling at his fighters. "You're looking good, Marine! You're looking good, Marine!" he kept saying, and all the men waved and smiled back at him. The veterans from down south all recognized Old Homer; they had seen him frequently up on line.

"Good hunting, Owen. Good hunting, young man," he called to me as I passed by him.

• • •

While waiting for our final orders, we sat in ditches on both sides of the road. Above us, the Corsairs soared in wide, slow circles, birds of prey, diving suddenly at the dark hills. The staccato of their guns and the thunder of their bombs echoed along the Sudong valley. Colonel Davis said they were flying support for Able and Charlie Companies, which were leading the battalion attack to retake positions abandoned by the ROK.

The colonel assigned Baker-One-Seven to a hill several hundred yards up the road, to its west. From where we stood, it looked like an enormous green wall matted with heavy pine trees and thick undergrowth. It rose sharply, and large parts of it were sheer rock wall. Through binoculars we followed its long ridgeline that sloped into the shadows of even bigger hills to the west. The ridgeline dominated the southern road, the way back to Hamhung and the sea.

The colonel told us that we were the battalion's reserve, and we should be prepared to return to the valley in a hurry if he needed us to back up Able or Charlie Companies. He ordered Captain Wilcox to leave Bill Graeber's platoon behind to set a blocking position on the road ahead of battalion.

Before we began the climb, I talked to Graeber. It was the first I'd seen of him since his reconnaissance with the captain yesterday. "Did you get a look at those Chinese prisoners?" I asked.

"I saw them being interrogated," said Graeber, the former military cop. "Good-looking soldiers, well fed and healthy. They had on regular Chinese Army uniforms and insignia. They didn't try to hide any information. Told the ROKs everything they wanted to know."

"Probably didn't want the torture treatment," I said. "Those ROKs can get mean when they ask questions." We had seen the South Koreans working over their prisoners outside of Seoul.

"Nope. These Chinks sounded as though they had memorized a script. Name, rank, serial stuff, plus unit number, size, weapons descriptions. They've been up in the hills north of here for two weeks already. They're waiting for us to come at them."

"They gave you all that information without persuasion?" It seemed strange that the enemy would be that forthcoming.

"They wanted us to know. Their generals want us Marine capitalist dogs to know what we're up against."

I said goodbye to my buddy and went to give my people a final check.

"Joe, another thing," Bill yelled after me. "The prisoners told us there are ten more divisions of them hiding in the mountains up ahead."

It was almost mid-afternoon. Battalion gave us hot chow and we refilled our canteens. The mortar ammo carriers took their six rounds apiece, eighteen pounds of dead weight that added to their weapons and small arms ammunition. It made little sense for us to carry personal gear to the top. Captain Wilcox told us to leave everything behind except weapons, ammo, and light packs with rolled sleeping bags and ponchos. We left the rest of our gear at the company supply point, which Gunny Buckley had set up at the bottom of the hill.

Only a few rounds of illumination had reached the supply point. The gunny told me that battalion had sent most of it forward to Able and Charlie. We would have to go short.

"Shouldn't need illumination tonight, though, Lieutenant," the gunny told me. "Baker Company is reserve. The Chinks won't get this far along. They'd have to get through Able and Charlie first."

The gunny wouldn't be making the steep climb up the hill with us. Captain Wilcox, noting the tough time Buckley was still having with his shipboard illness, gave him a detail of headquarters people to guard the company jeep and our excess gear.

While the men were loading up on ammo, I talked to Sergeant

Wright. "No sense for you to go up," I told him. "Your orders could come down from battalion any time now. Stay here with the gunny."

"I appreciate that, Lieutenant," responded Sergeant Wright. "But I want to stay with the mortars. If it's OK with you, that's what I'll do."

I nodded. "It's OK with me, Sergeant. I just don't want you wasting time getting back to your kids."

He said stiffly, "I'll stay with the section, Sir." He didn't like my favoring him. He went back to the mortarmen and told them to get ready to move out.

• • •

The sun was on its slide into the hills, and we marched north on both sides of the dirt road, up the wooded valley toward the hill that we would occupy for the night. The air smelled of pine trees. Weaver's 1st Platoon had the lead, then Kiser, company HQ, and the mortars. Lee had already put a section of his machine guns with each rifle platoon.

My men complained about the quality of the hot chow battalion had fed us at the field kitchen. After a while someone started singing, the cheerful teenager, Pfc. Fisher, who usually got the mortarmen going. "You Are My Sunshine." "Good Night Irene." A few choruses, then Kelly chimed in with a profane parody of the lyrics. Laughter. Ribald comment. The raggedy-ass Marines were on parade!

Colonel Davis stood in the road and looked us over as we passed. Captain Wilcox stood beside him. Scrubbed-down gear and squared away, Baker-One-Seven looked good in the bright November afternoon. The skipper looked good, too, and proud of his company.

The sky darkened ahead. The road twisted into the mountains, and as we marched we began to see South Korean soldiers streaming toward us from the opposite direction. Soaked with sweat, they ran through us without formation; many were without their weapons. Fright showed on their faces. They were the shreds of the 26th ROK Regiment who had been pushed off their hilltop positions before Able and Charlie could relieve them.

"Chinee! Many, many!" they called to us. Captain Wilcox came on the walkie-talkies and told us to stand by to move out in any direction. He added, however, that no Chinese were on the hill we were to occupy. The South Koreans were still holding there, waiting for us.

The din of fighting grew louder from the direction of Able's hill, forward on our right. Booming grenades blended with the sounds of rifle fire, automatic weapons, and mortars. Grenades meant the fighting was in close. In the ditches that ran beside the road we saw stretchers with wounded ROKs who waited for the meat wagons. Corpsmen from our battalion aid station took care of the South Koreans, giving them blood, water, and morphine. The ground beneath them was wet with blood, and low moans rose from the wounded.

A jeep from Charlie Company wove its way along the road, skirting the disordered ROKs. As it passed, we saw sticking out the back two pairs of feet with Marine Corps boondockers laced to them. Two WIAs from Charlie Company. Thick black smoke smeared the autumn sky to the north, and my mortarmen had stopped singing.

We left the road and waded through the boulder-strewn, shallow river. Then we crossed the railroad tracks, which emerged from a tunnel cut through a lower shoulder of the hill. Our guide, a South Korean officer, pointed us toward the trail we would follow, a few hundred yards north of the tunnel. The trail zigzagged up the southern face of the hill.

The terrain abruptly became steep and tree-covered. The bristly branches of the pines and the thick undergrowth grabbed at the men as they struggled under the weight of weapons, ammo, and gear.

It was an enormously difficult hill, a punishing, tormenting hill. We grasped at roots and branches to pull ourselves up. We leaned, doubled over, against its slope. Even in the cool mountain air the men sweltered under their brutal loads, and their dungarees became saturated with sweat. We cursed the whipping branches and the deep ruts in the trail and the rocks that had worn slippery. It was an eternal climb, and the NCOs made the men mindful of trip wires and mines, booby traps, and snipers.

Sergeant Dale's working party plodded down the trail, heading back to the valley. They were griping mightily as they passed by us, slipping and falling on the steep downward path. Dale told me that they had already humped one load of company gear up to the top and now they were detailed to carry more reels of telephone wire from Gunny Buckley's supply point. There wasn't enough wire on the hill to hook the company together.

We came to a stream that had gouged a deep cut into the mountain. Although it was less than a foot deep, the stream ran swift, and its four-foot banks were steep. A stout log spanned its width. I made my way over the log and judged that my heavily laden mortarmen could cross safely. Still, crossing was nerve-racking because as each man balanced on the log, he was a slow-moving target, vulnerable to snipers. Anyone on that log would be a prime target.

Sergeant Wright followed me over. Then, as the men edged their way across, he set them in a semicircular sniper watch.

I waited by the log as the men crossed. Only a few were left when it was Pfc. Grauman's turn. Grauman, my skinny teenager. He was a tense youngster, but he had come through OK as an ammo carrier in the fighting down south. He trembled as he inched toward me.

"You're doing fine. Doing fine, Grauman," I said as I reached out to steady the last few feet of his crossing.

At that moment we heard the stinging whine of a sniper's bullet as it passed between us. We both flinched and Grauman lost his balance. He slipped from the log and tumbled into the stream below. Its smooth stone bed was slippery, and the current sliced beneath him. With arms and legs flailing, and his awkward load weighing him down, Grauman bumped and slid downward, unable to gain his footing.

I was closest to him. Removing my pack, I raced along the bank, getting ahead of Grauman as he struggled and bounced downward. I grasped at him once but missed. Then I tripped on the steep slope and fell, nearly sliding into the stream myself. Another grab and I caught him by the packstrap. Seeing what had happened, Sergeant Winget had quickly crossed the log and was there to help pull us both up the bank.

The kid was soaking wet and shivering. "I . . . I thought I was a goner," he stammered. "You saved my life, Lieutenant." I thought he would cry.

"OK, Grauman," I said. I patted him on the shoulder. "You all right now?"

"Yessir. Yessir, Lieutenant. Thank you, Sir."

Sergeant Winget helped the lad get his pack on straight. "Didn't lose any mortar ammo, did you, Grauman? You lose any ammo and I'll send you back in after it," said the sergeant.

By the time we had Grauman on his feet and squared away Sergeant Wright and the mortarmen were ready to move out. They had peppered the area with their carbines, and the sniper was no longer heard. Kelly and Bifulk each claimed a kill. They were given profane acknowledgment and mock gratitude.

As we struggled higher, the big pines and the brush thinned. In a wide clearing, in sight of the ridgeline, Joe Kurcaba halted us and told me to dig in the mortars.

Captain Wilcox wanted the mortar section set up in battery, all three guns positioned together, rather than split off to the rifle platoons. Battery made sense this late in the day, but I didn't like the position the captain had assigned. It was near the extremity of the company's right flank, a distance of five hundred yards to the other end of our perimeter. I told Kurcaba my objection. He shrugged and told me to argue with the skipper.

I climbed the few yards to the ridgeline and tried to raise the captain on my radio. No response. The walkie-talkies would prove again what we had discovered down south; they were worthless on the hills.

We dug in where the skipper ordered. I showed Sergeant Wright where to position the guns and stack the ammo. It didn't appear that the rifle platoons would be near us, so we set up our own defensive perimeter. I wished that I had told Kelly to be on the lookout for any stray BARs that might have been lying around when we were passing through the battalion area. Stuck out by ourselves as we were, we could use the extra firepower.

The ROKs had dug good, deep holes before they left. By right of first claim, Corporal Burris took for himself a hole that had been lined for luxury with rice sacks. The squads turned to making gun pits out of the rocky soil and stacking the ammo.

Kelly went with me to walk Weaver's and Kiser's fronts and register the mortars for night defense. Because the walkie-talkies were so erratic, Kelly would be my sole link to the rest of the outfit.

Sergeant Richard had taken over Gunny Buckley's job of setting up the company CP, which was just behind the ridgeline, seventy-five yards along the line from the mortars. First Sergeant Caney was there, fussing with the portable field desk that he had set up in one of the big foxholes the ROKs had abandoned.

"Hey, Top," I asked the first sergeant, "why is the skipper putting the CP and the mortars so far out here on the flank?"

"That's where battalion wants us," he answered. "They might need us to get back down to the road in a hurry if Able or Charlie gets hit tonight. Or if battalion gets hit."

"It's a bad position, Top. We're dangling by ourselves out here. I don't like it."

"You should tell that to Captain Wilcox. You'll probably find him at the end of the ridge," the first sergeant said and went back to fussing over his desk.

Digging a hole a few yards from Caney was a second lieutenant I didn't recognize. He introduced himself as Bob Wilson, sent forward by regiment to be our air-ground liaison officer. He was a fighter pilot by trade, and he had flown support for us in the fight down south.

It was Bob Wilson's first night on line with a rifle company. I kidded him about the enormous size of his hole as he dug away, thigh deep in dirt and rocks. He gazed upward at the Corsairs that were searching the valley for prey. "I'd like this war a lot better if I could fight it up there," he said.

"Not me," I replied. "I'd rather be down here where I can jump into a hole when the shooting starts."

• • •

A trail ran just below the ridgeline on the forward slope. Kelly and I followed it and came upon the skipper. Garcia was with him, humping the big pack radio whose long whip-like antenna made a prominent target. This was the radio that kept Baker-One-Seven in touch with battalion, and its performance was far superior to the walkie-talkies used by the platoon leaders. Every few minutes it squawked for Captain Wilcox, and he would stop and take the handset from Garcia and talk to battalion.

Battalion was nervous that Able Company was still getting resistance from the Chinese up ahead. Captain Wilcox kept repeating that we hadn't made any Chinese contact, except for the earlier sniper fire.

When he got off the battalion radio, the captain said that he had been trying to reach me on the walkie-talkie. Battalion wanted me to send a mortar squad down to support Graeber's platoon. I suggested to him that it was almost dark, awfully late to split the section in unfamiliar terrain.

He gave me his "captain's word is law" glare. I told Kelly to go back to Sergeant Wright with the order to split off a gun and a squad and send them down to the 2d Platoon.

The captain gave Kelly the once-over, and I hoped he wasn't remembering the stolen locomotive. Kelly moved out on the double.

"We won't have many people left up here, Skipper," I said after Kelly had departed on his first mission as a runner. "This hill is getting bigger all the time."

"I've already mentioned that to battalion," the captain snapped. "But they don't expect us to have any trouble. Best I can figure, we're just parked up here to get us out of the way. The valley is too narrow for everyone down there."

I proceeded along the footpath that fronted the company's defensive line. Sergeant King had two squads of the 1st Platoon digging in on the north slope of the hill, forward of the CP and running west, toward Kiser's men. Their front was steep, in places a sheer climb that made direct assault unlikely. It seemed to me that we didn't need two full squads to hold that piece of the line.

Sergeant King told me that Lieutenant Weaver had stayed back at battalion, but King didn't know why. King didn't like our position, but he was digging as ordered. The platoon's other squad, Sergeant Dale's working party, hadn't returned as yet. I told him that I had seen Dale's people going down to the valley for a load of telephone wire. King wasn't happy with that information, either.

I didn't mention it to Sergeant King, but it seemed unusual that Weaver hadn't come up the hill with us. I wondered if something was wrong with him, if he had taken sick. Perhaps, I thought, Captain Wilcox would need to replace him.

• • •

Kiser's platoon had the extreme left flank. Hank was building his squads into a "U" formation, a horseshoe around the forward and reverse slopes. His center squad straddled the ridgeline, which sloped down to a tangle of pines and brush. The lower terrain was favorable to the enemy, providing concealment for a close approach. Archie Van Winkle, Kiser's platoon sergeant, worked downslope with a clearing party, cutting away smaller trees and brush to make fields of fire for the automatic weapons.

Hank had his three squad leaders gathered around him. Lieutenant Lee was there, too, and Sergeant Wallace from the machine guns that were attached to the 3d Platoon. They studied the tangle of forest and rocks that lay below.

Lee wanted Kiser's BARs and rifles to give his machine gunners more protection. Kiser argued that he was spread too thin already. I had heard this argument before when the two had worked together on the hills that approached Uijongbu. Hank would shift a few men around to satisfy Lee because the machine guns always gave him superb support. And it was difficult to argue with Lee's by-the-book logic.

I told them both where I intended to lay the mortars—on a line that extended north to south two hundred yards across the front of the forward squad, the one that straddled the ridge. Kiser, sensibly, wanted the mortars to reach out farther. Lee agreed with him. I explained that I didn't have that much range since my guns were already five hundred yards away. The accuracy that is critical for night fighting with the sixties deteriorates as range increases.

"Well, hell, then, bring a gun up here," Hank demanded. "That'll give us the range."

"Great idea, Hank," I said. "You want to tell that to the skipper?"

Hank shrugged. This late in the day not even the skipper could do anything about the situation, even if he agreed with Hank. It was battalion that had selected our positions.

Sergeant Richard had parceled out the available telephone line, and a wire team patched in Kiser's platoon to the command post. Pfc. Jack Gallapo, Kiser's runner, manned the field telephone several yards up the hill from where we stood. He yelled to me that the mortars were wired in, and that my two remaining guns were ready to register. I had him tell Sergeant Wright to stand by for registration fire orders.

I called the azimuth and range for the first mortar shot, seven hundred yards, as far as I intended to shoot. Gallapo relayed the message to Sergeant Wright, and in several seconds there was the black smoke, the stab of flame, and the muffled boom of an HE round exploding in the trees below us. A limb crashed to the ground. My first shot was long, seventy-five yards over, and far to the right. Gallapo barked my corrections into the phone. Another explosion, more earth and tree splinters thrown in the air, and the next round landed closer to where I wanted it. One more mark put us on target, and I brought in the number two gun fifty yards left. Now we covered a zone of one hundred yards left and right of the base round, and back into our forward fighting holes.

I could have used our third gun. If the Chinese attacked, we would need more coverage of both flanks. There wasn't enough daylight for battalion's big mortars, the eighty-ones, to lay down support for Baker-One-Seven. Artillery had not yet made it to the Sudong valley. We would have to make do with my remaining pair of sixties if the Chinese hit us.

• • •

Sergeant Van Winkle had put Glenn Galtere's fire team on the platoon's extreme right flank, tying into Sergeant King's line. Two of the men found a patch of soft earth at the base of a large white boulder where digging in was an easy five-minute job. Galtere's ground, ten yards away, was a web of tree roots interspersed with football-size rocks. His digging was slow and laborious, and it was well after dark before the job was done. Galtere had his evening chow then, a cold can of meat and beans and a couple of sips from his canteen. Sergeant Van Winkle had cautioned the men to go easy with the water.

• • •

I went back up the trail to tell the 1st Platoon where I had laid the defensive fires in front of Kiser. Sergeant King was even unhappier than before. There wasn't enough wire on the hill to string a phone to his platoon, and he had no contact with the company CP.

Little daylight remained when I came through the CP again. Kelly was waiting for me there. He had carried his dispatch to Sergeant Wright and reported that Sergeant Lunney's squad was on the way to Graeber's platoon. The rest of the section was dug in and squared away for the night.

There was no sound of fighting from the hills to the north that Able and Charlie Companies had taken. The Sudong valley was silent as dark came.

CHAPTER NINE

W hen Kelly and I returned to the mortar position, the tiny fires for heating the rations were smothered and a chill had already settled in. The men buttoned their field jackets and pulled up the collars. Their dungarees were still damp from the sweat of the climb, making the chill even worse. I asked Sergeant Wright if Grauman had been able to dry his clothes after the soaking he had taken in the stream.

"I had him build a little fire for them," Wright answered. "But then I had to send him along with Lunney's squad before they got dry. The kid's going to freeze tonight."

There was a gunner at both Winget's and Burris's guns; the remaining men were set in an arc of fighting holes to protect the two mortars. Grenades were placed on the forward edge of each hole, pins straightened. Our line of carbines wouldn't be much protection if the Chinese came, but it was all we had.

While Wright and I checked the positions, Kelly dug a long, shallow hole that he and I would share for the night. It was a hole for sleeping, not a fighting hole. When I slid into it, I complained that it was not long enough. Kelly responded that anyone six-feet-five was too tall to be an infantry Marine. "With respect, Sir!" he added.

Battalion had sent the password—Deep Purple—but did not order a fifty percent watch, which indicated that they looked for a quiet night ahead. I set the two sergeants, Wright and Winget, on watch; the rest of us went to our holes for sleep.

I took the photos from my helmet webbing and shuffled through them, thinking of Dorothy and the babies. Then I put my helmet at the edge of our hole and felt to make sure that the grenades were there. I went to sleep wondering how I would get my people down to the road in the dark if battalion needed us. Kelly squirmed and grumbled that I was taking up too much space, and we fitted ourselves against each other for as much comfort as the skimpy hole would afford.

• • •

First Sergeant Caney released Sergeant Dale's working party just before dark. The men had been laboring heavily since dawn and twice had climbed the hill carrying company gear. Dale led them over the ridge and down the reverse slope where they discovered a cluster of abandoned South Korean holes.

"This is it, you people," commanded the sergeant. "Get your weapons cleaned. Enjoy your dinners. Too late for candlelight and dancing girls, and the smoking lamp is out."

Since Lieutenant Weaver wasn't on the hill, Dale sent a man to inform Platoon Sergeant King of their position.

"Hey, Sarge, who gets the watch?" called one of the riflemen to Dale.

"You just volunteered," Dale answered. "You take the first watch until King tells us what he wants us to do. The rest of you people can sack out."

There were whoops of delight, except for the designated volunteer. "Yeah! Good duty!" "Semper Fi!" "No time like sack time!" "Break out my no-disturb sign."

In the fading light the men took apart their weapons and oiled and cleaned them. They opened their cold cans of meat-and-beans and chicken-and-vegetables, and each allowed himself a long swig of water. Then they burrowed into the luxurious ROK holes. Within minutes all hands were sacked out.

Sergeant Dale considered that his men had done a good day's duty. The air was brisk against his face as he zipped his bag all the way up, and the warmth felt good to his tired body. He figured that Joe King would come by soon to fill him in on the situation. He would allow himself to doze until then.

The rifleman that Dale had assigned to the watch put his legs into his bag and leaned back against the wall of the foxhole. He was weary and his eyes were heavy. He fought it for a time, but sleep finally overcame him and Sergeant Dale's men were left unguarded.

Dale's messenger found Sergeant King just before full dark. King was angry; too much front for too few men and too little light for him to properly set fields of fire. He needed the last minutes of dusk to get his left flank tied in with Lieutenant Kiser. He told the messenger to return to Dale with orders to set a defensive line along the rear slope of the hill.

By the time the messenger started back it was dark. He lost his way, but after stumbling around the hill for a time he came upon the company CP. There he found a buddy who said that no one expected the gooks to try anything tonight. To Baker-One-Seven, the Chinese soldiers had become "gooks," just as the North Koreans had been.

The messenger decided there was no sense in stumbling around any more and getting lost again. He found a spare hole and sacked in.

• • •

Darkness had caught Sergeant Lunney's mortar squad halfway down the mountain. The squad floundered through underbrush for a time before Lunney pronounced them lost. He told his men that they would stay where they were and make contact in the morning. He ordered them to eat their rations cold, then get into their sleeping bags and make the best of the night. He made no mention of keeping a watch.

Hugo Johnson asked Lunney if a couple of them shouldn't try to contact Lieutenant Owen. The sergeant thought that over and decided it would be safer to keep all hands together in one place.

• • •

It seemed I had dozed only a few seconds when Sergeant Wright awakened me. Joe Kurcaba was on the field telephone from the CP, wanting to know if there were any signs of the enemy on the slope behind us. I told him we had not seen or heard anything. Joe said that he had an uneasy hunch about the night. We had come to respect Joe's hunches; they were born of many Pacific campaigns. I told Sergeant Wright to awaken all of the mortarmen, then put them on fifty percent watch, every other man awake. Nobody was to be in the sleeping bags. I took the first two-hour watch.

I became drowsy and sucked on a piece of sour lemon candy, Charms. Kelly had filched a whole carton of them while battalion was feeding us that afternoon.

I crawled around our small perimeter and held whispered conversations with the men on watch. On the phone I checked with the CP again. Sergeant Richard, who had taken the phone watch, told me that nothing was happening. He was edgy, too, as Joe Kurcaba had been.

"Just talked to battalion," whispered Sergeant Richard in his thick Louisiana drawl. "It's quiet in front of Able. Charlie's quiet, too. Don't like it one bit, Lieutenant Owen. Too many gooks out there to be this quiet."

Richard said that there had been no communication with Grae-ber's platoon down on the road at the bottom of the hill. Nothing from Lunney's mortar squad, either. At the end of my two hours I roused Sergeant Wright to relieve me. Together we changed the watch, giving hushed orders at each hole. I checked with the CP once more; no enemy observed. The listening posts in front of Kiser and King reported negative. I squeezed in against Kelly again and dozed off quickly.

• • •

Pat Burris slept comfortably in the roomy, burlap-lined hole he had inherited from the ROKs. Suddenly, though, a loud command was shouted: "Out of your hole, Burris! Out of that hole. On the double!"

He kicked the sleeping bag off his legs, snapped his carbine to ready, and scrambled out of the hole. "And stay out of there!" The com-mand seemed loud enough to alert the entire mountain, but no one else in the mortar section stirred.

Burris crawled through the dark to Sergeant Wright's hole. "You want me? What's up?" he demanded.

"No, I don't want you," answered Wright.

"What did you call me for, then?"

"Whaddya talking about? I didn't call you. You getting shook al-ready, Pat?"

"Somebody just yelled for me to get out of my hole. You didn't hear somebody yelling?"

"I didn't hear a damn thing. Haven't heard a sound since I took the watch," Wright whispered.

"Hey, somebody called me out of my hole," Burris insisted. "The lieutenant didn't call me, either?"

"Nobody called you."

Corporal Burris was puzzled. He returned to his bunker and pulled his sleeping bag out of there. He spread it on the ground and put his legs into it. He would sleep outside tonight. He knew that someone had called him to get out of that hole. Or something.

• • •

In the brush below Kiser's platoon, Chinese assault squads waited in disciplined silence for the rockets and bugles that would signal them to attack. Their quilted uniforms kept them from shivering in the chill night. They already knew, in detail, how Kiser's defenses were set up and the location of each forward hole and our weapons. During the late afternoon their officers had watched Baker-One-Seven dig in, and they knew our line as well as we did. Under cover of darkness, the assault teams had crept soundlessly into their jump-off positions, within grenade range of the Marine line.

These soldiers were honored that they would be the first Chinese to attack American Marines. Marines, they were taught to believe, were selected from the dregs of capitalist imperialism, the scum of a criminal society. Marines were vile men, chosen for their depravity, and given license to rape and plunder. They were to be exterminated like snakes in the home. And like all oppressors, went the doctrine, Marines would turn coward and flee before the righteous Chinese liberators.

The Red soldiers were made even more confident by their easy wins the past week against the ROKs. It heartened them, too, that fifty miles to the west their comrades of the Peoples' Liberation Army had struck at American Army units and sent them into disorderly retreat. Paper tiger, the American Army. Bullies to be taught a lesson, the American Marines.

• • •

The sound of a rocket ripping through the air close above us jolted me awake and brought me upright in our hole. Kelly was up with me. A streak of fluorescent green crossed our line, followed by a red rocket from the other direction. Bugles blared and whistles shrilled down the Sudong valley. The luminous hands on my watch said 0030. Baker-One-Seven was under attack.

A sudden clamor erupted from Hank Kiser's side of the hill: The eerie chant, "M'line die! M'line die!" issuing from a chorus of Chinese voices, then the crash of mortars, the boom of concussion grenades, and the sharp sputter of burp guns. Seconds later there was the deeper sound of answering Marine rifles and BARs, joined by the pounding of our machine guns and the explosions of Marine grenades. The screams of wounded men soon added to the melange of sounds, along with profanities of rage in both languages. More rockets streaked above, splashing eerie tints of green and red. Enemy mortars walked the ridgeline, thundering along the company CP and raining clods of earth on my mortarmen. One of the first rounds landed past its designated target, the CP, and was a direct hit on the hole that Pat Burris had so recently abandoned.

An ammo carrier—Branek?—fired his carbine into the darkness. Sergeant Wright cursed at him and told him to cease fire. Winget and

Burris were at their guns, ready for orders. I yelled for Winget to throw illumination over Kiser's front. The field telephone gave its dull ring, and Kelly handed it to me.

Captain Wilcox was on the hook. He said that the line to Kiser had been blown out. There was no way we could get fire direction from that flank. He wanted illumination over there.

"It's on the way, Skipper," I said, just as the flare popped high in the air, over the left end of the perimeter, and the sky turned a garish blue-white.

Burris didn't wait for me to order the HEs. He already had three rounds up and headed for the registered target area. Winget had another round of illumination on the way by the time Burris's HEs exploded in front of Kiser's line. Kee-rack! Kee-rack! Kee-rack! We heard them go off from seven hundred yards away.

A string of enemy mortar shells, incoming, hit between our position and the CP. My phone line to the skipper went dead. I put Kelly's hand on our end of the wire and told him to follow it to the break and make a splice.

"Take a man with you," I told Kelly. "Take Perkins." Then I shouted, "Perkins! Get over here!"

Merwin Perkins came crashing over to us and threw himself to the deck. In the bluish reflection from the star shells his eyes showed big and white, as did Kelly's. Two scared Marines. Three, counting me. The night had quickly turned scary.

Kelly said, "Let's go, Perk," and they crawled on all fours, following the broken wire. Perkins said nothing. He went behind Kelly and they were gone into the night.

• • •

In front of Kiser's platoon our illumination lit the ground and revealed the Chinese attackers already pouring into the Marine positions. The following salvo of our HEs, one hundred yards out, landed without effect, well behind the Chinese assault. With the phone line to Kiser cut, and no help from the walkie-talkies, we could not adjust our fire to come in closer. Except for the illumination, our mortars were of no help, and we were short on illumination.

Chinese grenades exploded into the line and their burp guns blazed. The first wave of enemy soldiers rushed in, and the forward holes were buried in mounds of quilted uniforms. Clubbing and stabbing, the Chinese surged up the 3d Platoon's hill. Behind them were left dead Marines and wounded men who cried for the help of their corpsman.

Ed Toppel's hole was near the top of the hill, next to Lieutenant Kiser. The eruption of battle below awakened him. At the cries of "Corpsman! Corpsman!" he grabbed his aid bag and hurtled down the black slope toward the noise. In the dark he collided with Archie Van Winkle, and the pair tumbled to the ground.

As Van Winkle and Toppel got up, they found themselves caught in the midst of a forward squad of the onrushing Chinese. Toppel pulled out his pistol and shot into the enemy soldiers. By the light of muzzle flashes and exploding grenades he glimpsed Van Winkle firing his carbine on automatic and slashing his bayonet at the Chinese swarm. Then he saw the burly Van Winkle lift a Chinese above his head and hurl him into a group of enemy soldiers. They fell into a heap; Van Winkle and Toppel fired into them.

Van Winkle threw a grenade into the next squad of attackers and charged down the hill at them. He yelled for the shaken Marines to come with him, and they rallied with rifles and BARs. The enemy pulled back before his revived men and faded into the night.

Ed Toppel crawled from man to man, using the light of rifle flashes and exploding grenades to tend the wounded. He worked flat on his belly and was soon soaked with the blood of wounded men. Bullets grazed the slope and shrapnel whined past his head, but Toppel willed his hands to stop trembling while he worked and prayed.

Van Winkle readied the Marines near him for the next Chinese attack, putting his people into recaptured fighting holes. The men stacked Chinese bodies in front of the holes for greater protection. Somebody yelled to Van Winkle that his own shoulder was bleeding. The big sergeant felt his arm and found that a Chinese bullet had, indeed, passed through it and into his shoulder. Toppel was busy, so Van Winkle asked one of the riflemen to sprinkle the shoulder with sulfa powder and wrap it with the compress bandage from his aid pouch. He put the foil-wrapped morphine syringe in his pocket for later use.

Nearby, a man sat on the ground, sobbing and shaking. "My buddy. My buddy. Gooks shot his head clean off!"

The orange glare of a Chinese grenade illuminated the sobbing Marine. Van Winkle crawled to the man and grasped his arm, saying, "Come on with me, kid. You'll be all right." He rose from the ground and pulled the kid up with him. Together they headed for the center of the platoon position, where the enemy fire was more intense.

Farther up the hill Hank Kiser gathered together all the nearby Marines and prepared to counter the Chinese thrust. They were now hitting furiously at every point of his line. Communication with the rest of the company was lost; he had no means to call for supporting fire or reinforcements to plug the gaps and push back the attackers. He sent his runner, Jack Gallapo, up the trail to the company CP to restore contact. Then he mustered the few men he could find in the confused darkness and rushed down the spine of the hill where his center squad was losing ground to the rampaging Chinese. Immediately a storm of enemy bullets hit the small detail and forced it to the ground. Kiser hastily organized a meager line. Telling his men to hold there, he went in search of more Marines to help stem the attack.

The push on the center of Kiser's line, across the lower spine of the hill, was the enemy's main effort, and they quickly massed their grenadiers and assault squads to exploit the penetration. The first wave of their soldiers stormed forward but were dropped to the deck, casualties of the rifles and BARs that Kiser had placed above them. More of them charged through, climbing over the bodies of their fallen comrades. They were checked again, this time by a barrage of Marine grenades. More Chinese poured in, then more. One Marine foxhole went silent, and another. The Marines who gave way crawled up the hill, turning to fire into the relentless enemy and tossing scarce grenades. The Chinese pressed after them.

Kiser moved from man to man, building a base of aimed fire on the Chinese who kept coming on.

Archie Van Winkle now found himself on the lower fringes of the Chinese attack. He ignored his wounded shoulder and fired his carbine, one-handed. He called for nearby Marines to follow and launched his own attack into the flank of the Chinese who were moving up toward Kiser.

• • •

Lt. Chew Een Lee had dug in for the night near the 1st Platoon. Like Sergeant King, he had been skeptical of the platoon's defensive position, which paralleled the ridge to the right of Kiser's platoon. As Captain Wilcox had informed us, defensive alignment was sacrificed so that we would be able to move quickly off the hill when battalion ordered us to return to the road. Lieutenant Lee had grumbled to the skipper, "If they wanted us down there, they shouldn't have sent us up here."

With the first explosions, Lee sprang from his hole, prepared for battle. His carbine had the two banana clips strapped together, the sixty-round load, and he flipped on automatic fire. To his left he heard a detail of the enemy in the brush, maneuvering to hit Kiser's newly formed line from behind. He hastened toward the Chinese attack.

Lee called out in the Mandarin Chinese he had learned as a boy. The enemy soldiers immediately fell silent, suspicious of the accented dialect. Lee stood straight and yelled the few profanities he knew in his parents' language. The Chinese responded to the insult with a burst of a burp gun. It was wide of its mark. Lee threw a grenade toward the muzzle flash and hit the deck. A Marine who had followed him tossed another grenade. Lee scrambled to his feet with his carbine spraying full automatic and charged at the astonished Chinese. Two other Marines came in his wake, a BAR and a rifle at rapid fire that turned back the enemy probe.

In the darkness Lee collected all the Marines within sound of his voice and continued down the hill with them. He had gained the other flank of the Chinese uphill attack, and he spread his impromptu squad into a firing line. On signal, the Marines threw a volley of grenades, then poured their fire into the exposed Chinese.

• • •

Higher up the hill, Gunny Foster brought Sherman Richter's two machine guns from the 1st Platoon, and they commenced pounding down Kiser's slope. Withering fire and exploding grenades, now from both flanks and above, stymied the Chinese attack. There was a series of whistle signals, and the attackers fell back. They crawled over their dead but pulled their wounded with them as they backed down to the bottom of the hill and into the woods. They were supported by well-directed covering fire, and they held good order as they withdrew. When the Chinese were finally off the hill, the Marines ceased their fire and both sides went quiet.

• • •

While the assault on Kiser's platoon was in full fury, another enemy force had crept around the flank, onto the rear slope. Their intent was to make a jab up the hill while the main Marine positions were being hit from the front, then go for the CP from the rear.

Their rubber-soled sneakers let them move silently through the brush. There were thirty of them, and they aligned themselves for the jump-off. They had grenades, rifles, and burp guns at the ready, poised to wipe out the squad of Marines who were in foxholes no more than twenty yards above them—Sergeant Dale's men.

As the rockets streaked across the flanks and the bugles and whistles signaled the main attack, the Chinese below Dale sprang from the ground and went up the slope at a quick trot, a line of blazing burp guns at their front.

The attack carried them into the holes where Dale's people slept in their bags. Dale and two of his Marines were yanked out of their bags. The three were already dead; they had been burp-gunned and bayoneted through the bags—mercifully unaware of what had happened to them.

The Chinese let battle discipline lapse and paused over their first kills. Wasting minutes they couldn't afford, they scavenged among the bodies, clothing, gear, and food.

The pause gave the remainder of Dale's men time to kick free of their bags and scramble out of their holes and into the brush. Bellies low to the ground, they crawled upward through the dark, making for the ridgeline. Most of them had their weapons and shoes. They left behind a few rifles and a BAR, along with Sergeant Dale and two other dead Marines.

One of the Marines slipped away to inform Sergeant King of the situation. The others climbed fifty yards up the hill, then halted. Enemy fire blazed all around the sector. A fire team leader took over and spread the squad into a hasty defense. Two remaining BARs were set to cover the enemy approach and the rifles were tied in. The Chinese, having finished their plundering, trotted up the hill with fierce screams of "Sha! Sha! Sha!" ("Kill! Kill! Kill!"). Pulsing burp guns and a storm of grenades preceded them.

The man going for help ran into Lieutenant Lee, who had heard the Chinese attack coming up the rear slope and was headed in that direction. Lee grabbed two BAR-men and a few riflemen and sped down the slope through the dark. They reached Dale's survivors just as the Chinese moved in close.

The additional firepower from Lee's group went point-blank into the Chinese mass and slowed the uphill assault. Lee ordered a volley of grenades, which exploded amidst the forward attackers. The Chinese who were not felled turned back. Lee threw his last grenade and shouted insults in Chinese that followed them off the hill.

• • •

On the forward slope, in front of the 1st Platoon, another body of thirty Chinese attempted an assault up the steep incline. Cpl. James Jones's fire team was directly in their path. Mortars, grenades, and burp guns opened up on Jones and his foxhole mate, John Martz. The two men in the hole next to them were killed immediately, before they had a chance to fire their weapons. Above them a Marine machine gun went silent. Jones and Martz threw grenades at the enemy, which stopped their advance, but others pressed upward on both sides. Jones yelled to Martz to withdraw up the hill.

The two Marines made it to the shelter of a huge boulder that protruded from the slope. Jones had the fire team's BAR, and with Martz feeding him all of the ammo they had, he cleared the enemy before him. The Chinese took notice of the fire coming from their midst and bore their weapons on the big boulder. A stone chip ricocheted into Martz's eye just as he and Jones ran out of ammo. The two of them hugged the ground, hoping that the Chinese would not discover that they were still alive.

Up the slope, Sergeant King moved in a BAR to bolster the line. He sent a storm of bullets grazing into the enemy coming up the hill, skimming over Jones and Martz and forcing the Chinese to withdraw. As soon as the enemy had gone, Jones and Martz crawled to the top. Martz was blinded by the ricochet. Jones guided him to cover and then found Doc Mickens to take care of his buddy.

The next morning twenty-two Chinese bodies were counted where Jones and Martz had made their stand. There were four dead Marines there, as well.

When Jones turned Martz over to Mickens, the corpsman was busy working on Charley Baldwin, the machine gunner who had been positioned above Jones. Baldwin had fired only a few bursts when he heard the thud of a grenade landing in his hole. He vaulted out before it exploded, but the concussion caught him and rolled him several feet away. A Chinese bearing a Thompson submachine gun dashed forward, spraying the hole. Baldwin fired his pistol toward the muzzle blast and the Chinese soldier fell dead, sprawled over the machine gun. The Marine who had been in the hole with Baldwin was dead.

A second concussion grenade stunned Charley Baldwin, and he lost his pistol. He took a Thompson submachine gun from a dead Chinese to make up for the loss. Firing the Thompson, he backed up the hill. As he passed Mickens, the corpsman saw that the back of Baldwin's jacket was in shreds. A piece of shrapnel had caught him, and he was drenched with blood from shoulder to buttocks. Mickens told Baldwin to go to the rear, but there wasn't any rear to go to. The wounded machine gunner went farther up the hill and lay on his belly, his new Thompson at the ready if the Chinese came that far.

• • •

Sergeant King walked along his line, hole to hole. He was near the flank that tied in with the 3d Platoon when two enemy soldiers popped up, illumined by star shells. They were poised a few yards from the hole that was occupied by Glenn Galtere, and they were about to spray their burp guns, point-blank, into the BAR-man. Already two Marines had been killed at that spot, the two who earlier had found digging in so easy.

As King came upon the scene, Galtere was caught in the act of reloading his BAR and the Chinese had him in their sights. Galtere fumbled desperately for anything to defend himself—a grenade, a knife, a rock—as he waited the eternity it took for the two burp guns to open up on him, full automatic at ten feet.

From behind Galtere there came two shots from a Marine carbine. They ripped past his head. In the instant of muzzle flash, Galtere saw the two Chinese burp-gunners crumble.

An Arkansas drawl pierced the darkness, a few yards up the hill. "All right, boy. Mind you don't let these people get up on you. Ya'll are supposed to be holding this flank. Hear that, boy?"

"Loud and clear, Sergeant King! I hear you loud and clear," answered Galtere in a tone ardent enough for prayer. Galtere was not much of a believer, but he did some fervent wondering while he checked his weapon and prepared for the next Chinese rush.

• • •

The air liaison officer, 2d Lt. Bob Wilson, spent his first night in a foxhole on the forward edge of the Baker-One-Seven command post. He had selected a good position for his air-control work; the slope in front of his hole was too steep for the enemy to climb, and when daylight came he would have a long, unobstructed view up the valley.

When enemy mortars began to pound the CP, one round exploded just yards from his deep hole. Wilson, jolted from sleep by the ear-splitting noise, emerged from his bag and was just coming out of the hole when another round hit, close by. The shrapnel missed, but the concussion carried him through the air and landed him part way down the hill. He couldn't climb back up. The slope was too steep, and incoming mortars were landing close together on the ridge.

His only alternative was to go down into the valley. Wilson began to feel his way downward. He hoped he would be able to dodge the platoons of Chinese he knew were criss-crossing the wooded terrain below. And he hoped, too, that tomorrow would be a clear day so that he could hurl his death-dealing Corsairs at the Chinese mortars which were causing him these difficulties tonight.

Kelly and Perkins came back from the CP. Kelly showed me a strip of telephone wire. "Line was torn to shreds—too many breaks to splice," he panted. "Not a single line left coming in to the switchboard. There are gook mortars landing all over the CP. Everybody's dug in and buttoned up."

"What's the word from the skipper?" I wanted to know.

"He was on the radio to the colonel. Able Company's getting hit. Battalion's starting to get it, too." Kelly took a deep breath. "Captain Wilcox says for you to hold your position."

Bifulk's voice, on our perimeter, called out, "Who's there? Halt!"

The answer came up the slope. "It's me, Hugo!"

Sergeant Wright rushed to Bifulk's hole. "Password, damn it! Password!"

Hugo Johnson had already crashed into our perimeter, out of breath. "Overrun," he gasped. "Whole squad gone."

Whole squad gone! Lunney's squad! I shook Johnson by the shoulders. He was bent over, catching his breath.

"The squad's gone? What the hell do you mean?"

Sergeant Wright quietly told me to take it easy and let Johnson catch his breath.

"We didn't fire a shot down there, Lieutenant," was the first thing Johnson said when he could talk. "Damn Lunney. When he hears the gooks coming up the hill, he just yells out for us to get the hell out of there. Every man for himself. Then he was gone and everyone was gone. The gooks came through, blasting away with them burp guns so I took off and got back up here."

"Anybody hit?" I asked Johnson.

"None that I could see. Hell, we didn't stay there long enough for anyone to get hit. That yellow . . . never thought I'd see the day a Marine sergeant showed yellow."

"How about the mortar? Where's the gun?"

Johnson looked away from me. He said, very low, "I think the gooks got our gun, too."

The Chinese who had frightened off Lunney's squad were a team of scouts. They had stumbled across the squad's pile of gear before they knew the Marines were sleeping on the ground nearby. By the time their burp guns began spraying, the mortar squad—in response to their sergeant's panicked order—had already abandoned everything. There was no return fire, and one of the scouts went back to guide the assault force to the area. This would be a good place for them to try another stab up the hill.

I had lost a squad of Marines! And the mortar and the ammo! I feared that my men had been killed or taken prisoner. I feared that the Chinese would use my mortar against our own positions. I desperately feared reporting my loss to Captain Wilcox.

I stiffened myself and said to Sergeant Wright, "I'm going to see what happened to Lunney's people. And the gun." I heard my voice tremble.

"Yessir! I'll go with you," Wright stated.

"I need you here. You hold our people together right here."

"Aye, aye, Sir!"

Wright alerted the men and they crouched in a wide circle, ready to leap into their holes if the Chinese mortars started again. So far we had taken no small arms fire.

"I'm taking a patrol to get the mortar we lost down there," I told the men. I could make out their faces in the glow of the flares that lit the valley.

Second lieutenants were trained that combat leaders don't ask for volunteers—just order the men to do it! But right then, I couldn't ask these men to risk their lives to make up for my mistake. I felt that the blame for the loss of the gun and the squad was mine.

"I want three volunteers," I said.

All hands came forward.

"Not you, Sergeant Wright. I already told you."

The response from the men restored my spirit a bit.

"Burris, you stay here and call fire for the guns if the CP gets a line through to us."

"Perkins, stay by Burris. He can use you better on the gun."

"Fisher, you stick close to Sergeant Wright. Cover him if it gets hot up here."

"No, Hugo. I want you to get to the CP. Tell the skipper the situation down the hill. He'll want to get the word to battalion."

Kelly volunteered with a flourish, a mock sweeping bow. "Not you, Kelly. You don't volunteer. You go with me anyway." Kelly stepped beside me. There were snorts of laughter from the men. I wasn't trying to be funny, though; I was too scared to be funny.

Sergeant Winget said nothing. He stepped forward and took a place with Kelly and me. I pointed at Bifulk to join us, too. I wished that we had a BAR with us.

Sergeant Wright gathered an extra grenade for each member of the patrol. I told Burris to throw a star shell down the hill thirty seconds after we left the perimeter.

I placed Kelly five paces to my left, in the brush. Bifulk on the right, Winget coming behind. Carbines levered to full automatic, we stepped carefully, feeling our way in the dark, down the hill toward the Chinese who had taken my mortar.

My patrol froze when we heard the "pop" of the star shell that Burris put up for us. In its light we memorized a faint trail, a barely discernible darker strip of gray. The trees were thin and we saw no movement below us. When the light died we moved out again, stepping wide-legged and slow, hunched over our carbines.

We had traveled a cautious hundred yards down the slope when Kelly hissed, "Who goes there?" We all went to the kneeling position, weapons turned in Kelly's direction.

""Halt! Password!" Kelly demanded.

There was a long, silent pause. Then a voice came out of the darkness. "Me . . . Brown. . . ."

Kelly answered with a spray of bullets into the brush, from where the voice had come. Then he hit the deck, rolled, and poured in another line of slugs. "You dead!" Kelly yelled. There was no response from "Brown."

"Yeah! Me Brown. . .you dead!" shouted Bifulk as he triggered a parallel burst. First kill for the mortar section.

"Keep moving forward!" I yelled to my patrol.

We encountered no more Chinese on our way to finding the abandoned gear. There were no enemy soldiers in sight, but we heard them stirring somewhere below us. In the darkness I almost fell into a waist-deep pit, one of the holes left by the ROKs. Inside the pit was my missing mortar, all three parts strapped together, still in transport carry.

Sergeant Winget stumbled over the ammo. It was high-explosive, twenty rounds of it, piled a few yards from the pit. I was about to take the patrol and the gun back to our own perimeter when a Chinese concussion grenade landed in front of us. We hit the deck, and Winget and I rolled into the pit, falling on top of the mortar. The grenade fizzled, a dud.

Chinese burp guns opened. They passed close, above and around us, so close I felt their whir. The bile of fear returned, and with it the sickening shudder of will.

"You see anything, Lieutenant?" Winget was already peering over his side of the pit.

I forced my head up over the edge. Grenades exploded, then burp guns, three of them, came at us. The Chinese were in silhouette. Our carbines, on automatic, forced them to ground and they soon withdrew. As they left, I heard them calling to each other, no doubt mustering more men for another advance.

From the pit we had a clear view down the valley south into the battalion perimeter. Battalion was under heavy fire. The Chinese had emerged from the tunnel across the river from them, and they had set a line of rifles and machine guns behind the railway embankment. These guns were now firing into the perimeter.

I had a mortarman's dream target in front of me. The Chinese who were hitting the battalion were in direct sight of my mortar. The prospect was exhilarating.

"Set up the gun," I told Sergeant Winget. Then I yelled down to Kelly. "Don't let them get any closer up the hill. Bifulk, stay with Kelly."

A blast from a burp gun came in our direction, and Kelly called out, "We better not stay here too long. More of them are coming this way."

"Keep them busy, Kelly!"

"Aye, aye, Sir! You squared away, Bifulk?"

Bifulk half rose and threw one of his grenades down the hill.

Winget quickly had the mortar standing in the pit, bipod and baseplate clamped in place. He spread the legs and planted them toward the tunnel, in the direction of the Chinese line behind the railroad tracks. I squatted behind the base plate and cranked the tube down.

"You want the sight, Lieutenant?" Winget held the gun's bubble sight.

"No. We'll aim over the tube. Get the ammo. Gimme charge two."

Winget scrambled to the ammo pile. He grabbed an armful of shells and rolled back to the gun. He pulled the arming pins from two of the shells and stripped two bags of propellant from the fins of each.

I had the tube laid on the row of muzzle flashes that led toward the tunnel, the Chinese line. I cranked down for my guess at six hundred yards' range.

"Fire!" I shouted, and Winget dropped the first round into the tube. It did not fire.

Misfire! The propellant charge had failed to ignite, but the shell was possibly armed, primed to explode on contact. Misfires are the mortarman's nightmare, a lethal threat to anyone within detonating distance.

We had done the misfire drill many times; it was ticklish business, even in training. In the dark and under the fire of Chinese burp guns the task of sliding a live round from the tube and catching it in my hands terrified me. I had to fight the choking fear again. I tried to keep my hands from shaking and hoped that Winget wouldn't notice.

We both stood and Winget brought the baseplate to waist level, tipping the mouth of the mortar tube toward the ground. I placed my hands to catch the round as it slid free, before it could hit the ground and blow us both up. As the round slid out of the tube, the burp guns started again, accompanied by another flurry of concussion grenades. Kelly and Bifulk sent a return volley into the brush.

The misfired round was in my hands.

"Jesus! D-d-don't drop it," Winget's voice reflected the fear that he, too, was fighting to keep back.

Holding the extracted round by its tailfins, I tossed it far over my head down the hill. We heard it crash into the brush, but there was no explosion.

"Dud round. Try another one, " I told Winget. Kelly yelled for us to hurry up.

Winget asked me to wait while he checked the tube for an obstruction. He grabbed a long stick, which he shoved into the tube. He pulled out a cleaning rag, the cause of our misfire.

It was careless that we had not checked the tube for an obstruction before we fired. Winget said, "I won't tell anybody about this if you don't."

"Shut up, damn it!" I yelled at him. My fear showed itself in anger.

Kelly and Bifulk let go a burst of carbines and shouted again for us to get the hell out of there.

We had a round in the air, and while I watched to observe its impact, Winget readied more ammo. The first round fell short, but it was in line. I cranked down a turn of elevation and Winget dropped in round two. As we waited for impact, we could hear the enemy reforming among the trees, down the slope from Kelly and Bifulk.

"They're getting ready to come at us again," shouted Kelly. Another grenade exploded, short of where he lay.

Bifulk yelled down the hill, "You gooks better know the password."

"Knock it off, Bifulk!" rasped Kelly.

Down in the valley, along the tracks, the Chinese were extending their line behind the embankment and building up the pace of their fire into battalion. Our second round landed, a red blossom at the near end of their line, away from the tunnel. On target!

Winget forgot himself and thumped me on the back. "Goddamn good shooting, Lieutenant"

The exhilaration returned and coursed through my body. *Gung ho, Marine!*

"Fire for effect," I shouted, fear forgotten, exuberant. *Gung ho, Marine!*

Winget dropped the next two rounds in rapid succession, and I cranked down a quarter turn of elevation. Two more rounds and another quarter turn down. We shot all the ammo we had, and we blew up the enemy line. The muzzles of their weapons stopped flashing, and the railway embankment went dark all the way to the tunnel. Winget had dropped the twenty rounds in less than a minute.

Kelly yelled to me, "Here they come!"

Boommm! Boommm! Boommm! A flurry of grenades were thrown uphill at Kelly and Bifulk. Fire from the burp guns followed.

"Fall back on me," I shouted to Kelly and Bifulk.

Winget had the mortar—tube, bipod, baseplate, and all—tossed across his shoulder, and he was out of the gunpit, up the hill and away.

Kelly and Bifulk tossed their final grenades and pulled back. I rolled my two grenades, then followed Kelly and Bifulk. The Chinese, not deterred by the shrapnel of our grenades, chased up the hill after us, but we had disappeared into the black of the night.

Sergeant Wright heard us crashing through the brush. As we ran into the perimeter, he ordered a volley of grenades at the pursuing Chinese. All of the carbines opened up and the enemy fire diminished. There was a whistled signal followed by commands shouted in Chinese, and then the attack on the mortar section faded away.

I had my gun back! And the men of the lost squad had filtered back into our perimeter. No casualties. I heard Sergeant Wright tell the mortarmen that they had done themselves proud. I went to each hole and told them the same thing.

Kelly and Bifulk were laughing and creating the legend. "Me Brown. . .you dead!"

I cranked the handset on the field phone, and when I reached the CP switchboard, I asked Sergeant Richard to put me on to the skipper. I wanted to tell him that we had just saved battalion's ass, and that Baker-One-Seven had the best goddamn mortar section in the regiment. Just as I had promised him at Camp Pendleton.

CHAPTER TEN

C aptain Wilcox was gone from the CP when I made my call to him. Sergeant Richard put Joe Kurcaba on the hook for me instead.

Joe's voice was hollow and scratchy on the field telephone. He said, "Skipper went over to Sergeant King in the 1st Platoon sector. Gooks came up the rear slope and damn near busted through there. Your people holding OK?"

"Yeah," I answered. "Except there are lots of bandits moving below us. They could be heading for the road."

"Graeber's platoon is down there. Blocking the road into the battalion perimeter. I'll let battalion know," Joe said.

"Can you give me any people?" I asked. We're pretty thin if they come back up the hill at us."

"Negative on that," Joe informed me. "Skipper took all the people we could spare to fill in King and Kiser. Lots of casualties. Both platoons."

"Understood," I acknowledged and rang off. Flares and tracers lit the sky, and the sound of small arms fire, mortars, and exploding grenades grew from the valley below us.

• • •

Bill Graeber's platoon did not expect to fight the North Korean tank—a Soviet T-34—that barreled through them, its machine guns blazing and its powerful searchlight picking out targets. Neither the ROKs nor our own intelligence had warned of enemy armor. As a result, Jim Kovar's rocket launcher was not set up, and Graeber was not armed to repel the huge, clanking monster that sped through their line. Graeber's men held fire as the tank roared by, staying low in the holes on both sides of the road and along the railroad tracks. The best the platoon could do was to fix bayonets, prepare grenades, and wait for the enemy foot soldiers they expected would soon follow. None came. Graeber sent Sgt. Jim Bondurant to scout out the road ahead.

Bondurant bent low and went up the ditch along the road. He heard the muffled cadence of a formation marching toward him, an unlikely sound in the midst of battle. Until he heard an eerie chant from the formation—"Sha! Sha!" and "M'line die! M'line die!"—Bondurant thought it was a platoon from Able Company, on the way back to strengthen the battalion perimeter. But the flame from a jeep set afire by the North Korean tank illuminated three files of Chinese soldiers trotting in Bondurant's direction. When the Chinese were no more than fifty yards away, still in formation, Bondurant triggered a burst from his carbine at the leading rank. A few men went down.

Bondurant heard shouted commands, and the enemy files spread smoothly into two lines that approached him on either side of the road. Burp guns flashed and bullets zinged around him. He went to the ground and crawled rapidly along the ditch back to Graeber.

"Stand by for a ram!" shouted Sergeant Bondurant as he reached the platoon's line. "Forty, fifty of them! Coming right at us!"

Graeber was with his platoon sergeant, Gene O'Brien. Both of them peered into the darkness and tried to make sense of the enemy tactics. They had heard the Chinese open fire on Bondurant, and now they came into view, dressed in thick quilted uniforms and fur hats. They were in a wide skirmish line, hunched over burp guns as they advanced. The sharp bang and blinding explosions of their concussion grenades preceded them.

Before Graeber could yell the order, "Commence firing!" one of his BARs opened in the direction of the grenades. Bondurant, from the kneeling position, measured off short bursts of his carbine. O'Brien joined him, sending a line of tracers into the shadowy forms that came at them in quick bounds. Bill Graeber pulled the pin and heaved a grenade forward. Nearby Marines threw their own grenades, and their explosions resounded among the enemy soldiers who screamed in pain. The Chinese leader quickly shifted his attack to the other side of the road and the railroad tracks.

Sergeant Yeaman's squad was set up there, in the path of the new thrust, between the road and the tracks. He pushed Dick Bahr's fire team forward to slow the enemy advance. When he had them in range, Bahr ordered a volley of grenades.

This time the enemy was not to be stopped. They answered with their own grenades, followed by a squad of burp gunners who charged at Bahr and his men.

"Get the hell out of there," yelled Sergeant Yeaman to Bahr. "Pull back to the platoon."

Yeaman stood and emptied his carbine on the Chinese who were less than ten yards away. Bahr's fire team—three rifles and a BAR—followed their squad leader's example. They stood, emptied their clips, hit the deck again, and crawled rapidly back along the side of the road.

Corpsman Bill Davis was with the main body of Graeber's platoon, across the road from Yeaman's squad. Hearing the cry of a wounded man over there, he rose to go to his aid. A swarm of bullets enveloped him and he hit the deck. He knew that he could not get across the road alive. He listened with frustration to the wounded Marine who cried for his help.

• • •

Bob Wilson, the air-ground controller who had been blown out of his hole at the CP, found himself in heavy brush at the base of the steep hill. By the light of the battle he oriented himself to the road and the railroad tracks and started crawling. He didn't get far before he heard men moving close by, a large force of Chinese headed south on his side of the tracks. Armed only with his pistol, the earthbound aviator determined that he had neither tactical advantage nor sufficient firepower to oppose this superior force. Burrowing under a heavy clump of brush, he vowed revenge for this humiliation when later he could unloose the fury of his Corsairs.

• • •

The North Korean and Chinese tank-infantry attack, straight down the road and pointed into the battalion perimeter, had been poorly executed from the start. The Chinese infantry had jumped off too far behind the tank; they were of no use in exploiting the shock of its rapid penetration when it roared through the Marine line. Graeber's platoon further slowed the infantry phase of the attack. When the North Korean tank commander reached his objective, he found that he was without support. He jammed the tank into reverse and sped backward in the direction he had come, guns blazing as he went.

By the time the tank reached Graeber's platoon, the infantry phase of the attack had already been beaten off and withdrawn. The tank continued north, back to its own lines. Graeber rushed another fire team across the road to bolster Yeaman. Corpsman Davis went with them. The wounded man he had tried to reach earlier was already dead. The frustrated young corpsman put himself to work on another man who had been wounded in the fight.

• • •

One of the tank's first targets had been Gunny Buckley's supply point at the bottom of our hill. As it plowed through, the tank's heavy-caliber bullets chewed up the neatly stacked packs and cartons of rations. Two Marines were killed as they slept. The gunny recovered from the surprise and directed the remainder of his lightly armed men into a grove of trees above the position. Moments later, Chinese soldiers swarmed into the supply point. Seeing the treasure of packs and cartons, they stopped to loot, gathering up clothing and cans of rations. Fortunately for the gunny's tiny force, the Chinese were so intent on their booty that they paid no attention to the grove of trees only a few yards above them.

• • •

One of the early Chinese mortar rounds, perhaps the same one that had blown Bob Wilson down the face of the hill, was almost a direct hit on the hole occupied by First Sergeant Caney. The near miss had not caught Caney asleep; he was awake, crouched at the forward edge of his hole, on the fifty percent watch set by Captain Wilcox in response to Joe Kurcaba's earlier hunch.

When the first rounds exploded, Caney reached for his helmet. Before he could buckle it, however, there was a blinding flash only a few feet from him, followed by a noise that sounded as though an enemy shell had exploded inside his head. Its concussion threw him against the back wall of the hole; his helmet flew off.

It was a long time before Caney regained consciousness, and even then he revived only partially. Still, he was aware enough to know that his field desk, folded and secure, was safe in the hole with him; his meticulously maintained company records were unharmed. Caney rolled over and placed himself atop the folded-up desk. For the rest of the night he faded in and out of consciousness, hearing the explosions and screams of the battle that raged around him. He knew his carbine was somewhere in the hole, but he couldn't locate it in the dark and his helmet was missing.

• • •

After their effort to break through the mortarmen on the back of our hill, the Chinese made no further attempt on Baker-One-Seven. Captain Wilcox came to check on our position, feeling his way through the dark. He had Garcia with him, carrying the big radio, and a pair of riflemen for protection. The captain was weary and his voice was sad when he told me that the company had taken heavy casualties. He was angry, too, that we had been ordered to occupy this hill without a good estimate of the situation.

My elation over the retaking of Lunney's gun dissipated in the face of the captain's gloom and anger. When I reported the damage we had done to the Chinese outside of the railroad tunnel, he said, "Well done!" It wasn't a very enthusiastic "well done," though. He had other things on his mind.

• • •

With the first hint of light I took Kelly with me to walk the ridgeline. We went to the far right of the hill, looking down the slope that rose like a cliff above the railroad track, the river, and the road. The bottom was covered with heavy brush, and we saw no sign of the enemy.

As we were turning away, a bugle blared along the valley. Its notes were followed by a series of sharp whistle blasts, and suddenly there was movement in the brush all along the base of our hill and along the railroad embankment. Small groups of Chinese soldiers, in their green quilted jackets and trousers, emerged silently from the brush and headed toward the road below us.

"You seeing that, Kelly?" I asked. In the uncertain early light and mist I wasn't sure of my eyes.

"Jesus! Yeah, they're all over the place down there!" Kelly had his carbine up, sighting toward the Chinese.

"Hold your fire," I cautioned. "Let's see what they're up to."

More and more of the enemy soldiers padded out of the undergrowth. Thirty of them. Forty. More. As the light grew stronger, we were better able to view the strange spectacle below. Even more Chinese scrambled over the railroad embankment, reached the road, and made a formation of three ranks. After a few minutes I counted sixty of them. I had sighted their leader in my glasses, standing before the formation. He had blue piping on the collar and cuffs of his quilted jacket and a whistle hung from his neck.

The formation was two hundred yards away; our two carbines would do little damage. "Kelly, run back and bring up a couple of BAR-men. A machine gun if there's one anywhere near. On the double!"

"Aye, aye, Sir!" responded my runner. He slung his weapon and turned to run up the ridgeline toward the company CP.

I put my carbine to my shoulder, the officer in my sights. Suddenly, from the opposite hill came the burst of a Marine machine gun. It was accompanied by BARs and rifles. The shooting came from Able Company's position; they had been watching the formation take shape just as I had.

Able's fusillade devastated the Chinese. The ranks of green-quilted soldiers folded and crumpled to the road as the Marine guns flayed their lines. A few of the soldiers tried to scramble to the shelter of the roadside ditches, but they were picked off by the rifles.

I still had the officer in my sights and fired a round at his chest. When he went down, his arms flopped in the air. I gave myself the credit for the kill, but I knew that Able's people, on the other side of the valley, would take credit for the same prize.

Kelly had gone only a few steps on his mission when the firing started. He returned, assumed the prone position, and fired his carbine, single shot, into any of the Chinese soldiers who still moved. There were few such targets when Able Company ceased its fire.

• • •

Baker-One-Seven lost more men that night than we had in the five days of our campaign against the North Koreans, going up to Uijongbu. Captain Wilcox raised hell when he heard that Sergeant Dale and his men had been killed in their sleeping bags. He made it standard operating procedure that the company stayed out of the sleeping bags at night when we were on line. "Tell your people that they can put their feet in the bags and loosen their boondockers. That's as far as they go," he told us.

From then on, no matter how cold it became, we slept outside of our bags and our boots came off only to change socks.

• • •

First Sergeant Caney dragged the field desk out of his hole. He sat in silence, head down. Captain Wilcox approached him. "How you doing, Top?"

Caney did not respond, just stared at the ground.

Staff Sergeant Richard joined them. "First Sergeant took a close one, Sir," he informed the captain. "One almost landed in his hole last night. He was lucky not to get his head blown off."

The captain gently shook his first sergeant by the shoulder. No response.

"Send the first sergeant down with the wounded when we move them off the hill," ordered the captain.

"Aye, aye, Sir!"

"And, Sergeant Richard, you take over first sergeant duties for the company."

"Uh...er...yes, Sir. I'm not much good on the paperwork, Captain."

"You'll do OK until we get a replacement for Caney. Better get started on the casualty report to battalion. And the rations and ammo requisitions."

"Aye, aye, Sir," Sergeant Richard complied, his voice showing a distinct lack of spirit. He put his sniper rifle aside and opened the field desk to begin the odious paperwork chores. Baker-One-Seven never did get a replacement first sergeant.

• • •

I told Captain Wilcox that it would not be good for Sergeant Lunney to remain with the mortar section after his poor showing the night before.

"He let his men down, Captain. I doubt if they would follow him in another fight."

The company commander didn't question my judgment. "Too bad. He looked like a good Marine."

"Captain, he doesn't hold up under fire."

"OK. We'll send him back and let battalion decide what to do with him. You have someone to take his place? It's not likely we'll get enough replacements to fill in for all our casualties."

"Yessir. Corporal Johnson's a good man. He can pull the squad back together."

"All right then. Do it," the captain dismissed me.

Before I left, I tried to put in another word for Sergeant Wright. I suggested that if I accompanied him back to regiment, we might nudge his transfer along.

"Not a chance, Joe," the captain said to me. "We've got a whole new war going on."

I was disappointed for Wright. But it was the first time my skipper had addressed me as "Joe." He called me that from then on; he knew that my mortarmen had done a good job of fighting for him.

• • •

Sergeant Lunney had crept into our perimeter after the fighting subsided the night before. The rest of his squad had already straggled in on their own. They avoided Lunney.

When I returned from the CP, he was sitting glumly by himself. "Sergeant Lunney!" I called him to me.

"Sir!" The big, handsome redhead snapped to and presented himself.

I was angry with the man. He had endangered the lives of his squad. Without putting up a fight, he had abandoned a weapon to the enemy. I walked with him away from the section, so the men wouldn't see us. Then I faced him, and he stood at stiff attention.

"Sergeant Lunney, I am relieving you of your squad."

He looked straight ahead, but his eyes moistened.

"You let your men down last night. You abandoned your responsibilities. It's only good luck that the squad wasn't wiped out. They could all be dead. Or taken prisoner."

Lunney's voice trembled. "Lieutenant, it was pitch black down there. We were lost. I used my best judgment."

"I can understand getting lost," I said. "But you set no security. When the Chinese came through, you forgot your men to take care of yourself."

"Lieutenant, I panicked. I admit that. But if you could give me another chance . . ." Tears streamed down his cheeks, and he looked to the ground.

"I can't give you another chance. Your men don't respect you. You report to the CP. They'll give you orders from there."

His head bowed, Sergeant Lunney said, "I'm sorry, Sir. I'm very sorry."

"I'm sorry, too, Sergeant. Dismissed."

Sergeant Lunney walked back to the section's perimeter, gathered his gear, then trudged up the hill to the CP. No one said goodbye to him.

I felt sorry for the man, and I couldn't forget the times that fear had taken me close to the edge of panic, too.

• • •

Captain Wilcox put half the company to carrying our wounded and dead off the hill. We took the wounded to the battalion aid station and brought back ammo, rations, and water on the return climb. Most of the day Baker-One-Seven resembled two columns of worker ants, toiling up and down the precipitous trails.

I took a detail of my mortar section and several company headquarters people. One of the wounded we carried was Platoon Sgt. Archie Van Winkle. Although Toppel had him doped up with morphine for the trip, he remained semiconscious, alternating groans of pain with wisecracks.

At one point Kelly and I relieved the two men who carried the front end of his stretcher. Archie smiled dreamily when he saw me carrying him. "About time they found something useful for you second lieutenants to do, Lieutenant," he said with a weak laugh.

"Knock it off, Sergeant, or I'll drop you right here," I retorted, laughing back at him.

Shortly afterward our relief did drop him. On a slippery stretch of the trail one of the men lost his footing, letting the stretcher crash to the ground. Archie yelped in pain.

"Jesus, Archie! Sorry," said the man who had dropped the stretcher.

The badly wounded platoon sergeant gritted his teeth and made no further sound.

As we reached a level spot on the downhill carry, we came upon Chew Een Lee. He sat on a large rock, cursing mightily as he attempted to apply a pressure bandage to his right arm with one hand.

"What happened, Lee?" I asked.

Lee ignored my lapse of military courtesy. Through clenched teeth he answered, "Damn sniper got me. Broke a bone, I think."

He had been reconnoitering the area by himself, looking for Chinese stragglers. I helped him fix the bandage to his arm. The bleeding had stopped, but his broken arm hung loosely at his side.

"You want some help to the aid station?" I asked.

"I'll make it on my own," was the blunt reply.

"Suit yourself, Lieutenant Lee," I said to him.

I ordered the stretcher-bearers to saddle up again. After we were under way I looked back and saw that Lieutenant Lee was following the column, walking by himself.

One of the walking wounded was Gene Morrisroe, a machine gunner. He and Kelly had been buddies on Guam and joined Baker-One-Seven together as replacements after Uijongbu. Morrisroe was hurting, as were all of the walking wounded, but Kelly kept him joking as he helped him down the rough trail.

When we reached the aid station, Kelly said, "See you stateside, old buddy."

"You'll see me before that," Morrisroe replied. "I'll be back before you guys get finished. All those gooks we saw last night, they're not going away easy."

• • •

After a long, painful crawl down the mountain, we arrived at the aid station to find it already filled with casualties. Walking wounded overflowed the place. They sat on the ground or stood around, smoking and staring, pondering the battle they had just survived. The corpsmen worked with quiet efficiency, and they motioned our stretcher cases straight through.

The men clustered around Archie Van Winkle's stretcher. "So long, Sergeant," they told him, and "Semper Fi, Archie," and many profane words of admiration.

Van Winkle had a goofy grin from his last jolt of morphine. "At ease," he commanded them, then let himself doze off. It was the last we saw of him.

Leaving the area, we said goodbye to Lieutenant Lee. Bifulk stood at awkward attention. "Thank you, Lieutenant Lee. We're going to miss the hell out of you," he said.

"I will be back with Baker Company very soon," Lee responded. He said the same to each of the men as they bid him farewell.

• • •

Chinese snipers, lurking in the scrub growth above the battalion perimeter, kept the Marines scurrying low. While I saw to it that the men loaded up with cartons of rations and ammo for the return trip, Kelly scrounged the area for loot, ignoring the snipers. Only hours ago he had faced a row of blazing burp guns, and now he considered sniper fire a small hazard.

"Hey, you! Goddamit, get down! You're drawing fire," bellowed a major who was crouched in a foxhole. The order was directed at Kelly, who was pilfering through a pile of PX supplies.

"Sorry, Sir!" Kelly called back to the major. I watched him slip a carton under his dungaree jacket. "Sorry, Sir!" he repeated, and he made a zigzag run across the open area.

Sniper bullets followed him, spattering the ground and adding to the major's ire. "Get the hell out of here!"

Kelly reported to me when he made it to safety. "They got all sorts of good stuff over there, Lieutenant," he said, grinning broadly. "We ought to take the whole detail over there and load up. Candy. Cigarettes. Cigars. I think I saw some cases of beer."

"Never mind that stuff, Kelly," I told him. "We've got ammo and rations to take."

"And I got something special, just for Captain Wilcox," Kelly went on. With a sly wink he opened his jacket wide enough to reveal a carton of twenty-four Hershey bars. "This will make him forget about that locomotive me and Johnson swiped."

We had the men loaded and ready for the return climb. In a nearby jeep I spotted a carton filled with cans of pineapple. As our detail went by, I leaned into the jeep, swept up the carton, and slung it to my shoulder. My men had taken a great liking to canned fruit. Pineapple and peaches were best.

The arduous climb back to the Baker-One-Seven perimeter was lightened by laughter as the troops mocked the battalion "rear echelon pogues" who had hidden from the sniper fire. There were pleas for Kelly to spread the chocolate bars around, but he was true to the skipper and kept the carton intact. No one talked about the brutal fight we had endured the night before. Nor did we talk of our dead and the wounded men we had just carried off this steep, dark mountain that loomed above the Sudong valley.

• • •

We went to the CP, and as I reported to the skipper, Kelly gave him the box of chocolate bars, which was accepted with delight. Captain Wilcox was in a much-improved mood. His company had put up a hell of a fight and hadn't given the Chinese an inch. Back at battalion and regiment good things were being said about Baker-One-Seven.

Acting First Sergeant Richard had set up the field desk. He struggled over the roster, deleting the KIAs and transferring the WIAs to the charge of battalion. He muttered as he worked, and when I told him that the sixties had zero casualties he gave a satisfied grunt—less paperwork. Then he whispered to me that Kelly's offering of the Hershey bars to Captain Wilcox was a wasted gesture. The skipper was too busy to concern himself with the locomotive incident. First Sergeant Caney was no longer around to remind the skipper of such things, and Sergeant Richard was not about to. Too much paperwork involved.

Before we went back to work, I asked the captain if Lieutenant Weaver would return to Baker-One-Seven. He said that Weaver had been wounded last night within the battalion perimeter and wasn't expected to rejoin us. My immediate impulse was to ask Captain Wilcox to give me the 1st Platoon; my mortar section was in good shape and I wanted the experience of leading the rifles. But then I remembered the captain's fury at Inchon when I asked for a change, so I kept my mouth shut.

As we returned to the section, Kelly offered me a gift. "Got something here for you, Lieutenant," he said, reaching into his jacket. He withdrew a pair of banana clips, the carbine magazines that held thirty rounds each. Wrapped together with friction tape, they were a sixty-round load.

"Where did you get these, Kelly?"

"Lieutenant Lee gave them to me."

"These belong to Lee? He gave them to you?"

"Well . . .. uh, . . . well, they were going to take them away from him anyway at the aid station."

"You swiped them, Kelly?"

"I don't think 'swipe' is what I did, Lieutenant. It's more like . . . more like salvage, is what I did."

"OK, Kelly, you keep on salvaging. Just don't get me in any more trouble."

"Aye, aye, Sir!"

I snapped the banana clip into my carbine.

"I already got it loaded with tracers," Kelly told me.

• • •

Gunny Buckley had made his way to the top of the hill and was at the CP when Sergeant Wright and I went there to report the return of our ammo and rations detail. The gunny looked like hell, pale and drawn, and his face glistened with an unhealthy sweat. Even his proud handlebar mustache drooped at the ends.

"Looks like you had a rough time, Gunny," I addressed him. He sat on the edge of a foxhole, still breathing hard from the climb.

"Bad night, Lieutenant," he answered, looking up at me. "Real bad night. Gooks ran right through us."

I had heard that the Chinese hit the gunny's supply point at the bottom of the hill, but I didn't know the details.

"They shot us up real bad," Gunny Buckley continued. "At first I thought it was our own tank coming through. I wasn't ready, and I had two men already killed before their soldiers hit us. A whole platoon of them came at us on the run. Gooks all over the place."

"Jesus!" exclaimed Sergeant Wright, who was standing next to me.

The gunny went on. "Best I could do was get my people the hell out of there. No chance of putting up a fight. I lost another man getting away from them."

"What happened to the company gear?" I asked.

"The little bastards took everything. All the men's packs. Rations. All the communications gear and wire we didn't get up on the hill yesterday. Every goddamn thing we had down there."

The gunny shook his head sadly. "Three Marines dead. I lost three good Marines."

"Not your fault, Gunny." I could think of nothing more to say.

When we left the gunny, Sergeant Wright said, "I'm glad you didn't make me stay down there last night, Lieutenant."

It was fortunate that I had kept the pictures of Dorothy and the babies in the webbing of my helmet, instead of in my pack. The Chinese who drove Gunny Buckley's detail away from the supply point had thoroughly ransacked the area. Lost were our extra dungarees, skivvies, socks, and toilet gear. Letters, pictures, and paperback books were torn and strewn all over the area.

The skipper sent a working party down to salvage the gear. The jeep hadn't moved from where the gunny had parked it the previous afternoon. Inside was a dead Chinese soldier, slumped over the steering wheel, shot through the head. Gunny Buckley's men had put up a fight before they were chased off.

Baker-One-Seven went without a change of clothes for many more days, until the weather turned cold and we were issued cold weather gear.

CHAPTER ELEVEN

The Army field hospital that supported the 1st Marine Division was in an old schoolhouse on the outskirts of Hamhung, a two-hour ride away. An open truck brought Lieutenant Lee there, along with a load of other walking wounded. The school's playground had become a crowded parking lot for ambulances, jeeps, and trucks. Lee noted that no sentries were posted to guard the vehicles.

Lee was triaged and put in a room with other walking-wounded officers who awaited transfer to the fleet hospital in Japan. As soon as space was available, he would be flown out. There would be a few days' wait, he was told; the many serious stretcher cases already had clogged the air evacuation system.

Lee informed the Army doctor who examined him that he didn't need to be hospitalized—just put a splint on his arm, give him a sling, and he could return to Baker-One-Seven. The doctor applied the splint himself, but he told Lee that it would be a month before he would be fit for duty.

Lee rejected that prognosis. Damned if he would be put aboard the medical flight to Japan; he was going back to his troops.

The school's gymnasium had become an open ward for wounded troops awaiting passage to Japan. Some carefully hobbled about on crutches, others lay on the rows of canvas cots, smoking and recounting the battle of Sudong-ni. A few of them groaned with pain, but most expressed their misery with loud vulgarities.

Lee roamed the makeshift ward in search of Marines who would be fit enough to join him in an escape from the hospital. He found his man, Staff Sergeant Keller, a husky section leader from the battalion's 81-mortar platoon. Keller had been shot in the thigh, but he could limp his way around and he wanted to get back to his guns. He was delighted to sign on for a breakout with a crazy officer who would take all the blame if the scheme should fail.

Their escape was planned for early morning, before the doctors made their rounds and scheduled the patients for the Japan flight. Lieutenant Lee and Sergeant Keller met at an unguarded storeroom where earlier reconnaissance had found weapons, ammo, and web gear that had been taken from wounded Marines. The two equipped themselves, combat-ready, with an M-1 and a carbine.

The escapees strode purposefully through the passageways to the parking area, Sergeant Keller at a fast limp. No one chose to question the Asian-looking Marine lieutenant who had his arm in a sling and carried a weapon that appeared ready for business.

Outside they passed a cluster of Army drivers who were away from their vehicles, drinking coffee. Lee unslung his weapon, snapped the bolt, and glared menacingly at the drivers. Keller limped to an ambulance jeep that was pointed for the gate and squeezed behind the steering wheel.

The drivers muttered uneasily among themselves, keeping a wary eye on Lee's leveled carbine. When Keller started the jeep, one of them stepped toward it.

"Hey! Whaddya doin'? That's my jeep!"

Sergeant Keller gunned the engine and Lee jumped into the passenger side. He kept the muzzle of the carbine on the indignant driver, who dared come no closer. The jeep careened through the yard and out the gate. Keller floored the accelerator and they followed the MSR—Main Supply Route—signs, the road back to Sudong-ni.

Fifty yards away from the hospital compound Lee looked back to see two ambulance jeeps speeding after them. "Step on it!" Lee ordered. "They're after us."

Sergeant Keller made full speed ahead.

The northbound traffic was clogged with trucks carrying replacement troops and supplies. The red cross markings on the hood of the stolen jeep gave it right-of-way, and Keller took full advantage of it. The two meat wagons that followed had the same advantage, though, and it seemed to Lee that they were closing the gap.

A flat, uncluttered stretch of roadway opened before them, and Keller tried to coax more speed. The two pursuing ambulances also cleared the traffic and streaked closer. Suddenly a sharp curve appeared, almost a right angle, and there was neither time nor room to slow down or maneuver the elbow bend. The jeep went airborne and soared across a deep ditch.

In that moment of flight 1st Lt. Chew Een Lee braced himself and gripped the seat with his good hand. A single thought burned through his mind—instead of dying the proud warrior's death in battle, Chew Een Lee, the Marine Corps' first regular officer of Chinese ancestry, was to expire ignominiously, the victim of a vehicle accident.

The drivers of the meat wagons knew the road. They anticipated the turn, maneuvered it safely, and screeched to a halt. They saw that Lee's jeep had flipped off the road and landed, upright, in a thicket of heavy brush. And they watched, astonished, while Lee and Keller climbed out of the jeep and staggered to the road.

The ambulance drivers offered assistance to the two dazed Marines. "We need no assistance," said Lee. "Except for further transportation to the 1st Battalion, 7th Marines."

It didn't seem prudent for the soldiers to question the bloody-faced Marine lieutenant who had a loaded carbine in his one good hand.

"Yes, Sir!" the Army drivers responded. "We're headed up there anyway."

• • •

Battalion sent a series of replacement first lieutenants to take over Weaver's platoon, but they stayed only a few days at a time. Whatever was going on between battalion and Captain Wilcox, we didn't know. I felt that matters would be simplified if they just gave me the 1st Platoon, but apparently the captain didn't see it that way. And I didn't ask why.

• • •

Native farmers and loggers who lived up in the hills warned our intelligence people that the Chinese had gathered in strength, and that they were waiting to swoop down on us from the mountains to the north. Intelligence also determined that our regiment had destroyed the 124th Division of the Peoples' Liberation Army, the division that the Chinese generals had hurled at us at Sudong-ni. Someone calculated that 1st Battalion had killed 622 enemy soldiers in the battle; we wondered how they arrived at that exact figure. We had found hundreds of Chinese dead left lying around our own perimeter, and air and artillery had observed many more farther away. Because the early November weather was cool, the bodies were slow to decompose and release their terrible stench.

• • •

We left the Sudong valley, the battalions of the 7th Marines leapfrogging each other in the attack up the single-lane dirt road that wound north into the high mountain country. Charlie Company took the first point. They jumped off at dawn and they got clobbered before noon.

The Chinese tactics had us puzzled; sometimes they fiercely resisted our advance and other times they just faded away to the next ridgeline without firing a shot. That morning, by the time we reached Charlie Company's position to help them out, the Chinese had withdrawn. There were many Marine casualties, though, and we helped Charlie carry them down to the road for the meat wagons. Carrying casualties, like climbing and fighting in these steep hills, was difficult work. Soon we would be doing it every day.

As the hills grew steeper, the road narrowed and became more dilapidated. It was getting colder at night, and the men declared that they could smell snow in the air. Regiment issued heavier sleeping bags, but because of Captain Wilcox's order we couldn't get into them at night. We were also given scratchy winter underwear—long johns— and we sweltered in them the daytime. They were warm at night, though, when the chill settled in.

• • •

North Korean tanks surprised us again.

Baker-One-Seven took the point and marched for more than an hour without any sign of the Chinese—a single file of us on each side of the road, the men moving easily. Captain Wilcox had Kiser's platoon up front, then Graeber, the mortars, and the 1st Platoon. Gene O'Brien, Graeber's platoon sergeant, and I walked together, keeping an eye on the troops and talking as we went. It was a crisp fall day with the sun shining into the valley. We watched the skyline for signs of the enemy.

"Don't like this one damn bit, Lieutenant Owen," O'Brien said to me. He was a reservist, combat-experienced from the Pacific war. "It isn't natural for the gooks to let us move up this easy. We're walking into their trap."

"All I know is that MacArthur says the 1st Marine Division is to go for the Yalu River," I said. The Yalu was North Korea's border with China.

"You don't think the gooks will let us get that far without lowering the boom on us, do you, Lieutenant?"

"Hell no, I don't," I responded. "But just remember this, Sergeant, 'ours is not to reason why.'"

"Yeah, 'and into the valley of death rode the six hundred.'" Sergeant O'Brien remembered the Tennyson we had both learned in high school.

The troops were in good humor. They joked and laughed as we marched and made obscene comments about the things that were central to their lives: the chow, the terrain, the enemy, the lack of women.

"Second thing I'm going to do when I see my wife again is take off my pack," said one of the married reservists in the column.

"Oh, yeah?" came an answer. "By the time you see her again you'll forget what the first thing was."

"Hell, it'll be so long before we get back stateside you'll be too old for that stuff," someone else joked at the married man who was nearly thirty years old.

The frivolity ended suddenly with a fury of yelling and men scrambling away from the road ahead of us. Fifty yards up the column a Marine yelled, "Tank!"

"Jesus! Gook tank!" another man echoed.

Concealed under a pile of brush, in a deep depression off the road, was an enemy tank, its gun turret grinding as it revolved and the barrel of its cannon bearing directly on us.

"Tank! Tank!" screamed our startled troops. "Jesus! Get the hell out of here!"

Those up front jumped into the ditch on the opposite side of the road from the tank. One man turned and ran away. Panic followed. Several men ran toward Sergeant O'Brien and me, uncontrolled fear in their faces.

O'Brien grabbed one of the men as he dashed by us and threw him to the deck. I reached out for another and spun him into the ditch. Then another.

"Goddammit, stop!" I pointed my carbine at the men still rushing toward us. Their frightened faces showed confusion, but they stopped running. "Into the ditch! Bear on the tank!" I yelled at them.

The runaways leaped into the ditch and spread themselves out. O'Brien and I formed them into a firing line, their rifles and BARs pointed toward the menacing tank. Their fire would be useless against the buttoned-up steel hull, but the panic had subsided.

Sergeant Wright ran up to me. "Where do you want the mortars, Lieutenant?"

I wasn't equipped to fight a tank. My mortars were of little use against its armor, although a lucky hit might do some damage to its treads or the scope. The riverbed was behind us, and I told Wright to set the guns there.

Except for the side-to-side movement of its cannon, the tank showed no sign of life. Bill Graeber ran down the road toward us, crossing directly in front of it. As he passed by the tank, he rolled a

The Air Force drops supplies. Ammunition and rations came by parachute after the Chinese had cut the MSR—the main supply route. When the chutes blew into the hills, we fought the Chinese who tried to capture them. The silk chutes made good scarves and foxhole liners.

Chinese soldiers surrender after Marines take the high ground from them. When the rifle companies were locked in combat and far from the prisoner holding points at headquarters, guarding the captured soldiers was often impossible. PHOTO COURTESY FRANK KERR

A Marine catches some sack time. At Chosin we fought all day to take the high ground, and the Chinese fought all night to take it back. We slept when we could, minutes at a time, in ditches and holes scooped from the snow. PHOTO COURTESY FRANK KERR

On the MSR from Yudam-ni to Hagaru-ri Marines from headquarters and supply units fought off Chinese soldiers who raided the column. Only the wounded rode in the vehicles, and they, too, fought when the enemy came close in. PHOTO COURTESY FRANK KERR

On the breakout from Yudam-ni, the column waits for the rifle companies of the 5th and 7th Marines to clear the high ground ahead. It took the column three days and nights to go the fourteen miles to Hagaru-ri. PHOTO COURTESY FRANK KERR

Tanks gave us support coming out of Koto-ri. This looks like the hill where earlier Baker-One-Seven had its last big firefight. Lieutenant Kurcaba and Pfcs. Kowalski and Lupacchini were killed here, and Lieutenants Lee and Owen were wounded. PHOTO COURTESY FRANK KERR

Baker-One-Seven fought all day and all night to get from Hagaru-ri to the frozen, blizzard-blown village of Koto-ri. Here we slept in tents for a night before we jumped off again to link up with the 1st Marines coming up from Chinhung-ni. PHOTO COURTESY U.S. MARINE CORPS

The tactical air control party guided in the Corsairs—our flying artillery—in support of the rifle companies. Back row from left: Corporal Thomas, Pfc. Romp, Pfc. Pozega, Corporal Wright, Sergeant Hedrick, Pfc. Burns, and First Lieutenant Holland. Front row, from left: Pfc. Rice, Corporal Tinelli, and Pfc. Tebbs. PHOTO COURTESY JOE HEDRICK

Frank Bifulk, left, and Merwin Perkins aboard ship at Hungnam harbor, leaving North Korea. They were the only two men of the mortar section who were not killed or wounded. Only twenty-seven of Baker-One-Seven's Marines survived the Chosin Reservoir campaign. PHOTO COURTESY TOM LINEBERRY

These snapshots of Dorothy and the babies—Mike and Dinny—were two of the photos that I kept in the webbing of my helmet. I looked at them every night before going to sleep, and often during lulls in the fighting.

grenade underneath. It exploded without causing damage, and the tank did not respond.

Graeber resumed command of the men that O'Brien and I had lined up in the ditch. I scurried to my mortars.

Sergeant Wright had them set up one hundred yards from the tank. Pat Burris didn't wait for the command to open fire. As I crossed the dry, rocky riverbed, I heard a round come out of his tube. I turned to watch the shell explode several yards behind the tank.

"Up a quarter turn," Burris called to his gunner, Merwin Perkins.

"Up a quarter," answered Perkins.

Bifulk dropped a zero-charge round. Thunk!

I followed the high arc of the shell, almost straight up. As it began its descent, I was horrified to see Captain Wilcox with some of the company headquarters people sprinting toward the tank, near where the mortar round would land.

The shell exploded a few yards in front of the tank. Fortunately, it was just out of killing range from the skipper and his people. It jolted them, though, and they dove for the ditches.

"Cease fire! Cease fire!" I screamed at Burris. "God-dammit, you almost killed the skipper!"

Jim Kovar and his assistant rocket gunner, Bill Regan, were with Captain Wilcox. Kovar recovered quickly from the close explosion, rolled away from the ditch, and went to the kneeling position, the three-five tube on his shoulder. Only fifty yards away, a gigantic sitting duck in his sights, was Kovar's dream target, a Soviet T-34 tank. He waited for Regan to tap him on the back, the signal that the rocket was armed, ready to fire.

At the rear of the company column was Danny Holland and his tactical air team. At the first panicked cries of "Tank! Tank!" Danny ran forward, bringing his radio man. He had a flight of Corsairs on station, covering the day's advance. Within seconds one of his planes streaked in on the tank.

Also on the road with the battalion was the regiment's anti-tank team, hungry for action. They sped their jeep, towing a 75-millimeter recoilless rifle, up the road, skidded to a halt in front of Graeber's ditch, and spun their gun toward the tank. They had point-blank aim at their target.

The enemy tank didn't get off a single round. With an ear-splitting roar, only feet above us, the lone Corsair zoomed in and unleashed a rocket that was a direct hit. Simultaneously, the seventy-five gun fired in another direct hit. And as the Corsair flew by, Kovar fired off his three-five for a third knockout blow.

The tank jumped a few feet above its dug-in pit. When it settled, it was in flames. None of its crew emerged. Baker Company's second tangle with an enemy tank was a win.

All hands took credit for the kill. Danny Holland chalked one up for his fliers. The regiment's seventy-five recoilless crew were jubilant over their big hit. In Baker-One-Seven we gave the credit to Jim Kovar.

Bill Graeber raised holy hell with his platoon after Sergeant O'Brien told him about the men who had succumbed to panic. And the skipper chewed me out because my mortars had almost demolished him.

In two days of moving up the road into the mountains, the 7th Marines knocked off four of the Soviet tanks that the North Koreans had dedicated to support the Chinese army. The one we killed that day was the last of them; after that we encountered no more enemy armor.

•   •   •

The farther we went into the high country the more scarce the Chinese became. We knew that they were there, though. They revealed themselves in small groups that usually faded away before we could get close.

Each day we sent out patrols that consisted of a rifle platoon, along with a section of machine guns and a sixty-mortar squad with extra ammo carriers. Usually we were accompanied by forward observers—FOs—from the 105 howitzers or the battalion's heavy mortars. A tactical air team often came along, too.

Captain Wilcox relied on Kiser and Graeber for the longer patrols, a mile or so ahead of the company, into the hills. The 1st Platoon, with a new lieutenant almost every day, was used for shorter patrols, usually only squad strength. They checked the approaches to our perimeter so that the Chinese couldn't get in close enough for a surprise attack. Sudong-ni was an expensive lesson, and we did not repeat its mistakes.

One day our airplanes reported that they had spotted a large concentration of enemy concealed in the woods a few thousand yards northwest. Graeber's platoon went out to verify, and I accompanied him with two mortars. Sergeant Richard, seeking relief from his first sergeant duties, broke out his sniper rifle and attached himself to the patrol.

We were two hours out when we took scattered small arms fire on the approach to the enemy area. Graeber spread two squads in a skirmish line and led them forward. At four hundred yards I had Hugo

Johnson's gun drop several rounds in the vicinity of the shooting. I heard Sergeant Richard crank out a single round from his sniper rifle.

The enemy fire ceased after the one brief volley. When Graeber's line moved into the Chinese position, the enemy had vanished, leaving behind a cluster of shelters made of tree branches packed with dirt; they looked like mud igloos. There was a single dead Chinese, which we credited to Sergeant Richard and his sniper rifle. There was no other sign of casualties. Bill Graeber kidded me that the only thing I had accomplished with my mortar barrage was to lighten the load for my ammo carriers.

We searched the huts but found no papers or material that would be of value to the intelligence people. The dead man's pockets yielded a few scraps of paper and perforated Chinese coins. I took a coin as a souvenir and gave the rest of the contents to Graeber to turn over to intelligence.

We returned to the battalion perimeter and reported our observations to Major Tighe, the operations officer. He told us that there were increasing reports of heavy enemy concentrations on all sides of the battalion. However, General MacArthur himself was expressing impatience with the slow pace made by the 1st Marine Division in its progress toward the Chinese border. The Army was trying to light a fire under General Smith, our division commander.

• • •

While Graeber and I talked with Major Tighe, Sergeant O'Brien had the troops loaded up with rations, ammo, and water for the company. Kelly did his usual scrounging and uncovered a cache of canned fruit. He set aside two cases of peaches at the rear of the column, one for each of us to carry on the climb up to the perimeter.

The case of peaches was awkward to carry, and it slowed me down. Otherwise I might have been alongside Bill Graeber when a single Chinese mortar shell landed at the head of the column.

The shell hit downhill and a few yards off to the side of the trail. Its shrapnel had no effect, but its concussion was close enough to lift Graeber off his feet and hurl him against the trunk of a stout tree.

At the sound of the explosion, I dropped the case of peaches and ran forward. When I reached him, Graeber was on the ground, at the base of the tree, writhing in pain. The platoon corpsman, Bill Davis, knelt beside him, jabbing in a syrette of morphine.

"Maybe broke his back, Lieutenant," Davis said, looking up at me.

Sergeant O'Brien had spread the patrol off the trail, a precaution against more mortars landing on us. None came, though.

Bill Graeber gritted his teeth against the excruciating pain, and his eyes started to cloud over, the effect of the morphine. "Take over the patrol, Joe," were his last words before the drug took him out.

We eased him onto a poncho, put a man at each corner, and sent him back to the battalion aid station.

It was a blow to me, losing a good pal like Bill Graeber. My emotions were mixed, though. I was elated at the prospect that Captain Wilcox would give me Graeber's platoon. It seemed the logical thing to do because of my familiarity with Graeber's men.

• • •

First Lt. Chew Een Lee went directly to Baker-One-Seven, without reporting his return to the paper pushers at battalion. He was absent without leave from the Army hospital, and he didn't know if the MPs would be looking for him. Captain Wilcox was delighted to have Lee back with the company, even with his right arm in a sling. Colonel Davis was happy, too, when he heard about it, and he told Lee to forget about the administrative details; he would have the sergeant major take care of everything.

• • •

After I brought the 2d Platoon into the company perimeter, I turned the men over to Sergeant O'Brien and I reported to the captain. Battalion had already informed him that Graeber was knocked out of action.

Lieutenant Lee was at the CP with the skipper. Like everyone else, I was glad to see him. Regardless of his stiff, by-the-book ways, Chew Een Lee had demonstrated leadership under fire that inspired us all.

I wasn't glad, though, when Captain Wilcox told me that Lee was back just in time to replace Bill Graeber as 2d Platoon leader. I tried hard not to show my disappointment when I returned to my mortarmen.

• • •

Mail came while we were on patrol, the first since we landed at Wonsan. The letters from Dorothy said that the babies were fine and they were saying their prayers for Daddy. And Dorothy was going to Mass and Communion every morning at St. Cecilia's, praying that I soon would be home.

We had no paper for writing letters. During a break I wrote on the blank side of one of Dorothy's letters. It said, in part:

One of my replacements just broke out a mirror—first I've seen of myself since we left Hamhung, three weeks ago. What a sight! Believe it or not, I have not bathed, shaved, brushed my teeth, or changed my clothes since the Chinese first attacked us. I'd give anything for a bath and to put on clean clothes, but no one in the rifle companies has a chance at such luxury. We're all the same, a bunch of scroungy looking people.

This sounds like I have it rough, doesn't it? It's not too bad, Darling. We get a couple of laughs now and then, and I'm very fortunate having the outfit I have. They're a terrific bunch of people. And I don't have much time for thinking about things being rough.

Kelly found me an envelope, and I gave the letter to the sergeant major to mail the next time we went through the battalion command post. Long before the letter reached her, Dorothy was reading dire newspaper stories that were headlined "NATION FEARS FOR MARINES TRAPPED AT CHOSIN RESERVOIR."

CHAPTER TWELVE

Farther into the mountains lay the grim little town of Koto-ri. It stretched along the roadway, a string of shacks made of rough lumber and concrete blocks. Most of the buildings had been wrecked by the ROKs as they were being chased away by the Chinese. Our reconnaissance patrols entered the town and found that Chinese had now abandoned it as well. Koto-ri was ours for the taking, and it would become the base of operations for Chesty Puller and his 1st Marines, when they caught up with us.

Regiment put Baker-One-Seven aboard a convoy of trucks for a ten-mile ride up a narrow, winding road. The ride raised concern among the troops; it was their experience that there was no such thing as a free ride.

We were dropped off a thousand yards north of the town. We dug in a perimeter on a hill that was the farthest outpost of the division. Although we observed few Chinese, and those we saw were at a distance, our security was tight: Listening posts and trip flares out, tin cans strung on wires, mortars and howitzers registered on the approaches, and a fifty percent watch. That had become our standard operating procedure ever since Sudong-ni.

Our patrols resumed immediately. The Chinese tactics remained the same—a few volleys at long range, then fade away. Beyond Koto-ri these encounters increased, and each time we went out, the numbers of Chinese grew. Every man in the company knew that we were being sucked in, and all hands wondered why General MacArthur's staff in Tokyo didn't realize that.

The weather turned colder. Some of my men—Bifulk, Perkins, Veeder, Westberg—came from reserve units in Minnesota, and they were our weather forecasters. They sniffed the winds that blew down the high mountain passes and pronounced that cold weather was coming. "Gonna be colder than hell," was Bifulk's forecast.

• • •

The platoon that Chew Een Lee took over from Bill Graeber was a good outfit, but Lieutenant Lee was not satisfied with it. In his direct, by-the-book manner he made it clear to Platoon Sergeant O'Brien and the squad and fire team leaders that, henceforth, formations would be controlled much more tightly. Squads and fire teams would maneuver, or hold positions, with strict fire discipline imposed by Lee and the NCOs. When they weren't on patrol, Lee put his men through a rigorous training program of small unit tactics. They maneuvered all over the nearby hills and they bitched at the extra work. Lee paid little heed to the grumbling.

"Soon we will meet the enemy in force," he predicted to his men. "We will be ready."

It was an article of faith with Chew Een Lee that combat leadership came from the front. In the attack, he positioned himself with the most advanced squad, just behind the point. He wore a bright, fluorescent-pink vest fashioned of cloth panels that he had obtained from the tactical air team. The intended purpose of the brilliantly colored panels was to mark the forward extent of our lines for supporting aircraft. Lee wore his vest so that his men could locate him quickly during a firefight.

He still had a sling on his wounded right arm, and he carried his carbine in his left hand. He fired it from the hip, using it to shoot tracers that marked target sectors.

A few days after we began patrolling the country above Koto-ri, I took a mortar squad out with Lee's platoon. That day the Chinese departed from form and gave us a stiff fight. Halfway up a hill that was sparsely covered with shrub, they opened up on Lee. He was with the point fire team and, wearing his glowing pink vest, was very visible to the enemy as well as his own men. I expected to see him get hit, an easy target, but he did not go down.

I was with the main body of Lee's platoon. Sergeant Winget, at the bottom of the hill with a mortar, was within my view. I gave a signal to set up the gun and prepare for a fire mission. Then I raised my binoculars to search out the enemy position on the hill.

The Chinese were dug in above Lee. They had a machine gun and a line of rifles, more formidable than their usual defensive formations. They were expertly deployed below the crest, and their automatic weapons fired short, disciplined bursts. Tracers streaked, and bullets and shrapnel swept down the slope. They used Japanese rifles and Russian burps guns that were concealed skillfully in rock crevices and nests of brush, difficult to locate. Unlike ours, the Chinese ammunition emitted no telltale smoke when it was fired. In daylight their muzzle flashes were nearly invisible. We had faced that problem against the North Koreans down south, and we had learned to find enemy positions more by sound than by sight.

It took Lee some time to locate the machine gun that was giving the most trouble. When he found it he fired, one-handed, to put a tracer on it. His squads moved into skirmish lines, and the NCOs sent their own tracers to mark their sectors. The BARs and the rifles followed, sending a great volume of fire up the slope at the Chinese.

Winget waved to let me know that his mortar was ready. I aimed a tracer toward the machine gun and pumped my arm four times, four hundred yards. I saw the round leave the tube and followed its path. It disappeared over the ridgeline. Winget realized that he was too long and, without need of my correction, came up a turn. His second round was close, and I waved him to fire for effect. We seldom wasted ammo bracketing a target. Ammo carried up the hills was too valuable to be wasted on the niceties.

The enemy guns slackened as Winget pounded them. Lee's squads moved upward, responding to the NCOs' signals with short bounds, fire team by fire team. Five, ten yards at a dash, then to ground, bearing their fire on the enemy as the next fire team went closer in. It was the classic Marine Corps rifle tactic that Lee had drilled into his platoon during his extra training sessions.

A Marine went down and writhed on the ground. The platoon's corpsman, Bill Davis, dashed low across the slope and crouched at the wounded man's side. Another Marine fell and didn't move again. A buddy stabbed the dead man's rifle into the earth by its bayonet, then continued forward.

The Chinese found it difficult to defend against Lee's energetic tactics. Our coordinated mortar and machine gun fire kept them pinned to the ground. They were no longer able to apply aimed fire, and their effectiveness diminished as our riflemen pushed closer in on them.

Lee sent a squad crawling forward into grenade range. I signaled Winget to cease fire, and the mortars stopped exploding along the forward crest of the hill. The Chinese soldiers heaved a barrage of their potato-masher concussion grenades down the slope. The Marines threw a responding volley; our grenades were more powerful, filling the air with bits of hot flying steel. Both sides dove for holes. Another volley was thrown. Lee ran forward, waving the carbine overhead and calling for his Marines to follow. They surged for the top, screaming their gung-ho and rebel yells.

The Chinese withdrew. They pulled their wounded away but left their dead on the slope. Lee pushed his men over the ridgeline where they prepared to defend against counterattack. Attilio Lupacchini stood beside Lee, his BAR at the ready. Lupacchini had appointed himself Lee's bodyguard.

Sergeant Bondurant, the platoon guide, rifled through the pockets of the Chinese dead, gathering material for our intelligence people. I sent Kelly for a detail of the ammo carriers to bear the casualties. Bill Davis had two wounded men doped up with morphine and out of pain. And there was one dead Marine, already covered by his poncho.

When he was certain that the Chinese would not counterattack, Lee ordered us all off the hill. End of patrol. On the return march to the company perimeter, no one complained about Lieutenant Lee's excessive training methods. He walked along the column and thanked the men for their good work. I wondered to myself how many firefights Lee would survive, standing at the front of his troops clad in that brilliant pink vest.

• • •

Hank Kiser was also an effective combat leader, but his manner was far different from Lee's. Hank, too, led from the front—not the extreme front, as was Lee's style—but always forward enough to maintain direct control of his platoon in battle. He never seemed to get ruffled, and he wasn't a shouter.

He didn't need to shout; his runner, Jack Gallapo, a giant regular, had a booming voice that carried all over a hill.

"Get the 3d Squad up here," Lieutenant Kiser would say to Gallapo.

"Third Squad!" Gallapo would sound off with a thunderous roar that could be heard across a hundred yards of terrain. "Third Squad, get your asses up here! On the double!"

Hank had the ability to read quickly the enemy's defense when we were in the attack. Almost as soon as the Chinese opened fire on his platoon he would have his carbine up, putting tracers into their vital points. He was tall, easy for his NCOs to spot in a fight. Seldom did I see Hank on the deck, except under the most withering fire.

Once Hank and I were pinned down together. A string of tracers came at us as we scanned a ridgeline, looking for targets for my mortars. Then a burst of machine gun fire pelted the ground near us. We dove into a shallow depression made by an earlier Chinese mortar round. The hostile machine gun, with rifle fire added, zeroed in on us. Hank tried to raised his head; a bullet grazed his helmet, ripping its camouflage cover. We compressed ourselves into the bottom of our "hole."

With bullets swarming overhead, Hank and I made vows of perpetual goodness and purity if God would get us out of this one. Then we realized the absurdity of our response, and we broke into laughter.

Kelly used his initiative and called a mortar on the offending machine gun. Kiser's platoon brought every gun it had to bear and suppressed the Chinese who had pinned us down. Hank and I crawled out of there, none too proud of ourselves. Afterwards we reminded each other of the transgressions against God from which we had vowed to abstain forever.

• • •

Although I continued to push my mortarmen, I was quite satisfied with them. Only weeks ago these youngsters had been learning the parts of their weapons and how to fire them. Now they saw themselves the equal of any troops that the Marine Corps could put on the line.

The naive, boyish Perkins had turned out to be rock-solid in combat, and he showed a steady hand when his squad leader, Corporal Burris, put him on the gun.

Perkins's foxhole buddy was Frank Bifulk. Physically, they were a matched pair—short, powerfully muscled, and possessed of great stamina. The two were as devoted as brothers, and they squabbled, stole rations from each other, and wrestled continuously. No one had ever heard Perkins use a profanity, and Bifulk could not get through a sentence without uttering a string of them. I thought of Bifulk and Perkins as our "Katzenjammer Kids," named after the comic strip that featured two roly-poly, trouble-prone characters.

The gangly teenager, Fisher, was a pleasant surprise. He was very bright, quick to size up a situation and move in the right direction. Under fire I had noted that he instinctively positioned himself where his carbine could do the most good. I planned to make Fisher my next squad leader when I needed another replacement.

Sometimes I wondered how Dean Westberg kept going under the heavy mortarman's load. The skinny kid, with delicate features and the look of a research librarian, never faltered on me, no matter how steep the hill or how long the march. He had become very good on the mortar, too. When Hugo Johnson became squad leader, he made Westberg his number one gunner.

Branek had given me no more problems after the incident with the old man, when we were advancing into Uijongbu. Indeed, Branek seemed eager to impress me with his quick willingness to respond to orders. I thought he wanted to return to the runner's job if anything happened to Kelly.

I wasn't about to lose Kelly, if I could help it. As a highly trained regular, Kelly well knew the purpose and function of the sixty mortars, and how they were supposed to move in support of the rifle platoons. Steady under fire, he had a good runner's ability to convey a clear message to the skipper and the other lieutenants.

Kelly was an extra pair of eyes for me. He had an uncanny sense of the enemy's presence. Many times, even before the point squad of the lead platoon had sighted the Chinese, Kelly would give me a nudge and caution, "Lieutenant, keep a sharp eye. There are gooks close by. I can feel them." He was never wrong.

He was good protection for me, too. Whenever we moved up under fire, Kelly would call to me, "OK, I got you covered." And he would be the proper five-paces interval away, carbine at the ready, searching the terrain as he moved with me.

Grauman was still shaky. The night of Sudong he was with Sergeant Lunney's squad and had made his way back into our line by himself. He had crawled on his belly, terrified amidst the rampaging Chinese soldiers.

"I . . . I didn't think I'd make it back. Didn't know what to do, Lieutenant," he had stammered. "I'm sorry I ran away. But I didn't know what else to do down there by myself."

"You didn't run away. You did the right thing getting back to us," I told him. "Well done, Marine!"

That seemed to pick the lad up. But I told his squad leader, Corporal Johnson, to keep a close eye on him.

Hugo Johnson had taken over Lunney's squad with ease. His men had responded to him without question. They respected his experience, and they followed his up-front example when we met the enemy. They liked Hugo, too, and they wanted to make him look good as a squad leader.

Corporal Burris was a jewel, a natural leader who would quickly gauge the sense of an enemy encounter. In firefights he set an example of intelligent courage; he knew how to move his men and set them up tactically, taking advantage of the terrain to limit their exposure to the Chinese fire. With the exception of Kelly, perhaps, Burris was the best man I had for searching out targets. He had a sharp eye and a quick mind, and if he sometimes took too much initiative—moving up or opening fire before my order—that was a problem I could live with. I never worried about Pat Burris and his squad lagging behind.

Sergeant Winget remained my steady, solid workhorse. His squad was always squared away and ready to move out. He never faltered under fire, no matter how heavily we were being hit. He was the classic, stand-up Marine sergeant who bellowed out orders and encouragement to his men and showed them courage in the face of the enemy. I had not forgotten how Sergeant Winget had stood beside me when the Chinese charged at us that night at Sudong, and the strength that his presence had given to me.

Sergeant Wright and I agreed that the mortars had done well. "Never would have expected it, but these people have come a long way since Camp Pendleton," Wright said to me.

"Yeah," I agreed. "But I don't want them getting cocky."

"Not while they've got me snapping at them," responded Sergeant Wright. Sergeant Wright had turned out to be a fine Marine NCO. I mentioned that to the skipper every time I asked about his hardship transfer back to the States.

• • •

One cold morning the full company went out, a reconnaissance in strength. It turned into a terrible day.

We went west off the road and topped a long ridge. Before us was a wide plateau, an open meadow that stretched several hundred yards in every direction. Trees lined the other side of the meadow, a logical place for the Chinese to conceal themselves and observe our movement. The captain told Lee and Kiser each to send a fire team over there as scouts.

The weather had changed abruptly. Heavy clouds had begun to roll across the high plateau, cold and gray and wet. The temperature had dropped, and a chill wind from the north blew a drizzly rain at us. All hands broke out the ponchos, but the damp cold penetrated and we shivered in our lightweight clothing.

I had all three mortars set up and ordered a registration round on the distant tree line. Because of the low clouds, I was unable to follow the path of the shell, so I could not spot its impact. There was a muffled explosion, though, so it wasn't a dud.

"You see where that landed, Kelly?" I asked my runner.

"Didn't see a damn thing!"

I had Corporal Johnson's gun firing registration. "Drop another round, Hugo. Down one-zero-zero."

The round went up. I lost it in the clouds again, heard the explosion, but saw no smoke. *Where the hell were we hitting?*

"Kelly?"

"Nothing, Sir!"

Johnson threw another round. We were shooting blind. The thick, soggy air suppressed the smoke of the impact, holding it close to the ground and making it invisible. It was a phenomenon I had never before encountered. The solution to the problem was to observe from closer to the tree line, which I judged to be at six hundred yards range.

"We've got to get up closer," I told Kelly. "Let's go."

"Yeah, I figured that," said Kelly, who usually anticipated my thoughts. He slung the carbine off his shoulder and held it at the ready as we headed closer to the tree line.

We went out through Hank Kiser's front, and I moved Sergeant Winget's gun up behind the forward squad to maintain visual contact. Kiser's men were in the prone position on the wet ground, weapons pointed toward the tree line that was only faintly visible through the overcast.

"Where the hell are you going?" Hank asked me.

"I've got to get closer to register the mortars," I explained. "Can't see a damn thing through this rain and fog."

"Yeah. I sent out a fire team to scout that tree line. Watch out for them." Kiser told me. And he added with a laugh, "Don't expect me to come and save your ass if you get in trouble out there."

"You're a real pal," I said, and Kelly and I went out, running at a crouch. I hoped that the Chinese, too, found it difficult to see across this miserable, wet field.

We had gone only a short distance before firing broke out in front of us. One hundred yards ahead—maybe a hundred and fifty, it was difficult to judge in this murk—a cluster of dark, indistinct shapes moved toward Kelly and me. They were Kiser's four scouts, and Chinese bullets pursued them. Kelly and I dropped to the kneeling position, weapons up. Enemy tracers came from the misty line of trees.

I stood and waved my arm at Winget who was barely visible. I fired my own tracer toward the Chinese position, then pumped my arm six times—six hundred yards. Seconds later I saw the red flash of propellant gas from our mortar, and heard the hollow thunk! Although I was still unable to follow the shell's course through the clinging clouds, I heard it explode.

Kiser's four scouts neared us, now crawling on their bellies under the Chinese bullets. I signaled Winget to come down one-zero-zero. The sound of the round's impact was more distinct, although I still couldn't see it. Behind us the machine guns from Kiser's line began to clatter, their tracers sending long arcs over our heads.

One of the men approaching us caught a Chinese bullet. Shouting, "I'm hit! I'm hit!" he screamed in pain. Two of his buddies stood up, each taking an arm, and dragged him, face down, as fast as they could run. They ran hunched over, and as they passed Kelly and me, I saw the blood staining the back of the wounded man's poncho. His helmet had fallen away. Mud streaked his blond hair, and from the glimpse I had of the boy's face, I knew he was dead.

We weren't doing any good out there, so Kelly and I went back to Kiser's line with the three men who had pulled in their dead buddy.

• • •

More Chinese fire had broken out, far to our right, in front of Lee's line. They fired from a sharp, short hill that rose from the meadow. Lee wheeled one of his rifle squads to face the rise and maneuvered them forward. Burris's gun was with Lee, and he traversed the face of the hill with HEs before the squad moved up. The Chinese ceased fire and withdrew quickly, a familiar tactic. Lee stayed with the main body of his platoon and sent a fire team to reconnoiter the top.

When they reached the top of the rise, the four men walked along the ridge in search of the vanished enemy. Looking up, Lee saw his men silhouetted against the skyline and yelled for them to get down; they were perfectly outlined targets.

The Chinese saw them, too, and already had the ridgeline registered for their mortars. Their first round blew a Marine to pieces. The next barrage claimed two more. The fourth man dove from the ridge and leaped, rolled, and stumbled down the hill. He came to a halt at the feet of Lieutenant Lee.

Lee had seen three of his men killed needlessly, and he stood in silent fury. His good hand gripped his carbine so tight that his knuckles went white. "Stupid!" he hissed through clenched teeth. "Stupid! Stupid!" Over and over again. "Stupid!"

He turned to Gene O'Brien, his platoon sergeant. "See to it that this never happens again, Sergeant. You tell the men that if I see another Marine on the skyline, I will shoot him myself."

Lieutenant Lee strode off to be by himself until his fury and frustration subsided.

• • •

When I got into Kiser's line, he was on the walkie-talkie, the skipper on the other end. Hank's hand radio was functioning across the flat meadow, although mine wasn't. We never knew when the damned things would work.

"Skipper wants you to bring all your mortars over to Lee's front," Hank said to me when I approached. He handed me his radio.

The captain's voice came over the static. "Yeah, Five? Bring all your guns to Baker-Two sector. On the double. Out."

"Roger. Wilco. Out!" I complied and signed off. I handed the radio back to Hank. "Skipper's running us ragged today. I don't know what good we can do for him over there. I can't see where we're shooting, anyway."

"Goddamn gooks know where they're shooting, though," Hank said, and he went over to his corpsman, Ed Toppel, who was kneeling beside the dead man who had just been dragged in.

• • •

Lee's platoon was under machine gun fire as I moved across the company front with Winget's squad. We picked up Johnson as we went. The skipper was with Lee, trying to find the machine guns that were firing at us. Since the Chinese knew the terrain and the range, they were not using tracers. Their gunners skillfully traversed our line with plunging fire—heavy slugs raining down on our men.

"Think you can do anything to those machine guns?" the skipper asked as I ran up to him. He was easy to find, standing next to Lee, who was as usual wearing the fluorescent pink vest.

"Can't see a thing, Captain," I said. "I'll give it a try, if you want. But we're just wasting ammo."

Drops of rain spotted Captain Wilcox's big, round glasses. He gave me a long look and I thought I was about to get another chewing out. *What the hell! He asked for my opinion.*

But the skipper nodded. "Yeah, Joe, you're right. No sense shooting blind any more."

Then he turned to Lee. "Pull your people back and set them up at the edge of the field. I'll call in the coordinates to artillery. See if they can do us any good."

While Garcia was raising the artillery fire control center on the big radio, the skipper got Hank on the walkie-talkie and ordered him to pull back with Lee. He told Sergeant King to put a squad forward to cover the withdrawal.

When the skipper had artillery's fire control on the radio, he called in the coordinates for a registration round. The battery of 105–millimeter howitzers that supported us was dug in around Koto-ri, a mile and a half away.

Less than a minute later we heard the heavy ripping sound of their first round cutting the air over our heads. It landed a hundred yards in front of where Lee, the captain, and I stood. Stabs of flame, like lightning from a black cloud, leaped off the ground, and we felt the earth tremble from the explosion.

"Close, goddamnit! Too close!" shouted the skipper. Then, into the mike, he said "Add three-zero-zero. Repeat, add three-zero-zero."

The next round landed farther away, and we barely saw the stabs of flame. It was where the skipper wanted it. The enemy machine gun fire had stopped; the Chinese knew what would be coming at them.

"Repeat range. Give me concentration fire. Three volleys. On my command." The concentration fire would saturate the area where the Chinese were concealed. The captain waited to give the order to fire until Sergeant King had positioned the covering squad in front of us.

"Fire!"

Twenty seconds later the first rounds of the barrage landed, less than fifty yards away.

Short rounds! We dove for the deck, all of us, even Lee. The following rounds dropped among the front of the squad that the 1st Platoon had positioned to cover the company withdrawal. Screams from our own men, mud and flame, and crashing thunder. The skipper yelled into the radio: "Cease fire! Cease fire! Short rounds! Short rounds!"

Friendly fire. The worst thing that can happen in combat. Our dismal day turned to horror. Cries and moans and agonized screams pierced the black smoke that drifted over the broken ground. Doc Mickens and Joe King were already working among the wounded and mangled dead Marines. Bill Davis and Ed Toppel, the other platoon corpsmen, sprinted across the field to help.

Captain Wilcox yelled into the radio as the next line of shells exploded, now away from us, farther to our front. They had been in the air before the gunners could comply with the order to cease fire. They did us no further damage, but their noise added to the hellish scene.

I arose, shaken and not sure what to do. I saw Sergeant Wright at the edge of the field and called for him to bring the ammo carriers forward. We would use them to carry the casualties away. Joe Kurcaba had already brought the company headquarters people to lend a hand with the grisly work. We had four more dead and three wounded.

Kurcaba went to the skipper and said that we should get the company out of this place and back down to the road. The captain shook his head a few times to clear it and thought about Joe's suggestion for several seconds. Then he got Kiser and Lee on the walkie-talkies and told them to prepare their platoons to move back. He told me to walk a screen of HEs two hundred yards out to discourage any Chinese from following us. When I reported to him that the mortars were ready to fire the mission, I thought I saw tears coming down his face, although it could have been the drizzling rain. Eight dead Marines for the day. More wounded. And nothing accomplished.

The rain and sleet turned to snow—wet, sticky stuff that coated the ponchos covering the dead men. The troops struggled down a wet, slippery trail to the road, bearing the dead and the wounded. They were soaked through and spoke no words, except to blaspheme the goddamn fools who sent us out into this miserable, wet, cold country. We wore field jackets under the ponchos, but they had no lining, and our lightweight dungarees were the same ones we had worn while fighting in the steamy humidity of South Korea.

CHAPTER THIRTEEN

We were chilled through and bone tired as we slogged our way back to battalion. The men rejoiced that we were not ordered to climb another hill to set a night defensive perimeter. Instead, we bivouacked in a dry part of the riverbed that ran along the valley. The skipper passed the word that we did not need to set a security watch. The other companies of the regiment had caught up with us, and they were dug in on all the approaches to Koto-ri.

Battalion gave us hot chow. We filed past a big steel drum that was filled with boiling water that heated cans of C-rations. A "cook" stood with a pair of tongs and fished out a hot can of meat-and-beans for each man. There was steaming coffee, too. It scalded our lips when we put them to the edge of the canteen cups.

The bivouac was lumpy with rocks and boulders. We were still damp from the day of chasing the Chinese through the cold rain and fog, and we slid all the way into our sleeping bags. Then we wrapped ourselves in our ponchos and immediately fell asleep. I told my men to keep their boondockers on—just in case the enemy surprised us. Before I burrowed into my bag I turned into the wind that came down the valley. It was strong and cold and snowflakes spattered my face.

"Winter's here," I said to Kelly.

He was a long bundle, all wrapped up, lying next to me in the shallow hole he had scooped out of the rocks for us.

"I'm freezing my ass off," was his muffled reply.

We slept without interruption, the longest sleep since before Sudong-ni. But when we awoke at daylight a half foot of snow covered us and the sky was matted with angry gray clouds. I stuck my head out and was greeted by an icy blast of wind.

The men groaned, coughed, wheezed, and hawked big gobs of

phlegm as Baker-One-Seven came to life in the snow-buried river-bed. They scraped snow from their ponchos, wrapped the sleeping bags in them, and made blanket rolls. We didn't have gloves yet, and our fingers stiffened and froze as we tried to square away our gear. Word came down the line that the temperature was fifteen degrees.

Sergeant Wright came over to me, and I marveled at his squared-away blanket roll; mine looked like a bag of rags.

He expressed concern. "Sir, I think that every man in the mortar section has pneumonia." Wright's eyes watered and his face was sickly. "Half of them have requested sick call and the rest are just as bad."

Kelly was with us, shivering like a wet dog. "Why don't you ask Captain Wilcox to get us a day of light duty? Recuperation," he suggested.

"Yeah, Kelly," I answered. "And maybe ask if he can get us all trans-ferred back to Guam, where you came from."

"It was nice and warm on Guam," said my runner. He added a rasp-ing cough for effect.

"I'll get Doktorski to look at the men," I told Sergeant Wright. The headquarters corpsman, MacIntosh, had been injured on a climb and was no longer with the company.

At the company CP, Doktorski was already ministering to a line of sick Marines. He offered an APC pill to each of his patients. Then he gave them a swig from a canteen that was filled with diluted sick bay alcohol. The men walked away from Doktorski's treatment feel-ing slightly warmer, and some went to the rear of the line to repeat the cure. Kelly joined them and I went to the skipper.

Captain Wilcox informed me that our rest was over. We would move north out of Koto-ri as soon as the corpsmen finished sick call and we could get the company into formation. The skipper was shiv-ering cold, like the rest of us.

Gunny Buckley hobbled about, a sick, old man. His voice was weak as he ordered the headquarters people to get the company gear squared away to move out.

"How you doing, Gunny?" I asked.

"Ain't felt this poorly since the malaria hit us on Guadalcanal. Maybe worse than that," answered the gunny. His face was pasty and wet with perspiration in spite of the cold.

"You better get back to the aid station, Gunny. Let the battalion doctor take a look at you," I said.

"Nope, Lieutenant, with all respect," our gunnery sergeant replied. He leaned on a wooden staff, a broken-off tree branch. "Never missed a formation in all my time in the Corps. Ain't going to start now."

• • •

The column marched north into a cold, swirling wind that swept the road clear of snow. We put on the ponchos again, to help ward off the wind. They soon froze stiff and crackled as we walked.

The men were in foul temper.

"What kind of stupid bastards we got running this goddamn war?" came from the column.

"Don't worry about them guys running this goddamn war. They're sitting by a stove someplace, sticking pins in their maps."

"Yeah, and they'll get their pick of the cold weather gear before they send it up to us poor suckers."

"Guy in the battalion mess line said them rear echelon bastards are already wearing big fur coats and winter-issue boots."

"That's OK. We'll get that stuff next spring."

"Sure, what's left of it—by the time it gets to us we'll be needing jungle gear."

The worst suffering that day came from our feet. We had only thin cotton socks under the boondockers, little protection from the cold, especially as they were still damp under our leggings. We stomped away the pain of freezing toes and kept the blood circulating. There were complaints of numbness; some men said they felt as if they had pebbles in their socks. We didn't know about frostbite yet.

• • •

Chinese mortars fell along the head of the column, then some small arms at long range. Captain Wilcox called me forward to knock out the small arms. Then he passed the word to break for chow. The troops huddled together in the snow and opened cold cans of rations. A few small fires were made, but most of the troops spooned the meal down cold.

I put a mortar behind a steep rise, then crawled to the top, twenty yards up, to peer over the edge in hopes of locating the source of the enemy fire. I told Sergeant Wright to prepare for five hundred yards. When I turned around I saw that Kelly had a small fire going, kindled by propellant charges from the mortar shells. He waved a can of evaporated milk at me.

Evaporated milk, heated and mixed with powdered chocolate from the rations, was my favorite drink, a delicacy. Kelly had introduced me to it after he filched a couple of cans of the stuff on a trip through battalion. It was a rare find, and this was the only remaining can.

"Good man, Corporal Kelly!" I yelled down at him.

I returned to scanning the terrain above our halted column. Spotting a likely enemy position, I jabbed my bayonet into the ground as an aiming stake and turned to give Sergeant Wright the command.

As I turned, my foot dislodged a fist-size rock, which rolled down the slope. I watched it zig and zag and bounce, heading for Kelly's fire and the canteen cup that held the evaporated milk.

Direct hit! The rock rolled into the cup, knocked it over and splashed out the fire.

Kelly gasped. He looked up at me, suppressing rage at his clumsy lieutenant. "Will you watch where you put those big feet of yours!" he shouted. Then he added, "Sir!"

• • •

The snow continued throughout the day, blowing into our faces as we went north. Battalion halted us just before dark to defend a hill adjacent to the road. It was miserable work in the dark, climbing unknown terrain and digging in at the top. The skipper told Lee to spread a squad on each side of the column and clear the way to the crest. The remainder of the company followed their paths through the snow. The hill became steeper as we climbed higher, and the paths soon became treacherous, icy chutes.

Men slid backwards, fell, and crashed into each other. Weary Marines sprawled everywhere. They shivered in their frozen, damp dungarees, and their bare hands were raw from crawling in the snow. Still, they scrabbled and crawled, grabbing at the few thin trees to pull themselves higher.

The officers and NCOs earned their pay. When the men faltered we coaxed and cajoled, cursed and threatened. We pulled some men to their feet, and we spelled the machine gunners, mortarmen, and ammo carriers, carrying their heavy loads ourselves for stretches of the climb.

Captain Wilcox was up and down the hill with us, giving a hand and offering encouragement. "Keep it moving, Marine. Good man!"

We were fortunate that the Chinese gave no resistance that night.

The next morning Joe Kurcaba came bouncing up the road in the company jeep, blaring the horn and yelling for Baker-One-Seven to stand by for uniform issue. Two trucks followed him, carrying our new cold weather gear.

We each received a knee-length, pile-lined parka that had a hood to cover our heads. The parka was heavy; by itself it weighed more than all of the warm weather uniform we were turning in.

Then we were given winter-weight storm trousers, also heavy to wear, plus a new set of regular-weight dungarees to go underneath.

In addition, there were flannel shirts, new long johns, and heavy socks. The leather and canvas mittens we received had trigger fingers, with thin woolen gloves to wear inside.

And shoe-pacs, with felt inserts. Shoe-pacs would change the way we walked and bring us the crippling scourge of frostbite. They were big and cumbersome, twice the weight of our boondockers. They had thick, molded rubber bottoms with heavily cleated soles. The tops, from the ankle up the shin, were made of stiff leather that laced tightly. Shoe-pacs were clumsy for climbing and slippery on the ice.

The worst thing about them, however, was that when they were laced up, no air could circulate. On a steep climb or a long march our feet would sweat, no matter how cold it was. When we stopped moving, and the cold set in, the sweat-soaked felt inserts and socks would freeze. Long stretches of wet, frozen feet spelled frostbite.

We struggled around in the unwieldy cold weather gear for a while, getting used to the clumsiness and complaining about the extra weight. Then we set out on the day's march.

Later that morning the weather turned warm. By noontime, wearing the many layers of clothing under the parka—the storm gear, dungarees, flannel shirts, and long johns—we felt as though we were marching through a steam bath. We took off our parkas and slung them over the blanket rolls; yet it still meant extra weight to carry.

• • •

A draft of replacements arrived to fill in the ranks. Our casualties from chasing the Chinese into the mountains were light, less than ten percent over a period of two weeks. But there were the bad feet and the men who were injured in falls on the steep hills. And we lost several who came down with the flu or pneumonia as a result of the icy soaking we had taken above Koto-ri.

Some of the replacements were men who had recovered from their wounds at Sudong-ni. Charley Baldwin, the machine gunner, came back with tales of pretty nurses and the wild liberties he had enjoyed during his recuperation. Although they didn't believe much of it, the troops listened to the accounts with relish. Baldwin was wounded again, after only a few days back on his machine gun.

Kelly was delighted to see that his buddy from Guam, Gene Morrisroe, had returned to us. "Told you I'd be back," Morrisroe said to Kelly. "And I told you that there'd still be plenty of gooks left when I got here."

"Millions of 'em," Kelly agreed. "And more every day."

The new replacements were mostly reservists, men called up in

President Truman's July authorizations. They had arrived at Camp Pendelton after we formed up, and they were given intensive training in weapons and tactics before they went to the replacement drafts. When they came to us, they knew their stuff and they were in good physical trim.

One of the replacements, in his first day with us, saved Glenn Galtere's life. The 3d Platoon was in the attack, just short of the crest of an enemy-held hill. A few yards in front of Galtere a Chinese soldier sprang from a hole with a burp gun. Galtere was quicker than the Chinese. He swung his BAR from the hip and squeezed the trigger, expecting a burst that would blow the enemy soldier apart. Instead, there was a dull click. Misfire! As if in slow motion, Galtere saw the burp gun come up to level on him, so close that he could see the soldier's finger on the trigger. Galtere had learned at Sudong-ni that prayer might have value; now a quick one flashed through his mind. At that moment the replacement, coming up behind Galtere, cranked off a round from his M-1 rifle and drilled the burp-gunner through the chest. Galtere didn't know the name of the new man. Later he learned that his savior was one of the few casualties we had taken in that fight, a KIA in his first day of combat.

• • •

Yet another replacement first lieutenant came down from battalion to take the 1st Platoon. This one was Woody Taylor, a reservist who had volunteered for call-up as soon as the war began. He was a big, burly fellow, with a thick, bellowing Alabama accent. He knew combat from leading a rifle platoon against the Japanese on Okinawa.

Captain Wilcox had been using the 1st Platoon for squad-size working parties and short-range patrols. When 1st Lt. Woody Taylor showed up, he and the skipper had an immediate dispute over this practice.

The first day Woody was with us the full company went in search of a band of the enemy spotted by our airplanes. We moved in column into the hills, Lee's platoon at the point. The captain, the headquarters people, and my mortars were next in the column. The 1st Platoon, Woody Taylor, followed us, and Hank Kiser was the rear guard.

As we neared the base of a wide, bare hill, Garcia, the skipper's radio man, saw movement a few hundred yards off the right flank. Captain Wilcox ordered Sergeant Richard, the acting first sergeant, to peel off a squad from Taylor's platoon and scout out the situation. When Richard went back to the 1st Platoon, Taylor was down the column, talking to his men, getting acquainted. He wasn't aware that one of his squads had been detached until he heard firing on the right flank and saw a squad formation engaging a couple of Chinese soldiers as they scampered out of sight.

At the sound of the shooting Woody ran to the front of his platoon, ready to put them into combat formation. It was then he realized that he was one squad short, that the Marines doing the shooting a hundred yards away were his own men.

"Who the hell put my people over there?" Woody roared. His deep, thundering voice could be heard at both ends of our column.

"Captain Wilcox sent them over there to scout out the flank," Platoon Sergeant King answered his new leader.

"Well, to hell with that!" Taylor raged. He stormed up the column to confront the captain who was watching the flanking squad in action.

"Captain Wilcox!" Taylor called loudly to the skipper. He was red-faced and out of breath from the run up the column. "That's a squad from my platoon you sent over there on the flank."

"Yeah, Lieutenant. Saw a few bandits over there . . ."

"Captain, those are my men," Taylor interrupted. "My platoon moves on my orders."

Captain Wilcox glared at Lieutenant Taylor. I had seen that cold look many times before when it had been leveled at me. I figured that Woody Taylor would not be long with Baker-One-Seven.

Our new lieutenant and the captain stared at each other. Woody calmed down a notch. "Sir," he said, "I'd much appreciate it if you put any orders to my men through me. Colonel Davis sent me up here to run this platoon. That's what I reckon to do."

Taylor and the skipper were eyeball to eyeball, and the skipper realized that he had, indeed, violated the chain of command. "Yep, Lieutenant," he said, "you're right. That's your platoon. And I guess we understand each other."

"I guess we do, Captain," said Woody Taylor.

"All right, then. Carry on!" The skipper dismissed his new platoon leader.

We figured Woody Taylor was going to be one hell of a fighter. He was the last replacement officer to come to Baker-One-Seven, and he was with us to stay.

. . .

There was little fighting over the next few days as we made our way toward the town of Hagaru-ri. The Chinese had vanished again, although the natives continued to tell us that there were "many, many" of them still concealed in the hills.

After the first blasts of icy wind and snow, the weather turned warm again, like Indian summer back home, and the men became accustomed to the extra weight of the cold weather gear, which they carried in their packs. The shoe-pacs were still heavy and clumsy, though.

We set up a perimeter at the far north of the town, on the shore of the Chosin Reservoir. It was a long, broad lake, sparkling blue against the thick pine forests that clothed the surrounding mountains. On that sunny day when we first saw it, the Chosin was a tranquil body of shimmering water, a scene of magnificent beauty.

Colonel Litzenberg and Colonel Davis gathered together the officers of the battalion and described the grand strategy. It had come down from General MacArthur's headquarters in Tokyo, via the Army X Corps, of which we were a part, then through 1st Marine Division headquarters, and finally to us, the troops on the line.

The plan from Tokyo was for the Marines to continue north to the Yalu River, which was the North Korean border with China. East of us an Army division and some ROKs had already advanced that far against light opposition. Far to the west the 8th Army, MacArthur's main force in Korea, had received the same orders. There would be a grand sweep up the peninsula, brushing the few Chinese out of the way, and the war would be over in a week. Two weeks at most. Word was coming down that we would be home by Christmas.

Colonel Litzenberg and Colonel Davis knew better than that. They agreed with us that the farther away from the fight the planners were, the less they understood the terrain and the situation. Both of our commanders had been up on the line with us. They realized, as we did, that the Chinese strategy was to let us advance until our supply line had been overextended, then cut us off in the mountains.

Colonel Litzenberg took pains to tell us that General Smith had tried to dissuade MacArthur's staff from their plans to march to the Yalu. Indeed, our general had dragged his heels on our movement to the north. And he had insisted upon building up great stores of ammunition and supplies at several points along the MSR as we advanced along the single mountain road. Colonel Litzenberg told us that our general was in great disfavor at the higher Army echelons and that his Marines were disparaged for their "timidity."

• • •

We stayed in the perimeter north of Hagaru-ri for two days, and it was like being in a rest camp. The Indian summer weather was warm

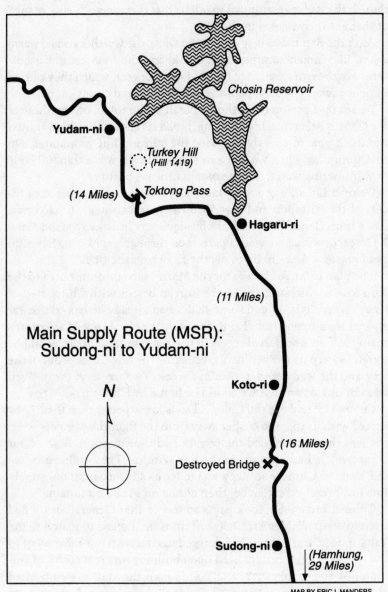

Chosin Reservoir

Yudam-ni

Turkey Hill
(Hill 1419)

(14 Miles)

Toktong Pass

Hagaru-ri

(11 Miles)

Main Supply Route (MSR):
Sudong-ni to Yudam-ni

N

Koto-ri

(16 Miles)

Destroyed Bridge ✗

Sudong-ni

(Hamhung,
29 Miles)

MAP BY ERIC I. MANDERS

and sunny. Battalion remembered to send up the PX gear—soap, razors, and toothbrushes—and we got ourselves cleaned up. There was little work, only short patrols to sweep the line and working parties to bring up supplies. All of our sick men returned to full duty, although Gunny Buckley remained unhealthy. Captain Wilcox suggested that the gunny turn himself in, that he was too sick to fight, but the gunny again refused.

A cold weather survival expert came from the Army and lectured us on how to live in sub-zero cold. Our Minnesota lads knew as much as the expert did about cold weather living. They told him that we had everything we needed to survive, except for the right gear. The expert responded that Tokyo was working on that problem.

And—what the hell!—we would be home by Christmas, anyway.

Mail came. Two weeks of letters and packages. The packages had cakes and cookies and an occasional bottle of booze, and these were passed around the squads. My dad sent me a stick of spicy pepperoni, enough for a good chunk for every man in the section. Sergeant Wright's wife had concealed a pint bottle of whiskey in a loaf of home-baked bread, and with the cookies and cakes and pepperoni, the mortars had a pretty good little party.

We went off by ourselves to read the letters. I had a dozen from Dorothy, who reported that the babies were in fine health and that they said prayers every night for Daddy. I took the pictures from my helmet and spread them near me. As I read the letters and looked at the pictures, I could feel the soft, chubby baby arms around my neck and I saw Mike and Dinny as they waved goodbye to me on that dusty lane back in Jacksonville. And I yearned deeply for my beautiful, golden Dorothy.

Frank Bifulk received a single letter. It came from his bride who said that the three months of being alone were too much to bear and that she was ending their marriage. Bifulk tore the letter into pieces and threw them into the air. He yelled at his foxhole buddy, Merwin Perkins, to leave him the hell alone.

I went over to talk to Bifulk. He was sitting on the edge of his foxhole, sharpening his fighting knife.

He glared up at me as I approached. "Just stay out of this, Joe," he spit out. "You don't know nothing about it!"

I ignored the use of my name. "Why don't you go see the chaplain? Maybe he can help," I suggested.

"The chaplain don't know nothing about it, either," Bifulk replied and went back to sharpening his knife with furious strokes.

"Keep an eye on your buddy," I told Perkins as I left the two of them.

"Yes, Sir, Lieutenant! I'll do that. He's gonna be all right, though."

• • •

The regiment had two chaplains.

Reverend Craven, the Protestant, was a former Marine enlisted man from the Tennessee hills. He was a big man with an easy-going manner, and by no means a rear echelon type of chaplain; the rifle companies were accustomed to seeing him when we were being shot at. Often, when things were quiet, he would come up to us and call the troops together for the most informal of services. Soon he would have a circle of Marines around him, singing out familiar old Bible Belt hymns. He never gave a long sermon, just a few minutes of old time religion. Then he would mix with the troops, asking about home and reminding them to write back to the folks.

The men asked Reverend Craven if it was true that we were going up to the Yalu and, after that, whether it was true that we would be home by Christmas.

"It's straight dope that we're headed due north and right up to the Chinese border," Reverend Craven told the men. "But only the Lord knows about getting you boys home by Christmas. That's the best I can tell you."

Father Griffin, the Catholic chaplain, was a young priest right out of the seminary. At first he had been taken aback by the profanities and vulgarities that were the prevalent language of his flock of Marines. He adapted quickly, though, and, like Reverend Craven, he had the reputation of showing up when there was a firefight going on. During the lulls, when he came up to us, he always said Mass for the troops, and he insisted that Joe Kurcaba and I attend. Before Mass he heard confessions and advertised himself to the troops as "the easiest confessor in the history of Catholicism."

The troops checked with Father Griffin to confirm that we were headed north to the Yalu, as they had with Reverend Craven. And whether we were going home for Christmas.

"Colonel Litzenberg himself told me that our objective is the Yalu River," the young priest would answer. "But I don't know whether God has made up His mind yet when we're going home."

To the men in the rifle companies, the "word" wasn't straight dope until the padres said so.

• • •

Colonel Davis came up to Baker-One-Seven to inform us that we were moving out again. Tomorrow morning we would advance up the west side of the Chosin Reservoir. Our objective was the town of Yudam-ni, fourteen miles away. This was not a patrol, our battalion commander told us. It was an attack and we should expect the fighting to get serious.

When he finished briefing the officers, Colonel Davis asked me to bring Sergeant Wright to him. The hardship transfer order had finally come through, and our colonel wanted to say goodbye, personally, to a good Marine NCO.

It was a great moment for Sergeant Wright. All of the company officers were there when the colonel expressed his appreciation and best wishes to my departing sergeant. Captain Wilcox and the lieutenants added their own "well dones." Sergeant Wright had done a good job of whipping the mortar section into shape and keeping them squared away.

The mortars had a farewell party for their sergeant, who had been with them since the first day at Camp Pendleton. The rifle platoon corpsmen came by, Mickens and Davis and Toppel, each bringing a canteen of sick bay alcohol. The skipper and Joe Kurcaba joined us in a few toasts.

When he was ready to leave, weapon and gear all squared away like a parade-ground Marine, Sergeant Wright approached me. His eyes glistened; probably mine did, too.

"Sir, I think we did some good with these people," he said. "I want to thank you for giving me the chance to serve in your outfit."

"Thank you, Sergeant Wright. You are a fine Marine NCO. God bless you and your family."

Sergeant Wright snapped a salute at me and strode off. I would never see him again, and I would miss him very much.

CHAPTER FOURTEEN

The weather turned ugly again as we formed up to resume the attack to the north. A bitter cold wind greeted us, filled with a stinging, gritty snow.

It was my birthday. After the troops were squared away, I crouched in the ditch alongside the road and took some time to go through my snapshots. I thought of Dorothy teaching the happy birthday song to the babies and how they would try to sing it. I saw their little pink cheeks and blue eyes and Dorothy's golden hair. And Dorothy and I would go out with friends that night and raise hell and laugh. *What if we really did get home for Christmas?* I tucked the photos back into the webbing of my helmet.

• • •

Our objective was Toktong Pass, a rocky peak that was the highest point on the road to Yudam-ni. It was six miles ahead, and we stepped out in parallel columns spread along each side of the twisting, frozen-dirt road. Rifle platoons from Able and Charlie Companies covered our flanks from their positions in the endless snow-covered hills.

We moved out in colorless dawn. The men beat their hands against their sides after the finger-numbing ordeal of strapping their gear and checking weapons in the cold darkness. We were helmeted, shapeless figures in long, hooded parkas, showing only a small patch of face to the wind.

"Nothing but Chinamen from here to Mongolia," Kelly muttered to me. He walked backward for shelter against the wind. "I hope them chink bastards are as cold as we are."

There were some listless profanities aimed at the cold and the snow that coated us white. Until we caught up with the Chinese again, the weather was our enemy.

A newspaper reporter came along with Baker-One-Seven that morning. He went up and down the column, asking the men for their opinion of the war and their purpose in fighting it. The troops knew that if they talked to the reporter their names might appear in their hometown papers. Therefore, they gave fanciful accounts of their noble purpose, their love of democracy, and their fight against Communism.

A few of them, though, expressed their true opinions. Bifulk, especially cynical since the "Dear John" letter from his teenage bride, declared, "I'm here because the goddamn president of the United States would put me in jail if I didn't report for duty."

The troops lost patience when the writer tried to whip up enthusiasm for the upcoming tangle with the enemy.

"I want some good photos with you guys today," the reporter said, coming up to Kelly, Pat Burris, and me in the column. "You boys want to get your pictures taken? Real, up-front action stuff, you know."

Pat Burris recommended, "Why don't you just run up ahead and see if you can get the gooks to crank off a few rounds at you? That'll give you some good pictures."

"Yeah!" came Kelly's gravelly voice. "Or leave your camera with us. We'll take your picture when they take you back to battalion on a poncho. Now, shove off!"

The Chinese opened up on us as we approached the top of Toktong Pass. They were embedded around a high spike of rocks, and they took us under fire at two hundred yards. Their machine guns and rifles were sporadic at first, tracers seeking targets. They soon intensified.

Hank Kiser's platoon had the lead, and they quickly formed a firing line off of the road. Hugo Johnson's mortar was with them, and I soon heard his raucous directions and rounds thumping out of the tube.

The enemy fire became heavy; about fifty Chinese were dug in against us, and they were serious about defending this place. Chew Een Lee took his platoon off the road to extend our firing line. Captain Wilcox came forward with Garcia and the big radio and set up in the ditch just behind Kiser. I marveled at his easy, ambling gait during firefights; he always stood straight up.

The static of the SCR-300 radio added to the pounding of our own machine guns and BARs. Rifles cracked, Johnson's mortar thumped out the HEs, and enemy bullets zinged through the air and spun off chips of boulders. Soon came the urgent cries, "Corpsman! Oh, God, Corpsman!"

And the fear came, as it did to me with the onset of every fight. The corpsmen cries, the booming explosions and the whine of bullets, blood-drenched parkas. *Dear God, not this time, please!*

Platoon Sergeant King, from Taylor's platoon, crouched among some large boulders above me. He shouted down that there was a machine gun near the spike of rocks that marked the Chinese main position. I willed myself to climb up to get a better look. The fear submerged and the cold was forgotten.

I sweated heavily with the strain of climbing a steep, snow-buried hill with weapon, pack, parka, shoe-pacs, and the several layers of clothing. Kelly was with me, and we slipped frequently and fell to our knees, then scrambled up again.

Progress was slow and we attracted enemy attention. Bullets whined close by, and we made desperate bounds over the snow, up the slope, and into sheltering boulders.

Just below us Pat Burris had found a rock-rimmed pit for his gun, and I soon had him throwing HE into the rockpile. Our mortars had little effect; the enemy positions were skillfully emplaced. Even with artillery support it would be a long, hard day taking Toktong Pass away from the Chinese.

We were joined by Bob Wilson, the tactical air officer. He and his radio man, Tony Tinelli, had hauled their heavy radio up the near vertical climb under thickening fire. By now the Chinese realized that we were an observation post, and they concentrated on us. They filled the air with bullets that ricocheted off the boulders and threw off chunks of granite.

"Why the hell can't you people find your own position?" Kelly growled at Tinelli.

Bob Wilson brought in the Corsairs that were on station to cover our advance. I called down to Burris to lay in a round of white phosphorous to mark the Chinese guns, and the fliers came in on the column of white smoke.

They flew in low, barely above us. Their great, racketing noise overpowered all other sound as they flashed by. On the first passes they fired their machine guns and cannons. These had little effect; the Chinese were dug in too well.

They followed with a napalm run, a spectacle of awesome and terrible beauty. The pods slid from the planes, tumbled across the ground, then exploded. Black smoke billowed and red flame leaped against the white snow, and seconds later we felt the blast of heat that consumed the ground two hundred yards away. Chinese soldiers were aflame, running about in frenzied circles. They threw themselves, flailing, into the snow.

There was sudden silence. The Chinese ceased fire and our own weapons were quiet. We were stunned by the power of that close-in, flaming strike.

There was no further resistance at Toktong Pass. When we reached the top of the open slope, we found several charred Chinese bodies. Other than that, the position was empty; the enemy had withdrawn in good order with their wounded and their weapons.

We congratulated Bob Wilson and asked him to convey a "Well done!" to his Corsairs for making Toktong Pass an easy fight. We would come back to this place again, when it would be known as Fox Hill. That would be a much more difficult fight. And there would be fewer of us by far.

Before we moved out again, Sergeant Winget came up the road. Winget was my section chief now, and he had been at the rear of the column with the third gun.

"You remember that newspaper guy? The one who was gung ho to see a firefight?" Winget asked, laughing. "Soon as the gooks opened up on us, he dove under the company jeep. Stayed there the whole fight."

"Give him your name and home town," I told my big sergeant. "He'll make you a hero."

• • •

The road to Yudam-ni writhed like a snake through the mountains, and its frozen mud surface was even narrower than the road up to Hagaru-ri. Much of it was covered with ice, a difficult passage for the company jeep, which pulled a trailer filled with the day's ammunition and the company gear.

Sergeant Richard drove most of the time when his services as scout and sniper were not required. It was also his job to perform the first sergeant's function as keeper of the company records—an account of personnel, rations drawn, and ammunition received. He was less than meticulous in that duty.

"I'm not much good at paperwork. Never was. Don't know why the captain gave me this godawful job, anyhow," the old salt, Richard, complained to anyone who would listen. Captain Wilcox, who heard the complaint every day, ignored it. He knew that Sergeant Richard would carry out any duty assigned to the best of his ability. And replacement first sergeants were not forthcoming to the rifle companies.

Gunny Buckley should have been driving the jeep, staying off his feet rather than grinding out the marches and climbing the hills with us when we were in the assault. The gunny looked sicker every day, and we thought he should be relieved and sent back to the hospital. Captain Wilcox, though, said that this would be the gunny's final duty before he retired from the Corps and he wasn't going to send him out with a whimper.

So Gunny Buckley limped up and down the company column, yelling at the troops to keep their intervals and encouraging the laggards. He struggled up the hills in firefights, leading the ammo bearers. And it was the gunny who signaled the end of every break on the march with his stentorian call, "Saddle up! Saddle up, Baker Company! Saddle up and move out!"

He had to use the big wooden staff when he walked and his once-proud mustache drooped at the ends, but he was still our gunny.

. . .

The Chinese showed that they would not hibernate from the war because of the cold weather. The farther we advanced, the stiffer was their resistance. The hills continued to grow steeper and each climb we made, encumbered with the heavy clothing, became its own ordeal. Most of our fights were platoon-size, Kiser or Lee or Taylor maneuvering up a slippery, snow-covered slope to dislodge a force of the Chinese who fired down at us on the road. When the skies were clear, the Corsairs flew support for us, which made our work easier.

Much of the time, though, we couldn't get air support and, after Toktong Pass, we were beyond artillery's range; the big guns were still back at Hagaru-ri. The platoons fought up to Yudam-ni on their own. Our sixties and the eighty-ones from battalion, hundreds of yards behind us, were a help, but the rifle squads and the machine guns did the heavy work. It was close-in and deadly fighting. After each hill stretchers were brought down to the road, many with ponchos covering the bodies.

. . .

The road edged the sides of the mountains, often clinging to cliff-like slopes. On one hairpin turn of the road, the Chinese had set up a block. As the company column reached the first leg of the hairpin, we were scathed by machine guns and rifles concealed on the opposite leg. There was no cover or concealment on the bare road and no room to maneuver above or below them. The solution to the problem was to call in the battalion's eighty-ones, but these were not quickly available. Air couldn't help us in this tight terrain.

Colonel Davis was at the head of our column, with Captain Wilcox. When the Chinese opened up from across a chasm three hundred yards away, the skipper called me up front.

"Think you can knock out those guns?" Captain Wilcox asked. He and the colonel crouched, their acknowledgment of the machine gun slugs that tore into the slope above our heads.

"Yessir!" I answered, crouching alongside my two commanders. I wished that they would kneel or lie flat to make smaller targets of themselves.

"Kelly, bring up Johnson's gun," I commanded. Hugo was with Kiser's platoon leading the column that day. They were just behind the bend.

"Aye, aye, Sir," snapped my runner in a way to impress the colonel.

Colonel Davis and Captain Wilcox continued to scan the opposite slope. "Eleven o'clock," said the colonel, indicating a slight movement in an outcropping of boulders.

"Yes, Sir! I have it," I told my colonel as I located an enemy machine gun through my own binoculars. "And another one at ten o'clock, fifty yards higher, Sir."

"Good eyes, Lieutenant," said Colonel Davis.

There was sudden commotion behind us, the sound of Marines singing as they double-timed up the road. Kelly was leading the mortarmen forward, and he had them sounding cadence with his parody of the Army marching song, "Sound Off."

How can a mortarman survive,
Following a man who is six foot five?
Sound off!
Put your rifles and machine guns away,
The sixty mortars are on the way!
Sound off! Sound off!

There was no ditch, so Hugo could not take cover from enemy fire while setting up his gun. He and Dean Westberg spread the bipod on the rear edge of the flat, open road surface. I stood behind the gun as they worked quickly. The volume of bullets increased.

"Eleven o'clock, Hugo," I said. "Give me three-five-zero." I fired a tracer from my shoulder.

Westberg had a mortar round ready. Hugo, with his sharp-shooter's eye, spotted the target and said, "Three-five-oh plus a hair."

He laid the tube in the direction of the machine gun and cranked his elevation. "Fire!" he said to Westberg.

The round thumped out and we followed its arc, ignoring the Chinese bullets that were bouncing off the frozen surface of the road and the slope behind us.

The first round was a direct hit. *God bless you, Hugo Johnson.*

"Next target at ten o'clock, Hugo," I yelled. "And give me another half turn down." I fired another tracer at the second position.

Hugo shifted the bipod, cranked down, and yelled, "Fire!" to Westberg, who had a round poised to drop. While it was in the air, we saw the Chinese machine gunners abandoning their positions; their fire had ceased. The round landed close, but the enemy soldiers had already fled.

"Cease fire, Hugo," I told him. "Good shooting. Secure the gun. Well done!"

Captain Wilcox called out for the company to continue the march.

Colonel Davis approached the gun. He had a big smile. "You tell your men their shooting is right on, Lieutenant," he said. He glanced at our choir director, Kelly, and added, "But tell them that their singing is way off key."

• • •

Colonel Litzenberg was proud of the nickname that was given to his 7th Marines. The newspapers called us "The Ridgerunners," derived from the tactics we used. The rifle companies of the regiment leap-frogged each other as we took the high ground, the ridges that commanded the road. The tactics were effective, but they exhausted our men, who were cold and poorly fed as they climbed and fought.

Colonel Litzenberg was no stranger to the forward troops, and he was aware of our fatigue. Like General Smith, the division commander, he had slowed the advance to maintain security, in spite of Tokyo's orders. The more we stalled, the stronger came the pressure from General MacArthur and the rear echelons for the Marines to press forward.

"Litz the Blitz," our troops had named our gray-haired, grizzled regimental. We saw him often; he would get out of his jeep and walk our column, chatting with the men.

"How's it going for you, Marine?" He would fall in beside a rifleman who hunched against the cold as he walked.

The teenager would note the silver eagle pinned to the camouflage cover on the colonel's helmet. "Very good, Colonel, Sir!" he would reply to this old man.

"Son, are you warm enough with that new parka?"

"Sometimes, Sir. But it's awful heavy."

"How about those shoe-pacs? How do you like them for marching boots?"

"They're too heavy, Colonel, Sir. And they're either too cold or our feet sweat in them."

"You're right, son," was the colonel's reply. He wore the same burdensome parka and the shoe-pacs that his troops endured. "You tell your buddies that I have complained to the top and maybe we'll get us some sensible cold weather fighting gear before long."

The colonel came alongside the 2d Platoon's corpsman, Bill Davis. Noting the red cross on Davis's sleeve, he asked, "You carrying some cold weather medicine in that canteen of yours, Corpsman?"

Bill Davis wore two canteens. One was filled with straight sick bay alcohol; he used it for purifying wounds and for cleaning his hands when he reached into open flesh. The other canteen had water-diluted alcohol, the all-purpose body warmer that many of the troops now carried.

The young Davis wasn't sure that he should reveal to his regimental commander that he was carrying "hootch." He patted the canteen with the one hundred percent stuff in it. "Colonel, I use this for treating the wounded men."

"How about that other canteen?" demanded Colonel Litzenberg. "I've never met a corpsman yet who didn't have the right medicine."

"Yes, Sir!" Davis complied, nervously. He handed his second canteen to the colonel, who unscrewed the cap and took a healthy slug.

"Good medicine, Corpsman," said "Litz the Blitz." "When we get back to the states, I owe you a good stiff one. Carry on!"

"Aye, aye, Colonel," acknowledged the corpsman, and since he had the canteen out, he took a dose of his own medicine.

• • •

The cold weather was as formidable an enemy as the Chinese. The troops, never prone to minimize a problem, declared that temperature readings were down to thirty below, fahrenheit. There was a thermometer back at regiment, and the daily action reports confirmed the troops' judgment. Rarely did the reports exceed zero degrees, and there were lows of twenty below.

When we weren't on the move, we were freezing cold and we spent much of our energy trying to get warm. Battalion had warming stations—big pyramid tents with kerosene stoves in them—which we rarely used because they were far from our company perimeters. Up on the line we had only our own body warmth, which we tried to keep enclosed within the parkas. At night, in the foxholes, the men pressed together to preserve whatever warmth they could generate.

We wore woolen caps under the helmets that kept our ears from freezing. The hoods of the parkas went over the helmets and provided some protection from the bitter winds, but they obscured our peripheral vision. We seldom removed the knitted gloves that we wore under the canvas mittens. Bare fingers, we found, froze to metal; they froze to weapons, bayonets, buckles—whatever we touched.

Chow was usually a can of half-frozen rations, although we learned to carry the next meal inside our clothing, close to our body heat, so it wouldn't freeze solid. In daylight, when we weren't under enemy observation, we made small cooking fires. The unused mortar propellant charges served to make a quick starter flame. The mortarmen did a good business trading the propellant charges for cigarettes and fruit rations.

Down on the road, if there was a vehicle nearby, we filched gasoline, then poured it over any dirt or gravel that we managed to scrape from under the snow, and that made a skimpy but adequate flame. We learned that trick from one of our reservists who had been in the Army in Europe, the Battle of the Bulge in 1944.

The cold ration diet caused stomach disorders. We alternated between constipation and diarrhea. It was common to see a man suddenly scamper from the column to the nearest tree or boulder, then desperately unbuckle, unbutton, and slide down several layers of trousers, long johns, and skivvies before he let go. Many times he wouldn't make it; the resulting stench became part of the air we breathed and, frigid as it was, we were grateful for the cleansing wind.

Weapons froze and seized up when we used lubricating oil on them. They slowed or jammed when we didn't. The machine guns and BARs were most affected; on first firing they would hesitate two or three seconds between rounds, then slowly build up to their regular rate of fire. Hair tonic, with alcohol in it, became a fairly effective substitute lubricant. At first the hair tonic was hard to come by, but soon battalion began sending it along with our ammo and rations.

The cold forced the corpsmen to change their way of doing business. With the first sounds of a firefight they would take several syrettes of morphine and put them in their mouths. This kept the morphine liquid until the syrettes were jabbed into a wounded man's flesh to relieve his pain.

The corpsmen were the only ones who worked with bare hands in the severe cold, and they found a way to keep their fingers nimble while tending a wounded man. The heat of the man's blood did the trick, or his guts, as they were stuffed back into the belly.

• • •

Tokyo made a big public relations splash out of Thanksgiving dinner for the troops. Every soldier and Marine in Korea was to have a hot turkey-and-trimmings dinner. The cooks, bakers, and messmen worked for days to prepare the meals and put them on galley trailers to go forward to the rifle companies. It was especially important, in Tokyo's public relations scheme, that the front-line troops be shown enjoying the bounties of Thanksgiving. The war was going so well, the rear echelon hucksters proclaimed, that General MacArthur could afford to give the men not only the traditional meal, but also the day off.

The Chinese didn't take Thanksgiving Day off. They gave us a stiff fight on a wretched hill, a few miles short of Yudam-ni. Colonel Litzenberg told us that after we took this one, Yudam-ni would be wide open. He and Colonel Davis were up front with us when we attacked.

It took us several hours and some casualties to fight to the top of the corrugated terrain, a mean jumble of giant boulders, felled trees, snow, and slippery ice. The Chinese defended stubbornly, but we had good support from the battalion's heavy mortars and our own sixties. After we pushed the enemy away, Able and Charlie Companies barreled up the road and went into Yudam-ni with little trouble.

While we were taking the hill above them, the rest of the battalion had all eaten their Thanksgiving dinners, hot and bountiful.

We had our dinner in frigid darkness at 2300. Captain Wilcox ordered us to come down from the hill, one platoon at a time. We filed into a tight little valley, just off the road. Waiting for us there was a truck with a galley trailer, its sides pulled up, and the cooks standing proudly amid mounds of festive food. Gunny Buckley had the lights on the company jeep illuminating the area.

Most of us had lost our mess gear, but a smiling, back-slapping mess sergeant from battalion gave us aluminum trays. The cooks in the mess line were solicitous of the grimy, tired Marines who filed before them.

"What'll you have, Mac? Take all you want. Plenty of chow for all hands."

"You want more turkey, Mac? How about a couple of these oranges for later?"

We sat in the snow and on the big boulders with the overflowing trays. We relished the feast before us, but we had not reckoned with the cold. The temperature had sunk far below zero again, and our food began to freeze before we could set a fork to it. The giblet gravy congealed and became an icy coating over the chilled turkey and mashed potatoes. The cranberry sauce became sherbet. The oranges froze as hard as baseballs.

I found a place on the hood of the company jeep, next to the corpsman, Bill Davis. Both of us spooned beneath the icy coating in search of morsels that hadn't yet frozen. A bullet zinged the air a few feet above our heads—a Chinese sniper from somewhere up the valley wall.

"Screw him," Bill Davis said, in response to the sniper's attempt, and he kept digging through his frozen turkey. Somebody turned off the jeep's lights, and the sniper didn't bother us again.

When we went back to our positions on the hill that night, we were still hungry. We knew that battalion and the rear echelons had done their best, though, to give us a Thanksgiving dinner. Afterward, when we had to fight through this place again, we found turkey carcasses strewn everywhere and we remembered it as "Turkey Hill."

CHAPTER FIFTEEN

The village of Yudam-ni was another scattering of small, grim buildings and huts. It joined two primitive roads on the edge of the Chosin Reservoir. The reservoir was now frozen solid, and we set watches along the shores to guard against a Chinese attack across the ice.

The 11th Marines came up from Hagaru-ri to give us artillery support. The engineers had made the road passable for the big guns, and they also scraped a small landing strip for the Piper Cubs that were used for spotting targets and for courier duty. The cargo planes were too big to land there. They dropped rations and ammo to us by parachute.

The 5th Marines came on trucks to join us at Yudam-ni; we now had two regiments there, almost ten thousand men. Word came down that our mission had changed. Rather than continue the push north to the Yalu, we were to mount an attack to the west, fifty miles across another mountain range. The Chinese were pressuring the 8th Army's flank over there, and the 1st Marine Division was assigned to relieve that pressure. Gone were the home-for-Christmas rumors.

Except for tentative probes, the Chinese had not attacked our positions since we arrived at Yudam-ni. And although there were firefights on our daily patrols, most of our casualties resulted from the cold weather.

Despite our efforts to keep the men in clean, dry socks, we were losing the fight against frostbite, which resulted from damp, cold feet. The men would complain of pains or numbness in their feet, and when they limped badly, we sent them to the battalion aid station. Many never returned. Some had waited too long to turn themselves in; by the time the doctors saw them their toes had become purplish black and had to be amputated.

Each night, when Captain Wilcox made his final perimeter inspection, he had Gunny Buckley with him carrying a knapsack filled with clean, dry socks, a pair for each man. I had my men remove their shoe-pacs, exposing their feet to the numbing cold as I looked for discolorations. Then, on with the clean, dry socks. It was strange duty, close-up inspection of bare feet in the below-zero cold and deep snow.

We also gave the men instructions to wiggle their toes to keep their blood circulating when they weren't moving. It was a bizarre command, heard from the NCOs during a firefight: "All right, you people, keep your toes wiggling!"

In spite of our efforts, though, frostbite claimed its victims, and after Chosin there were men who would never again walk right.

• • •

Because the ground was frozen hard, digging good fighting holes was nearly impossible. Digging became a matter of chipping a shallow pit in the unyielding earth beneath the snow, then barricading it with rocks or tree branches. If any dead Chinese were found on the hill, we added their stiff corpses to the barricades. To make level places for their guns, the mortarmen took turns at the concrete-like dirt with entrenching tools and combat knives.

After digging in at night and registration fire, there was the ammo detail. This involved sending a working party down the hill to the road where battalion delivered our nightly supply of ammo. The ammunition, however, was often defective, especially the illumination. This meant that we had to draw a double allotment, and it was sometimes necessary for the ammo bearers to make two runs. Each night I faced near mutiny from the weary troops who made these agonizing climbs. Our perimeter echoed with their curses and snarls as they slipped, slid, and fell along steep, icy slopes under their punishing loads.

• • •

The night after the 5th Marines arrived, the Chinese threw everything they had at Yudam-ni. Their all-out attack started with a heavy barrage of mortar fire. Then came the red and green rockets and the flares and bugles, more than we had ever heard and seen before, and thousands of their soldiers poured through the mountains. They hit with simultaneous force at all of the Marine positions west and north of the village. Baker-One-Seven was not directly involved, but we had a clear view of the fight from our hill across the valley.

Every one of the big guns that the 11th Marines had emplaced on the low meadows of Yudam-ni opened up to protect the ridgelines. The sky filled with the arcing red streaks of the artillery shells, and the hills blossomed with their fiery explosions. Star shells popped high in the air, their stark blue light casting unearthly shadows across the snowy ground. There were tracers from both sides, brilliant lines of red and orange, flashes of grenades, the flaming bursts of the machine guns, and burp guns and rifles winking like swarms of fireflies.

The Chinese attacked in massive numbers, an overwhelming weight, but they also endured terrible casualties. Several times they pushed the Marines off their ridges. Each time the Marines re-formed, and they had artillery support behind them. Their counterattacks sent the Chinese reeling back. The battle went back and forth all night. When the Chinese bugles sounded at daybreak and the fighting broke off, there was little ground lost. The Marines still controlled the high ground around Yudam-ni, but they had paid a price of hundreds of dead and wounded men.

• • •

Across the reservoir that night, east of Yudam-ni, there was another display of pyrotechnics. We had heard that our Army was over there, units from the 7th Division. Miles away, from our hill, we saw the sky light up above their positions. The Army was under Chinese attack, too. We didn't know how desperate their battle was.

• • •

Dawn showed at Yudam-ni, another gray sky with dense, snow-filled clouds. It was twenty below zero, according to regiment. It was even colder up on our hill where a stiff north wind blew. A thick fog sat in the valley, shrouding the village. The fog was the exhaust from hundreds of trucks and jeeps that had to be started up every few minutes to keep the engines from freezing.

Coughing and cursing, we arose from holes gouged in the snow. We hunched and shivered, dreading another day of the icy ordeal. The sleeping bags that had been wrapped about our legs for the night were rolled into blanket rolls, secured by means of canvas straps that had small metal buckles. It was the agonizing first chore of the day. Our mittens were big and thick, and we couldn't buckle the frozen straps with the woolen gloves on. So we had to expose our fingers to the numbing cold, and they quickly stiffened and pained. The blanket rolls were slovenly.

Gunny Buckley came hobbling along with word from the skipper that squad cooking fires were OK if we kept them in defilade, behind the skyline.

"Defilade from which side, Gunny?" called out Bifulk. "Last night there were Chinks everywhere around us. We surrounded again?"

"Just stay off the skyline, Bifulk." The gunny forced a laugh and then struggled along the icy trail to the next position.

The men were cold and aching even before we mounted out, and a day-long, company-size patrol was still ahead. Heavy fighting, too, judging from the intensity of the Chinese attack last night. A wireman, stringing a telephone line from battalion, said that at least three Chinese divisions were coming at us. Thirty thousand troops. As it turned out, there were many more than that.

• • •

We went along the high ground to cover the 5th Marines' left flank as they made the main attack to the west. We had already patrolled the rough terrain that the 5th had to cover, and we knew they had a difficult time ahead.

We climbed through heavy snow. The cold was forgotten as we struggled upward in our awkward gear. The skipper had placed Woody Taylor's platoon up front. Headquarters people and the tactical air team followed Taylor, then the 2d Platoon, the mortars, and Kiser's platoon. Lee's arm was festering badly, and he was back at the aid station on Captain Wilcox's orders. Sergeant O'Brien had the 2d Platoon for the day.

The road was an hour behind us, and we had encountered no enemy. Kelly, though, insisted they were there. "Gooks all around us. I can feel them up there. Lots of them."

I saw no sign of them until we took a chow break.

On the break the men sprawled on either side of the trail that the forward squads had stomped through the snow. They fumbled with their ration cans. Body heat, trapped inside several layers of clothing, had kept them warm.

"Up there! Look!" Kelly nudged me. A ridgeline at five hundred yards southwest was lined with Chinese soldiers peering down at us.

We all saw them at the same time, and the men scrambled to the ready. Before our mortars began to thump, we heard heavy fire from the front of the column. Captain Wilcox passed the word on the walkie-talkies that we were under attack. Form a perimeter and stand by to repel boarders!

Woody Taylor rammed his platoon forward. He formed skirmishers and went up a slope at the far end of the column, a move that, for the moment, took the pressure off the remainder of the company.

The Chinese maneuvered down from the ridgelines all around us. They ran across the snow in squad columns, then formed firing lines among the boulders or prone in the snow.

Hugo Johnson spotted a moving column at three hundred yards. Holding the bipod, he led his target with the tube and, on command, Westberg dropped a round of HE. We watched the shell arc, then saw it fall precisely in the middle of the Chinese squad.

There was no explosion; the direct hit was another dud. The Chinese squad, unharmed, continued its move through the snow. We cursed in disgust. Johnson spit a gob of brown tobacco juice in the direction of the Chinese.

When the Chinese first hit us, Captain Wilcox was up forward, the tactical air control party with him. Sgt. Joe Hedrick, who was leading the air liaison that day, was not able to bring the Corsairs to our immediate assistance. They were working full time in support of the main effort, the 5th Marines' attack two thousand yards north of us.

The captain came back from the forward line to set up the CP in the middle of the perimeter. Taylor hadn't been able to reach the high ground ahead of us and was working his way back, holding off the Chinese from that end. O'Brien's platoon had set up along our left flank, and Kiser made a semicircle around our rear. I took the mortarmen who weren't on the guns, along with all of the company headquarters people I could find, and strung them in a line to cover the right flank, a tie between Taylor and Kiser.

Pat Burris's gun was behind Kiser's line, and he and Jack Gallapo, Kiser's runner, spotted targets for the mortar. Under heavy fire they both stood, acting as aiming stakes, and called range to Perkins and Bifulk on the tube. Gallapo nailed a machine gun at two hundred yards, relieving much of the enemy pressure on that sector.

We had no machine guns of our own in my stretch of the line, but the mortarmen and the headquarters people had taken BARs from the early casualties, so we had some fire power to defend against a direct assault. Chinese mortars began to fall on us and on the CP, which was fifty yards behind us. A round exploded close by and lifted me off the ground. I was dazed for awhile, and when full awareness returned, Kelly had me by the arm, leading me toward the CP.

"Where are we going, Kelly?" I didn't understand why we were heading away from the line.

"Get a corpsman to look at you. I thought you were a goner back there." He pointed to my parka flapping around my knees; it had shrapnel holes in it. "They don't get closer than that to tearing your balls off. It's a good thing you got me around, Lieutenant."

The corpsmen at the CP were far too busy with the seriously wounded to tend my mild concussion. The casualties lay in blanket-covered rows. Doktorski, Davis, and Toppel went from one to the other; they jabbed morphine, slowed bleeding, cleaned out holes blasted in flesh, patched them, and wrapped them up as best they could. The corpsmen had their mouths filled with syrettes of morphine, and their bare hands were bloody. They worked with enemy mortars exploding, bullets stabbing the air two feet above them. Weak, frightened voices called for their help.

Doc Mickens, from the 1st Platoon, took some shrapnel, then later a .25–slug in the leg while he was patching WIAs on Woody Taylor's line. The stretcher-bearers dragged Mickens to the CP and laid him in the line of casualties. Next to him, damning the Chinese in his Arkansas drawl, was Platoon Sergeant King, who had been blasted by grenades and hit by a burp gun. Raul Rendon, a machine gunner with the platoon, lay there, too, a leg shot up. The 1st Platoon was rapidly being depleted, and it was having a hell of a fight holding their end of the perimeter.

Bob Fisher had taken charge of the stretcher-bearers, a dozen men who were not on the firing line. They crawled or scurried low to the ground, sliding wounded men on stretchers, or dragging them by the parkas to the makeshift aid station that the corpsmen had set up. It was hard work, and hazardous, running through enemy fire, hunched down, hauling wounded men who screamed terribly at the rough handling.

"Keep it moving, you people! Keep it moving!" Fisher yelled at his detail. "Hey, Grauman! Veeder! There's a man down over in Bahr's squad. Move out. On the double!"

The afternoon light faded and we worried about whether the ammo would run out. The Chinese had fully encircled us. Their volume of fire was just enough to keep us pinned down. They would wait for dark, then swarm over our lines. They had plenty of people to do the job.

Our bayonets were fixed and our grenades ready. Every man had a target sector, and we kept fire discipline to conserve ammo. We began to settle in and wait for dark.

As bullets zinged, grenades exploded, and Marines cried for help, someone yelled out that Captain Wilcox had been hit. He had taken a bullet in the face, and a piece of shrapnel had shattered his arm. Joe Kurcaba took over as our skipper.

When he got the word that Captain Wilcox was down, Joe and I were scouting the perimeter; the skipper had wanted a new estimate of the situation. My senses had revived and I wished that Joe would get closer to the ground. No matter how much enemy metal was in the air, Joe would repeat, "If I get down I might never get back up again."

As soon as we heard about the captain, we ran to the CP. We found him there, his head wrapped in a big white ball of bandage, unable to speak. His blood-soaked sleeve dangled beside him. He kept struggling to get on his feet when the docs put him down on his spread-out poncho. After a while the morphine kicked in and the skipper nodded off, groaning softly.

Sgt. Gene O'Brien, of the 2d Platoon, was hit while setting up a machine gun, and Fisher's people dragged him into the aid station. Bill Davis, the corpsman, took a piece of shrapnel through the mouth; two of the wounded he had been tending were killed by the same blast. Doktorski and Toppel were the only corpsmen we had left. They shot Davis with morphine, wrapped him up, and laid him on his poncho, next to Mickens.

• • •

Before they stabilized their line around us, the Chinese had pushed the 1st Platoon back almost to the CP. Just as Joe Kurcaba came to take over command of the company, Woody Taylor stormed in, demanding that we get the hell out of there.

"The gooks have all the high ground. They've got us surrounded," he boomed. "They're going to pick us to pieces tonight."

Joe Kurcaba answered him quietly. "We need air support to run interference for us. Then we might be able to make a break for the road."

"They better get to work mighty fast," said Woody. "We only have a few minutes of daylight left."

• • •

All afternoon Joe Hedrick, the air controller, had attempted to get a piece of the air support dedicated to the 5th Marines. Now in the remaining minutes of daylight he caught a flight of four Corsairs in search of action. The 5th Marines' attack had run into far greater resistance than expected, and it had been called back. The Corsairs wanted to use up their ordnance before dark, so they were looking for targets of opportunity.

Joe Hedrick gave them their opportunity.

The Corsairs' first strike went along the ridgelines where the Chinese were looking down our throats and taking potshots at us. Hedrick aligned the next run over Kiser's platoon and down the valley that led back to the road, a mile away. Kiser had the air marker panels in the snow, and he was ready to break out as soon as the planes flew over to shoot up the Chinese who were facing him. I took all of my mortarmen, except one man to carry each gun, and we moved up to add more BARs and rifles to Hank Kiser's push.

The four Corsairs streaked low above us, pointing themselves at the Chinese positions less than a hundred yards away. They dropped their earth-shaking big bombs, and then they scathed the long, deep valley with rockets and heavy-caliber slugs. The Chinese took cover and we moved out.

Kiser's platoon, with my mortarmen bolstering their center, charged forward. The sharp thrust, quickly following the air strike, gave us momentum. Kurcaba formed the rest of the company in two parallel columns, with the wounded and dead carried in the center. For the remaining few minutes of light, the Corsairs continued their covering passes in front of the column.

As darkness descended, our progress slowed. We slid and stumbled down the steep valley. Stretcher-bearers strove, vainly, to protect the wounded from rough falls. We put flankers out on the slopes on each side, and the forward elements took little Chinese fire. Woody Taylor's platoon fought off a few trailing attacks, but these were not serious attempts to stop us. The enemy seemed to be letting us slip from their grasp.

• • •

I lost Grauman that day, the lad who had tried hard to be a good combat Marine. He was running toward me, carrying a helmet filled with grenades taken from the wounded, when a bullet tore through his throat. The shot didn't knock him down at first, just threw his head back, and I saw a fountain of blood spurt from his neck. He staggered a few steps, then fell face forward in the snow, which quickly turned red. When I got to him, he was already dead.

I lost Branek, too, in that fight. He and his squad leader, Pat Burris, were fighting as riflemen when he took a round in his arm, enough to put him out of action. He was a help bringing out the walking wounded, though. Branek had shaped up since the incident down south, and he had done a good job of fighting for us. I hated to lose him.

• • •

It took hours more for Baker-One-Seven to make its way the mile down to the road. Colonel Davis brought elements of Charlie Company out to meet us. We loaded our dead and wounded on waiting trucks and sent them back to Yudam-ni. The Chinese had cut off the MSR between Yudam-ni and Hagaru-ri, the colonel informed us.

• • •

While we formed up for the three-mile march to Yudam-ni, Frank Bifulk chomped on a frozen Hershey bar.

"Where'd you get that, Bifulk?" asked his buddy, Merwin Perkins.

"Captain Wilcox," replied Bifulk.

"Captain Wilcox gave you his chocolate bar?"

"Not exactly gave it to me," Bifulk explained. "After he got hit I was helping him get out of his pack. And there was this Hershey bar in there."

"You stole it!" accused Perkins. "Our captain gets wounded and you steal his stuff from him!"

"Well, what the hell!" said Bifulk, still gnawing at the frozen chocolate. "His face was all shot up and he couldn't eat it, anyway. That ain't stealing."

"Gimme some," demanded Merwin Perkins, the company chow hound.

• • •

On the march back into the Yudam-ni perimeter, past midnight, the men were silent, spent from this cold and brutal day. And Captain Wilcox had been a good skipper.

CHAPTER SIXTEEN

Lieutenant Lee and Gunny Buckley had not been with us on that disastrous patrol. Lee had stayed behind to get his wounded arm cleaned. The gunny didn't go because Captain Wilcox had finally ordered him to sick bay. The docs diagnosed him with severe pneumonia and put him under a pile of blankets in the aid station. We never saw our gunny again.

Lee was waiting for us when we staggered into the Yudam-ni perimeter. Many of the men limped with the first stages of frostbite, and there were some walking wounded who had elected to stay with the company. Undisguised tears ran down Lee's face when he saw the column make its way in.

• • •

The Chinese attacked Yudam-ni again that night, with even greater force than the night before. The 5th Marines and the other two battalions of the 7th Marines took the brunt of the onslaught, fighting until dawn when our Corsairs swooped in to help push the Chinese back. The pressure on Yudam-ni had grown more serious. Nobody knew how many Chinese soldiers were out there, waiting to let loose on us. We only knew that the hills around Yudam-ni were swarming with them.

• • •

Joe Kurcaba formed us up in the first light while the Corsairs were blazing at the enemy hills. He told us that we were going to the aid of Charlie Company, which had been posted on Turkey Hill to guard the MSR. Last night, after we had marched away from that area, the

Chinese had poured out of the hills and surrounded Charlie. Charlie was fighting for its life when we went to pull them out.

Able Company went along our left flank, proceeding on the high ground that paralleled our push down the road. We took fire from the hills to the west, but it was scattered and we quickly moved through it. Colonel Davis, forward observers from artillery and the eighty-ones, and the tactical air team were all with us. The air officer told me that we had Australians flying support that day.

Able had hard fighting on the ridgeline leading to Charlie's embattled perimeter. They hammered through it, though, and gained a position that led down a long spine into the perimeter. A substantial enemy force stood between them and what was left of Charlie Company.

Baker-One-Seven suffered a few WIAs from long-range harassing fire as we attacked along the road. Lee had the lead, and when he came in sight of Turkey Hill, he halted the column and spread his platoon off the road in a firing line. Joe Kurcaba told me to set up all three mortars behind Lee.

Through my binoculars I had a good view of Charlie's perimeter, four hundred yards away. They were a tight circle not more than seventy-five yards across, halfway up the north slope of Turkey Hill. Chinese machine guns and rifles infested the hill around them, firing at any Marine who moved. Charlie's people were thoroughly pinned down.

Lee put his machine guns on the Chinese who were firing into Charlie's perimeter from the lower slope. My three mortars had the same target. Able's machine guns and mortars raked the hill above the perimeter.

Soon our tracers lined the sky, and puffs of black smoke from the mortars dotted the rocky hill. Then the big shells from artillery and the battalion's eighty-ones started to fall, and the hill rocked with their explosions. Chinese soldiers scurried for cover.

My classmate Jim Stemple led Able's assault down the ridgeline and into the Chinese. The enemy soldiers had their heads down from the heavy covering fire, and Stemple's platoon tore into them. Through the binoculars I observed one squad of Stemple's Marines led by a giant of a man in a flapping parka who swung a huge, double-headed axe. The Chinese soldiers, seeing this great, maniacal devil charge at them brandishing a bloody axe, abandoned their positions in terror.

I gave Kelly a look through my binoculars. "Christ!" he exclaimed. "I'd run, too, if I had that ugly monster coming at me with an axe."

The Chinese quickly lifted their siege of Charlie Company and made a rapid retreat from Turkey Hill. As they fled Able Company's downhill assault, they had to cross Baker's line of fire. Woody Taylor's platoon had come up to extend our line, and every weapon we had was trained on the Chinese as they ran to the protecting slopes, on the other side of the valley.

"Turkey Shoot at Turkey Hill," our people called it. We were at rapid fire with the mortars and machine guns, the BARs and the rifles, even Kovar's rocket launcher. Few Chinese made it all the way across that gauntlet of exploding flame and steel. They dropped in heaps, even before the Australian planes came down on them.

We hadn't worked with the Australians before, and they were out to prove that they were as gung-ho as our own Marine pilots. They came roaring low along the valley, from behind us, and when they passed above Lee's glowing pink vest they dropped even closer to the ground.

"They're low enough to cut the Chinks' pigtails off," Kelly quipped. The planes had their guns blazing, and the Chinese went down in bunches. The Australians made two passes. At the end of their second low-level assault there were no Chinese soldiers left to shoot at.

It took almost every able-bodied man that Charlie Company had to bring down their dead and wounded. Their overnight defense of Turkey Hill had cost dearly.

• • •

There were more heavy skirmishes over the next few days, with more enemy facing us every time we went out. On one long day, in numbing cold, we attacked south and tried to fight through the Chinese who blocked the MSR to Hagaru-ri, fourteen miles away. We were two battalions strong and we fought all day, side by side on both sides of the valley. By dark we had made only four miles, and we had to turn back. It was late at night when we came back into the Yudam-ni perimeter, and the Chinese were making another mass assault against the 5th Marines, on the north and west. By now the rifle companies of both regiments were down to half strength, or less.

• • •

We lost the corpsman, Doktorski, leaving only Ed Toppel to take care of the company.

I lost Sergeant Winget and Pat Burris to frostbite. Both of them asked me to let them stay with the outfit, but they hobbled badly and would slow us up. They bitched at me when I ordered them to the aid station, and I was sorry to lose them.

Bob Fisher caught a round in the foot; the cold numbed the wound and he limped around with us for a day, but he couldn't keep up. I sent him to battalion for evacuation. I was short of men, and now we had to depend on the rifle platoons to carry ammo for my mortars. They did so with a minimum of grumbling; the sixties did a good job of supporting the rifle platoons.

• • •

Joe Kurcaba returned from a meeting with Colonel Davis and the other company commanders to tell us that the Marines were pulling out of Yudam-ni. We were heading back to Hagaru-ri where a battalion of the 1st Marines and some Army troops had a stronghold. Out battalion, One-Seven, would attack west of the MSR to break through the Chinese, who held almost all of the fourteen miles to Hagaru-ri and the high ground that commanded it. In parallel columns the battalions of the 5th Marines would hit along the MSR and the hills east.

The enemy did not hold Toktong Pass, the highest point on the route. Fox Company of the 7th Marines occupied that vital terrain. They had fought off two regiments of Chinese attackers for three days and nights to keep it in Marine hands. Toktong Pass was now known as Fox Hill; it was our main objective, eight miles away through mountains and thousands of Chinese soldiers.

• • •

Able Company took the lead for the battalion attack. The Chinese put up their first stiff resistance at Turkey Hill, which they had occupied in strength after we pulled Charlie Company out of there.

Able had a brutal fight. The enemy knew the terrain as well as we did, and they set a formidable defense. Able had to work through a tangle of deep gullies and thick woods. It took them several hours to fight up the steep, slippery slopes to the top. Casualties were heavy, and all day the stretcher teams struggled to bring them off the hill. Many of Able's walking wounded elected to stay with their own squads after the corpsmen patched them up.

Colonel Davis sent my sixties over to add support to Able's attack, but for most of Baker-One-Seven the climbing was worse than the fighting. We passed through Able when they took the crest just before nightfall. The stop and start climb in the extreme cold had made it an exhausting day.

As soon as we finished digging in and fired night registration, Joe Kurcaba summoned the company officers to the CP. Colonel Davis

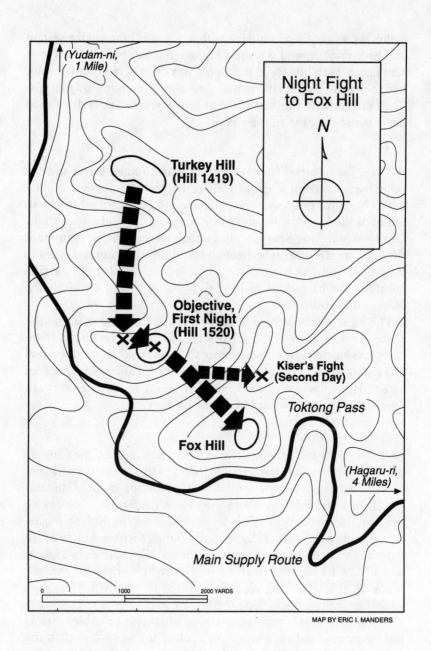

(Yudam-ni, 1 Mile)

Night Fight to Fox Hill

N

Turkey Hill (Hill 1419)

Objective, First Night (Hill 1520)

Kiser's Fight (Second Day)

Toktong Pass

Fox Hill

(Hagaru-ri, 4 Miles)

Main Supply Route

0   1000   2000 YARDS

MAP BY ERIC I. MANDERS

was there. He was clean-shaven in contrast to us shaggy-faced company lieutenants, but his features showed the same deep lines of strain and exhaustion that marked us all.

The colonel traced a stick in the snow to indicate an audacious plan of attack. Baker would jump off under cover of darkness and lead the battalion in a surprise attack against the Chinese who were positioned between us and Fox Hill.

Since we had been unable to break through in several daylight attempts along the road, the colonel reasoned we could go overland in the dark to reach the objective. As Marines did not ordinarily attack at night, the Chinese would not expect us; surprise was the essential element of the attack.

Our direction would be marked by star shells fired at three-minute intervals. Silence was vital; hopefully, we would walk through the defenders without being seen or heard. Joe Kurcaba gave Chew Een Lee the point.

A blizzard had whipped up before we formed the company. The men were lethargic from cold, physical exertion, and lack of rest. They grumbled their disbelief that we were about to launch an attack through trackless mountains in the dark and the blowing snow. Before starting out, we had them jog in place, to check for noisy gear and to get the blood moving.

Lee's platoon was ready, in column at the line of departure, and my mortars fell in behind Lee, followed by the company CP and the other two platoons. Colonel Davis and his command group followed Baker, although the colonel spent most of the night forward with us.

Then came Able, now as battered as we were and down to half strength. Charlie was next with only fifty men. The column's rear guard was a composite of men from the depleted How Company, 7th Marines, and replacements sent up from headquarters and artillery units. In all, Colonel Davis's patched-together One-Seven numbered less than five hundred Marines. Still, it made a file nearly a half mile long, an unlikely body to sneak through the encircling Chinese forces.

The first star shell went off far to the south, silhouetting a range of high ridges. Chew Een Lee raised his good arm and signaled us forward. The column of five hundred Marines followed him into the stormy night.

Simultaneously, we heard every weapon on the Yudam-ni perimeter commence firing. Artillery and heavy mortars pounded the slopes. Small arms and machine gun fire built to a crescendo. We hoped that the massive demonstration of firepower would divert enemy attention from our path.

Lee and his men had to plow through the heavy snow to break the trail and, at first, made it easy going for those of us who followed. The second star shell went off, then the third, all at three-minute intervals. We had no difficulty with our bearing. Soon, though, we came to a dip in the terrain, and Lee's view of the guiding light was obstructed. When he hadn't seen a burst for several minutes, he called a halt to read his compass. The column stopped, producing the inevitable accordion effect. In the darkness men stumbled into each other. Some fell into the snow beside the trail. Muffled curses were quickly squelched by whispered warnings from the NCOs.

When we moved again, we went up a steep grade. The trail became icy, packed by the feet of those ahead. Men slipped to their knees, staggered up, and slipped again. The sounds of falling and the involuntary grunts of pain and frustration grew steadily, in spite of our attempts to remain silent.

After a time we started downhill, and the star bursts were visible once more. Downhill the icy trail was even more treacherous, especially for the mortarmen and machine gunners with their cumbersome loads. Some of the men tried to sidestep their way, slowing those who came behind. Others ventured off the trail to make their own way in untrammeled snow. They had to be brought back into the column. In the dark and blowing snow they could easily become lost.

Exhaustion was telling on us. The falls became heavier, and it took longer for the men to pull themselves up from the snow. Curses and grunts of exasperation grew louder. We stumbled up the hills and we slid down them. We stopped and started, climbed and slipped.

Under the heavy parkas our bodies sweated with the strain, but our hands and feet were frozen numb. The windborne cold attacked with terrible fury. When we stopped for bearings, we stood silent and motionless. Because we needed to maintain silence, we could not slap our hands against our sides or stomp our feet for circulation. The cold gnawed at our toes and fingers and ate into our bodies. The sweat we had generated while climbing froze against our skin. We shivered violently. Men muttered through clenched teeth: "Let's move out, goddamnit. We're freezing to death here."

During one long halt the frustration spewed out of Joe Kurcaba, down the column. "Find out what the hell we're waiting for. Pass the word."

Each man relayed the message up the file, and their hoarse whispers threatened our silence. When the word reached me, I broke the verbal chain. I climbed forward along the column until I came upon Lee.

In front of Lee there was only swirling snow and darkness. Not a distinguishable terrain feature was to be seen, not a tree or a rock to bear on. Lee sent two men to the limit of visibility and bore his compass on their dim shapes. He was still wearing the sling but he had taken the mitten off his good hand to grip it.

"Haven't seen the star bursts in ten minutes," Lee whispered to me. "Tell them back there that we can't go any faster unless we want to walk in circles. Or over a cliff!"

I returned along the side of the column. Many men had collapsed in the snow, curled into balls like Eskimo dogs. NCOs moved among the fallen, prodding and kicking, urging them to their feet. I collided with another Marine churning forward through the snow. Both of us fell, and as we wearily recovered, I realized that I had knocked down Colonel Davis.

"What's the holdup, Lieutenant?" was all my battalion commander said. Then he continued breaking through the snow to the head of the column.

Time had no meaning. We labored through infinite darkness in ghostly clouds of snow over an icy path that rose and fell but seemed to lead nowhere. We saw only the back of the man ahead, a hunched figure in a long, shapeless parka, whose every tortured step was an act of will. We carried on with the only strength that was left to us, Marine Corps discipline.

Over the noise of the wind we heard Chinese soldiers speaking. They were no more than twenty-five yards away, but we could not see them. Undoubtedly, they heard us, too, but in the blinding snow they mistook our column for one of their own. Certainly the Chinese commanders would be positioning troops in response to the big attack down on the MSR. The first encounter of the night went unchallenged.

The nearby Chinese voices had an adrenalin effect. Realizing that we were within grenade range, we were charged with energy, and our minds cleared. Gone was our wearied stumbling. The men became sure-footed, alert. The nightmare passage we had endured through the dark, frigid storm was ended. We had reached the enemy. The men held their fire and watched for signaled orders. No unlikely noise gave away our presence.

Lee kept his men moving in a column, climbing a rise. We were a file of dark shadows, at ten yards distance indistinguishable as friend or foe. A man lost his footing and fell with a thunderous crash, but he uttered no sound that would identify him. In the wind we caught the whiff of the garlic that often gave away the Chinese positions. The Chinese stopped talking among themselves. The only sounds were the scuffing of Marine shoe-pacs on the icy trail and the wind that howled above us.

Suddenly, a harsh Chinese voice broke the silence. A challenge or a command, it came from the crest of the steep rise ahead, no more than fifty yards up. We could see no one up there.

Lee signaled his squads into skirmishers, extending to both sides. Quietly he led them forward on hands and knees. The enemy's first shots came as our riflemen topped the rise. A torrent of oaths and fire erupted from the Marines as they poured across a small Chinese position. An enemy squad had been sleeping on a wide shelf of ground that jutted from the hillside. Most of them were shot in the brief firefight; one was bayoneted in his hole. A few ran off into the snow.

There was no longer any need for silence. Lee and his NCOs bellowed orders to re-form the skirmish line, then sent the riflemen in pursuit up the hill. Light, disorganized small arms fire rained down at us. Our mortars set up on the shelf that Lee's people had just taken. Joe Kurcaba came forward and ordered the other platoons to attack on Lee's left flank. Colonel Davis reached us just as a barrage of grenades announced Lee's arrival at the next Chinese position.

The night exploded with the flash and sound of the fight. The Marines had the advantage of surprise and momentum. They fought with fierce energy, now released from the hours of cold and misery. The Chinese could do little more than try to escape. Their position was a wide plateau studded with large granite boulders. The snowy field was pocked with small holes and rocks from which startled Chinese emerged. Many of them were unarmed, and most ran off to the south.

Those with weapons attempted to fight. The night was against them. Under the ghostly blue illumination from the mortars, teams of parka-clad Marines using automatic weapons, bayonets, and grenades blasted through the Chinese who stayed to face them. A few of the enemy tried to fight back with rocks; one used a huge tree limb. All were eliminated.

A squad of mortarmen brought up their weapon to prepare for a counterattack. A few yards from their new position shadowy figures dodged among the boulders. One of the shadows called, "No shoot! We Cholly Com'ny. We M'leen." A volley of carbine rifle fire took him down.

Farther forward, the Marines ferreted out Chinese soldiers who were still concealed in holes and crevices. Lee called to them in their language, urging surrender. Some came out working their weapons and were quickly killed. A few of the weaponless responded with their hands up. They were taken prisoner and sent back to battalion for interrogation.

Baker Company quickly secured a perimeter. Despite the prodding of the NCOs, many of the men fell asleep. Others nodded off while in the act of repeating their orders. Colonel Davis walked the line with the platoon commanders. He assured that the officers and NCOs were prepared against counterattack and ordered twenty-five percent watch, one man in four awake. No counterattack came.

Dawn arrived, gray and cold, and we jumped off on the second phase of the breakthrough. Able and Baker attacked on line, headed for Fox Hill, a thousand yards away. Minutes after we moved out, Kiser's platoon, on the left, walked into heavy small arms and machine gun fire from a ridge on his flank. The sixties responded with HE on the ridge, and Kiser's people broke through deep snow to mount the hill. When they neared the ridgeline, we lifted the mortar fire, and the platoon drove through the enemy position on its own fire power.

We were astonished by our first view of Fox Hill. The snowfield that led up to the embattled company's position was covered with hundreds of dead Chinese soldiers. Many of them seemed asleep under blankets of drifted snow, but their bodies were frozen in spasms of pain. There were jumbles of corpses in padded green uniforms. A white-clad column had fallen in the formation that had attracted the attention of Fox Company's machine gunners. Craters of dirt and snow made by the big guns at Hagaru-ri were rimmed with bodies and parts of men. Thick bands of dead Chinese lay at the base of Fox Company's perimeter.

We stood in wonder. Men bowed their heads in prayer. Some fell to their knees. Others breathed quiet oaths of disbelief. Tears came to the eyes of raggedy Marines who had endured bitter cold and savage battle to reach this place of suffering and courage.

Someone let loose a wild cheer, and we broke forward in a jubilant run. Across the snow-covered and corpse-filled battlefield, the Marines of Fox Company waved brightly colored banners, the blue, yellow, and red remnants of the parachute drops that had sustained them for nearly a week.

Around their perimeter Fox Company had constructed barricades of frozen Chinese bodies. From behind these walls of dead the Marines had mounted their weapons and maintained the fight against an enemy whose numbers never ceased. Now the men of Fox Company arose from behind these gruesome piles to join us. Arm slings and blood-soaked compresses were common among them. Men hobbled about with makeshift leg splints. All hands were haggard and dirty, as were we.

We exchanged profane greetings that did not conceal the love that we Marines felt for each other.

• • •

The sun came out later and Marines appeared along the skylines to the north. Then we saw Marines marching down the MSR toward us. There were columns of riflemen at first, followed by a long trail of vehicles and artillery pieces. Our Corsairs swooped in close, their crooked wings wagging in salute. The 5th and 7th Marines had broken out of Yudam-ni.

• • •

Hank Kiser lost his runner, Jack Gallapo, as we mopped up around Fox Hill. One of Jack's buddies, responding to a spasm of diarrhea, was nailed by a sniper. Gallapo went to help the man who cried in pain as he flailed about in the snow he had just soiled. He pulled his buddy to cover, but the sniper's next bullet caught Gallapo in the lower back.

A fire team went for the sniper and killed him. Gallapo was hurt badly, though. He yelled that his left leg was numb and that his testicles had been shot off. Ed Toppel berated Gallapo for getting shot in the ass, but he assured him that the vital equipment was still there. We put Gallapo in a tent with Fox Company's wounded.

Ed Toppel, the only corpsman left to us, was hit in the leg sometime that day. It was a flesh wound, painful at first, but the cold deadened it. Toppel was not about to turn himself in. He patched up his own leg, chomped on a cigar, and limped about, taking care of his Marines.

• • •

Glen Galtere, the BAR-man from the 3d Platoon, had been promoted to company runner by Joe Kurcaba. Galtere's good fortune in firefights had continued, but the shoe-pacs gave him a bad case of frostbite. We had to leave him behind.

We had lost scores of other good men. Sergeant Bondurant. The corpsman, Doktorski. Sergeant Swandollar, the big squad leader from the 1st Platoon. Sherman Richter, the machine gun sergeant. Dean Westberg and Jim Veeder, workhorse mortarmen.

Hugo Johnson was a severe loss to me. He and Kelly were the only NCOs I had left, both corporals. We were in the high spire of rocks that topped Fox Hill. As we studied the mountains that lay between us and Hagaru-ri, a sniper's round took Johnson in the shoulder.

"Damn!"he shouted when the bullet struck and we all went to the deck. I cut away his pack strap so we could get to the wound, a deep hole within a bloody smear of flesh. "Damn! Damn! Damn!" Hugo grimaced. He couldn't move the arm. Kelly and I put on the compress, but Hugo didn't want the morphine that was in his first aid pouch.

"It'll be all right soon's I get moving about," he said through clenched teeth. "Be all right, Lieutenant."

"Yeah, Hugo, but you're going to the aid station." I knew he would ask me to let him stay with the mortars. With one arm dangling uselessly, though, he wouldn't be worth much to us. "Take him down to the road, Kelly."

"Well, goddamn, Lieutenant!" exclaimed Corporal Johnson, his eyes blazing at me. And, "Damn! Damn! Damn!" as Kelly helped him down through the rocks and snow to the road where many other wounded Marines waited for the meat wagons.

Sergeant Richard had been hit twice, but he was still with us. In the fight for Toktong Pass, going north, he took some shrapnel in his arm and shoulder, but Ed Toppel fixed him up. Later, on one of the Yudam-ni patrols, a bullet got him in the leg. The battalion aid station made the repairs and let him come back to the company. Hank Kiser and I told Sergeant Richard that it was a good thing he had come back; he was still acting first sergeant and the company records needed tending. He told us how he intended to go back to rear echelon and shanghai a real first sergeant for Baker-One-Seven. The paperwork was as great an ordeal for Sergeant Richard as was the fighting or the cold.

Richard and Gunny Foster were the remaining senior NCOs. Foster kept the machine guns but became the company gunnery sergeant when Buckley had turned in. All of the platoon sergeants had been hit, as were most of the squad leaders. We had corporals and privates stepping into leadership billets, but they were combat-experienced Marines and they knew the work.

• • •

The Marine column that came out of besieged Yudam-ni had hundreds of jeeps, ambulances, and trucks, as well as the big guns of the artillery regiment. Many of the trucks were filled with wounded men, and some were stacked with the corpses of our KIAs.

While the rifle companies secured the high ground, the column crept along the road, often grinding to a halt. The stop-and-start pace made it vulnerable to bands of Chinese who infiltrated to the road. The walking wounded who could carry a weapon were turned to as riflemen to protect the column. Every man who could walk, hobble, or limp was ordered off the trucks. The only riders were the serious cases, the gut wounds and blinded men, those with severe leg wounds, and men with frostbite so bad they would need amputation. Many of the wounded died in the trucks; some froze to death and some were shot by the infiltrators. The fourteen-mile ride was three days and nights of grim survival.

Bob Fisher, who could hardly feel his wounded leg anymore and was worried that he would lose it, was ordered off the truck and given flank guard duty. A limping sergeant shoved a rifle at him and ordered him to "Fix bayonet, lock-and-load, and stand by to repel boarders."

Fisher managed to keep pace with the slow-moving column by grabbing the rear of a truck to pull himself along, hopping and stumbling. Rows of feet, still in their shoe-pacs, protruded from the rear of the truck. As he struggled to hold on, Fisher realized with horror that the feet sticking out above him were those of dead Marines.

He didn't have to hold on to the truck for long. A Chinese raiding party swarmed out of a draw near the road and hit the column from the side. Fisher slid into a ditch and came up firing his M-1. The same sergeant limped by with another rifleman and dropped some bandoleers of ammo clips into the ditch.

"You lads hold right here," said the sergeant. "You don't let them gooks come close to the trucks. I'll keep the ammo coming." The sergeant hobbled off to the next cluster of Marines, farther along the ditch.

The walking wounded fought off the Chinese and did not let them get to the trucks. It was like that all the way to Hagaru-ri.

• • •

Pat Burris was unable to walk, but he could handle a rifle. He perched himself on the front fender of a truck and helped guard the column from there.

Father Griffin, the young chaplain for the 7th Marines, came along the column and found Burris shivering at his exposed perch on the truck. The padre reached into one of the deep pockets of his grimy parka and pulled out a small bottle of whiskey.

"You look as if you could use this," the priest said to the frozen corporal.

Burris cut the seal with his fighting knife and emptied the tiny bottle in one swallow. He felt the warmth course through his body. "You're a godsend, Padre."

"Thank you for saying that, son," answered the chaplain. "This is not the way I had expected to be doing His work." Then he moved on down the column, looking for more frozen Marines.

A firefight erupted when the Chinese made an assault on Burris's part of the column. Burris could only sit on the fender, open to enemy fire, and crank off rounds from the M-1 rifle he had been given. Bullets pinged off the hood of the truck, and one smashed the windshield behind his head. The driver popped out of the other side of the cab and returned fire, steadying his carbine on the roof.

Along the line Burris heard Father Griffin shouting directions to the men who fought to protect the trucks. With language that would have made an Old Corps gunnery sergeant blush, the padre rammed his fighters into position and they turned back the attackers. Burris figured that, under the circumstances, God would overlook the profanities shouted by the young priest.

Later the Chinese took the column under mortar attack. Pat Burris, still perched on the truck's fender, caught a piece of metal in his foot, and other bits of shrapnel peppered his body. It was Father Griffin who came along again, cut off the boot, and patched the wounds as best he could in the cold darkness. And he gave Burris another small bottle of whiskey. Burris thought of it as holy water.

CHAPTER SEVENTEEN

The rifle companies of the 5th and 7th Marines stayed in the hills, guarding the MSR as the column pulled into Hagaru-ri. The garrison of the town came out to meet the bedraggled Marines who had run the fourteen-mile gauntlet of fire and ice. There were trucks and jeeps with their windshields shot away and their hoods and sides peppered with bullet holes and gashed by shrapnel. Wounded men were stuffed in layers in the backs of the trucks; others were lashed across the hoods or tied to the fenders. There were many more trucks filled with corpses than had started the journey.

As the walking wounded came within sight of the town, someone commanded them to fall into ranks. Maybe it was the limping sergeant who gave the command, the old salt who had set the defenses along Bob Fisher's stretch of the column; it could have been Father Griffin. Or Sergeant Winget or Corporal Burris or Corporal Johnson.

The wounded men, and some who were unharmed but who staggered from exhaustion, formed up into three files, shouldered their weapons, and marched in ragged step. Slowly the tread of their thick, rubber-soled shoe-pacs on the icy road became a steady, sure cadence, and the haggard and hurt Marines put their heads high.

Captain Wilcox, who couldn't carry a weapon, was in the forward ranks. His arm was in a huge cast and splinted so that it was horizontal to the deck; his head and face were a cocoon of bandages. But holding himself erect, he picked up the cadence and marched standing straight into Hagaru-ri.

A battalion surgeon took time away from the hundreds of wounded men he tended in the Hagaru-ri aid station to witness the column's arrival. "Those bastards! Those magnificent bastards!" were the words the doctor used to describe the worn and torn Marines from Yudam-ni.

• • •

Except for the road we had opened, Hagaru-ri was under siege, surrounded by many thousands of Chinese soldiers. They had been held off by a battalion of the 1st Marines and hundreds of rear echelon people who had reverted to riflemen. For three days and nights the cooks and bakers, the truck drivers and artillerymen, the office pinkies and technicians, dug in alongside the infantry Marines. They threw back every thrust the Chinese made against the Hagaru-ri perimeter.

American soldiers were there, too, Army technical support people who picked up rifles and BARs and went up the hills and filled in the Marine lines. Wherever there were gaps, the artillery threw in massive bombardments. During daylight hours, the Corsairs flew in low with bombs, rockets, and napalm that helped to hold the attackers at bay.

The three divisions of Chinese who had tried to isolate the 5th and 7th Marines at Yudam-ni, plus those who had besieged Fox Hill, followed us south, and now they added their numbers to the encirclement of Hagaru-ri. The single road south, the MSR to Koto-ri and our only way out, was cut off. The hills that flanked that road were high and steep, and there were as many Chinese embedded in them as there had been at Yudam-ni.

• • •

The engineers, with their heavy earth-moving equipment, had dynamited the frozen ground and leveled an airfield large enough for cargo planes to fly in and out of Hagaru-ri. Air Force pilots flew the big, clumsy planes, loaded to the gunwales with replacements, rations, and ammo. For the return trip they filled the planes with the most seriously wounded.

When they landed and took off, they had to fly low, between the hills that lined the valley. The planes became slow-moving targets for the Chinese guns in the hills, and every one that left Hagaru-ri was perforated with bullet holes. The men on the ground marveled at the courage of the Air Force pilots who kept flying in and out of there.

• • •

Baker-One-Seven was the last rifle company of the 7th Marines to come into the Hagaru-ri perimeter. When we had fought to within sight of the town, we were ordered to a hill overlooking the road to become the rear guard. We watched as beneath us the hundreds of vehicles and all of the other rifle companies of both regiments crawled along the road. After they all had passed into the shelter, we faced into the frigid wind, set our weapons, and made sure that the Chinese did not attack again.

"Why the hell us?" Kelly asked plaintively. "We do the up-front fighting all the way until there's a place to get warm. Then they make us stay out here so we can freeze our asses off some more. Ain't fair, Lieutenant. Ain't one bit fair."

"Quit your bitching, Kelly. You volunteered for this lashup."

"Yeah, but I'm putting in for a transfer. Soon as we get out of this cold I'm putting in for Guam again. Or any other place in the Corps where they don't give you frozen chow three times a day."

"Sure you are, Kelly. And we'll all go with you."

Toppel's leg was hurting. We had a tiny fire going at a patch of trampled snow that served as the CP. While Joe Kurcaba walked the perimeter, I tended the radio to battalion. Kelly was with me. Toppel lay in the snow trying to keep the weight off his bad leg. To cheer him up, Kelly mixed him a canteen cupful of "snow cream," a mixture of powdered chocolate from our rations and clean snow.

Toppel grunted with pain as he moved the leg away from the fire. "Shouldn't let it get warm," he said. "When it starts to thaw out, it hurts like hell."

"You should have turned in, when we were down on the road," Kelly replied, handing Toppel the freshly whipped concoction. "One of those meat wagons would've given you a ride all the way into the aid station."

Toppel snapped at him. "You see what happened to some of the wounded down there in the column? They were sitting ducks in those ambulances, just waiting for the gooks to shoot at them. I'm staying up here where it's safe."

"OK, Doc," said Kelly, preparing a new batch of snow cream. "We'll let you stay with us. You just keep that sickbay alcohol coming."

Through my glasses I saw a column of riflemen marching toward us out of Hagaru-ri. There were two files of them, moving at a brisk pace along both sides of the road. They wore crisp white parkas and their arms swung smartly. Because they were clean-shaven and energetic we assumed that they were fresh replacements flown in to the air strip. We found out later that these clean and jaunty troops were British Royal Marines who had fought their way into Hagaru-ri from the south. They, too, had found the MSR blocked, and they had punched through Chinese forces far superior in number to them.

They were the 41st Commando, a unit that roughly compared in size to one of our own rifle companies. Like us, these Marines had suffered heavy casualties.

The Royal Marine column halted and spread into ditches along the road near our CP. A freshly-groomed young officer strode toward Kelly, Toppel, and me. With the young officer was a grizzled sergeant, whose proper military bearing could have come straight from the pages of Kipling. The sergeant had a meticulously trimmed, broad mustache that would have stirred Gunny Buckley's envy. Like the lieutenant, the sergeant was dazzlingly clean and squared away.

My binoculars hung around my neck, which is how the lieutenant distinguished me as an officer. Certainly there was little other difference among Kelly and Toppel and me. Our parkas were all stained with blood, food, gun oil, and dirt. Our filthy faces were matted with bristly beards that bore icicles of mucus and spittle.

The lieutenant concealed his disdain for our appearance, braced himself, and delivered a broadhand salute. "I say, Sir, we're ordered to extend a patrol beyond your lines here. I'm to set up the covering machine guns, and I would be most grateful for your suggestions."

I appreciated the British lieutenant's courtesy, and if I had possessed a razor I would have shaved on the spot to make myself more presentable.

Before I could answer, however, Toppel sounded off, "We don't give a goddamn where you set up your goddamn machine guns. Just do it so we can go someplace and get warm!"

The proper British lieutenant and the proper British sergeant were startled by such gross insubordination. They looked with disgust at Toppel, who was still lying in pain beside the fire. They did not know—and perhaps it would have made no difference—that this was the second day Toppel had been carrying a bullet in his leg.

The lieutenant looked from Toppel to me. I wondered if he thought I would shoot Toppel, then and there, to atone for the lack of courtesy. Certainly that is what the sergeant expected to see.

"Very little enemy out there since last night," I said to change the subject. "But come on. I'll show you where our guns are. You may want to use those positions."

The Royal Marine lieutenant and his sergeant followed me to our machine gun positions, and they checked out the fields of fire for their own mission. As we walked the line together, we exchanged observations about fighting the Chinese. The British lieutenant knew what he was talking about.

His sergeant kept looking back toward the CP where Toppel still rested by the fire. He was probably thinking how he would like to have Toppel in his charge for a bit of proper training.

• • •

Early the next day we marched into Hagaru-ri. Joe Kurcaba told us to find spaces for our men and let them sleep until we moved out again. By the time we arrived, though, there was no room in the tents. But there was shelter from the wind and we did not need to worry about Chinese attacks—luxury enough for men who had lived endless nights and days on cold, windswept ridges, much of that time under enemy fire. I found a quiet spot for my diminished mortar section. The men crawled into their bags, which they zipped all the way up, and we slept dead to the world.

Kelly awakened me with the information that the Marines were preparing to leave Hagaru-ri and that all materiel which could not be carried would be burned or blown up. Kelly had found a mound of PX supplies where cartons of cigarettes, cigars, and candy bars were there for the taking. My luxury-starved mortarmen piled out of their sleeping bags and followed Kelly to the treasure trove.

Other outfits had already discovered the bounty, but plenty of cigars and Tootsie Rolls remained. We stuffed them into our empty packs and the pockets of our parkas and went back to a tent that Gunny Foster had found for us. Soon the tent was filled with cigar smoke and the sound of a dozen Marines sucking hungrily on the sweet Tootsie Rolls.

Someone said that mail was waiting for us at Hagaru-ri, and I went to battalion to see what I could find. We hadn't heard from home since starting up to Yudam-ni. If we had received mail, though, no one knew where it was. I returned to my sleeping bag and broke out the pictures of Dorothy and the babies. Still wearing my clumsy mittens, my parka, and all my stinking layers of clothing, I shuffled through the photos and remembered my beautiful Dorothy and the soft, clinging arms of the babies.

• • •

Our corpsman, Ed Toppel, found a place in a tent. Its warmth thawed out his wounded leg, and the pain from the bullet still lodged in his flesh became excruciating. He was unable to walk, and Hank Kiser told him to turn himself in. Toppel was still chomping on a cigar and bitching that he did not want to leave the company when two of the riflemen assisted him to the aid station. Since we were fresh out of corpsmen, Joe Kurcaba sent Acting First Sergeant Richard to battalion to procure another one.

• • •

Cpl. Dick Bahr, from Lee's platoon, went in search of food more substantial than Tootsie Rolls. He found an Army mess tent where he was welcomed by the mess sergeant and given his fill of flapjacks, which he smothered in maple syrup. When he had finished stuffing himself, he was offered a gallon of the syrup to take along. Bahr put the big metal tin in his pack, thinking of the march that lay ahead.

In the mess tent Bahr met soldiers who had come down from the east side of the Chosin Reservoir, parallel to our move down the western edge. They had a tragic story to tell.

While the Chinese had hit us with three divisions of their mountain fighters at Yudam-ni, they had sent another division, ten thousand men, to attack the Army troops across the reservoir from us. The Army had gone up the east side with a force of only two battalions, so they were far outnumbered when the Chinese slammed into them. The night pyrotechnics that we had witnessed on the east side of the reservoir had been the enemy's opening assault on these troops.

It was a surprise attack, and a devastating one, for the soldiers had left Hagaru-ri unaware of the enemy's strength and disposition.

Unlike our General Smith and Colonel Litzenberg, who had resisted Tokyo's demand for rapid advance, the Army leaders on the ground were unable to challenge General MacArthur's orders to speed north to the Yalu. The Army outfits that went east of the reservoir were hurriedly patched together and poorly equipped for their mission. The artillery and tanks that were to support their advance were not organized in time to accompany them when they moved north out of Hagaru-ri. The heavy weapons that aided the Marine breakout west of the reservoir were not there for the Army. And many of the soldiers in that fight had not yet received cold weather gear; scores of them froze to death.

It was the Army's bad fortune, too, that a large number of its officers and experienced NCOs had been knocked out of the battle at the outset. The two senior commanders, a colonel and a lieutenant colonel, were killed at the front of their troops. Most of the company commanders and the platoon leaders went down. In a short time the casualties of all ranks outnumbered the able-bodied, and some of the wounded had to be left behind. Platoons and squads dwindled to a few men and coalesced into small bands that fought until their ammunition was gone. Those who could walk or crawl then made their way back across the frozen reservoir to the Marine lines at Hagaru-ri.

For the soldiers it was a disastrous fight, but it had one good effect. The Chinese division that had mauled them was aimed at the attack on Hagaru-ri. The fight the soldiers put up on the east side of the reservoir had slowed their advance, and that bought valuable time for the Marines. When the Army survivors made their way into Hagaru-ri, those who could still carry on were reequipped and formed into a provisional battalion that became part of the 1st Marine Division. They fought alongside us for the remainder of the campaign.

• • •

Baker-One-Seven attacked south out of Hagaru-ri before dawn the next morning. Even as we jumped off, the Chinese were winding down a night attack on the other side of the town. It was their heaviest attempt yet, but they made no penetrations because the 5th Marines were now on the line with the garrison. Fires burned everywhere—the burning of supplies and equipment that would be left behind the breakout. Their smoke blended with the exhaust from the hundreds of vehicles that would form into column when the 7th Marines cleared the MSR to Koto-ri. The cold measured twenty-five below zero, and it felt even worse after our night in the unaccustomed shelter of the town.

Battalion sent a new corpsman to us. He was a replacement just flown into Hagaru-ri. His youthful face was clean shaven, his uniform was brand new, and he seemed out of place among the scruffy, filthy-faced men of Baker-One-Seven. He looked scared, too. Later, though, I saw him tending a wounded man, and the kid knew his business.

In the attack, we leapfrogged with Able and Charlie Companies, taking one piece of high ground after another. The Chinese were not ready for us as we engaged them up in the hills west of the road. Many of the soldiers we encountered were frozen to death; others had feet so numbed by the cold that they couldn't walk. They wore only canvas sneakers on their feet and had thin cotton gloves. Those who couldn't run away stayed in their holes, firing their weapons at us until we overcame them. We shot them dead because we could not care for them, nor carry them with us, and we could not leave them unguarded in our rear. We had great respect for the fight they always put up, and their courage, and we told ourselves it was better for them to be put out of their misery.

Colonel Davis stayed with the assault platoons all day as we rolled up the Chinese along the ridgelines. The men all knew the colonel, and it gave them great confidence to see him exposed to the same risks that they faced.

Also with us were FOs from the eighty-ones and artillery. For once we had all the heavy support we could ask for. The big guns, which were laid in back at Hagaru-ri, blasted the terrain ahead of us until we came within a few hundred yards of each objective. The eighty-ones took over then, their big HE shells pinpointing individual Chinese positions. There was little work for my sixties that day, and my ammo bearers groused that they had to carry their loads of ammo for so long.

Chew Een Lee came close to getting nailed. Kelly and I were following behind him as he led his platoon in an assault against a position that appeared to have already been destroyed by the eighty-ones; there were no signs of live Chinese. As always, the bright pink marker panels strapped to Lee's back and chest made him an obvious target. A Chinese soldier, who had survived the bombardment, rose from behind a felled tree. His rifle was pointed straight at Lee. I yelled a warning and swung my carbine at the enemy soldier. Before I could get off a round, a tight burst exploded from Lupacchini's BAR. The enemy soldier collapsed over the tree trunk, his rifle falling into the snow. Lupacchini approached and prodded him with his shoe-pac.

"We got him OK now, Lieutenant," said Lee's self-appointed bodyguard.

"Well done, Marine," Lee said to Lupacchini, and the two of them continued through the position.

"That's the kind of protection I'd like to get," I told Kelly.

"You'd have been dead a long time ago without me," Kelly responded.

"Yeah, Kelly. What would I do without you?"

• • •

When it got dark, the colonel pulled us off the hills and ordered the company to proceed along the road toward Koto-ri. Baker-One-Seven had the point of the advance on the right side of the road. One of the companies of the 2d Battalion was on the left side. In the dark our advance became a chaotic nightmare.

At first we thought we were in for an easy time. The Chinese let the advance party continue along for several hundred yards. The company came forward in loose formation, flankers out to the right. We progressed slowly, trying to maintain visual contact. All of the troops, it seemed, were sucking on Tootsie Rolls as they went, and we were as silent as a rifle company could be, moving in the dark.

The Chinese opened up on us without warning. Mortars, machine guns, burp guns, rifles, everything they had and all at once. We scattered off the road and took cover. There were cries for the corpsman up and down our broken column; the new corpsman had plenty of work that night.

Confusion set in. Squads and fire teams were split off from their platoons. My abbreviated mortar section had been together when the Chinese took us under fire, but now I didn't know where they all were. Kelly was still with me, and Perkins and Bifulk had their mortar. I shouted for the rest of them to assemble on me, but my calls were mingled with the shouts of the other lieutenants and the NCOs trying to regroup. The Chinese kept up their heavy fire, and we were having a difficult time organizing a response.

Joe Kurcaba walked up and down the road, yelling at us to get squared away and start some return fire going. Tracers streaked all around him, but I had to stand up when he came by me.

"Joe, I don't know where anyone is," I informed my company commander.

"You got any ammo left?" Joe asked. "Put what you got up there where those goddamn tracers are coming from."

Joe Kurcaba continued down the road, organizing the defense. I went down on all fours and told Merwin Perkins to set up his gun and put HE on the side of the hill above us.

Perkins and Bifulk had eight rounds left. Kelly and I each had a couple. We fired off most of what we had before the Chinese zeroed in on us.

"I'm hit! I'm hit! Goddamn, I'm hit!" screamed Frank Bifulk.
Dear God, not Bifulk!

"I'm hit! I'm going back to the aid station." Bifulk went flat to the deck beside his mortar. Perkins dropped in the remaining rounds, then rolled flat, too.

I crawled over to Bifulk. The Chinese pelted the ground around us; there was no shelter for me to pull him into.

"Where are you hit, Bifulk?"

"My gut. They got me in the gut."

"Let's see." He had curled up and I turned him on his back. Perkins and Kelly had moved a few yards away, and they fired up the slope with their carbines. The Chinese fire had slackened; our HE had done some good.

I could hardly see as I felt for blood under Bifulk's parka. The front of his clothing was dry, but a large chunk of ice-crusted dirt, chipped off the ground by shrapnel, had become embedded in his parka. There was no blood.

Thanks, God!

"You're OK, Bifulk. Just a chunk of ice. You'll live."

"I'm wounded!" He grimaced with the pain in his gut. "I'm going back to the aid station. I got a right to."

"And where do you think you're going to find an aid station?" We didn't know where the aid station was, whether it was in the column following us or still within the Hagaru-ri perimeter.

"What a screwed-up outfit this is," Bifulk said, cursing. I helped him to his feet, and for some time he walked doubled over. But he stayed with us.

• • •

Dick Bahr's squad, moving farther along the road, encountered a group of Chinese troops emerging from a culvert. In the ensuing firefight a grenade fragment pierced Bahr's knapsack and tore open the gallon can of maple syrup that was inside. The impact of the close hit threw him to the ground. Dazed slightly, he felt gingerly for wounds. His mitten became smeared with sticky fluid, which, in the dark, Bahr thought was blood. He felt no pain, though. Still, the night was frigid and Bahr had learned in past fights that the deep cold often delayed the pain from a wound. He got up, figuring he would go on until he met a corpsman.

Although Dick Bahr was happy to learn he had not been wounded, he was a very angry Marine when he discovered the damage that the enemy had done to his maple syrup. Later he reported the outrage to Lieutenant Lee. It was one of the few times anyone had seen Lee laugh.

• • •

Cpl. Ron Moloy led his fire team toward a hut still standing a hundred yards off the road. Seeking warmth, Moloy opened the door of the hut and peered in. A Chinese soldier lay on the dirt floor. Moloy thought he was dead and stepped inside over him. The enemy soldier came to life and rose to put his burp gun on Moloy.

Pfc. Charles Keister had followed Moloy. When he saw the Chinese move, he triggered a burst from his BAR. The enemy soldier collapsed to the deck again, this time dead for sure.

The noise of Keister's BAR in the tiny hut startled Moloy. "Jesus, Keister, watch where the hell you're shooting that thing!" he shouted at his BAR-man.

"Aye, aye, Corporal," answered Keister to his fire team leader. "I'll get your permission next time."

．．．

Father Griffin, driving his jeep in the column, took a bad hit that night. A Chinese mortar exploded in front of him, and the jeep swerved off the road. The padre was hit with shrapnel in his face and upper body, and his assistant, Cpl. Matt Caruso, pulled him away from the vehicle. A swarm of Chinese suddenly rushed toward the road, tossing their grenades and firing burp guns. Caruso threw himself over Father Griffin, who was unconscious. Chinese bullets stitched Caruso's back, but the padre received no further wounds.

A squad of Marines drove away the enemy band, killing several. Matt Caruso was dead. The Marines put Father Griffin on a truck that took him to an aid station when the column reached Koto-ri the next morning. He was one of the hundreds of wounded who were flown out of another air strip that the engineers had blasted from the frozen ground at Koto-ri.

．．．

Acting First Sergeant Richard never got the muster role straight after that night of fighting. Many of the men who left Hagaru-ri with us became separated in the confusion, and they never found us again in the jumble of men and outfits heading into Koto-ri.

Others were wounded and picked up by ambulances that followed the forward companies; these men were not reported until several days afterward. The graves registration teams were close to the forward fighting, too, and they picked up bodies as they came along. The corpses were identified by their dog tags, but that information did not get to the company until much later, when the fighting had ended and Baker-One-Seven had a real first sergeant.

The company now numbered fewer than fifty Marines, counting all the men we still had with us when we came into Koto-ri, as well as all our stragglers that we could find. The corpsman who had been issued to us the previous morning was not to be found. Someone said he had been killed along the road during the night.

I had only seven men left, Kelly, Perkins, and Bifulk among them. Hank Kiser's platoon was reduced to a dozen people. Lee and Taylor had about the same number, and only a couple of the headquarters people remained.

Koto-ri was similar to Hagaru-ri. It had been under attack and defended by one battalion of the 1st Marine Regiment, plus an assortment of headquarters and technical personnel and some Army detachments. There was an artillery base there, and the garrison had erected a tent city to shelter the troops who came down with the column from Hagaru-ri.

Baker-One-Seven went into the tents, and we were soon given a hot meal from the field kitchen. Joe Kurcaba told us that we would jump off again at first light the next morning and that we should give the men all the sleep they wanted.

A few minutes later Joe came back to roust out Chew Een Lee and me. The Chinese had occupied a hill north of the village, and they were using it to put harassing fire on the tail end of the column, which was still coming down from Hagaru-ri. Regiment told battalion and battalion told Kurcaba to send someone out to clear the hill. Kurcaba told Lee to get the job done, and he told me to take my mortars along to help.

It was a bare, high hill a half mile north of the town. Lee and I didn't understand why the troops in the column didn't clear their own flanks, but we followed our orders.

Lee formed a line of attack to go straight up the hill, after preparation fire by Gunny Foster's machine guns and the two mortars that remained to me. Lee signaled his men forward, and I followed closely behind, bringing Perkins's gun with me. Bifulk, on the other mortar, dropped a steady line of HE in front of our advancing rifles and BARs.

Bifulk had a full ration of ammo, and he used it liberally. As we neared the top of the hill, I signaled him to cease fire; his rounds were landing close to our own rapidly moving troops.

We took the crest, and most of the enemy soldiers who hastened down the reverse slope were shot. With my glasses I observed the Chinese setting up a heavy mortar in the valley below.

"Perkins, set up your gun!"

"Aye, aye, Sir!"

"Seven-zero-zero yards, HE. Aim on me."

Perkins was ten yards behind me, the bipod of his gun already jammed into the ground. He repeated the fire order as he cranked in his elevation. Kelly, who was beside him, ripped the propellants off the shells.

"Fire when ready." I was watching the Chinese mortar crew going through the same procedure on their gun. *A mortar duel!*

Thunk! went Perkins's first round. The Chinese hadn't dropped one into their tube yet. I watched our round arc, fall, and send up its black smoke plume. Fifty yards short.

"Half turn down, Perk," I called. "Fire for effect!"

"Half turn down. For effect!" answered my gunner. The rounds immediately started thumping.

A round puffed out of the Chinese mortar, but I lost its direction. Wherever it landed it did the Marines no harm.

Our HE hit directly in front of the Chinese gun, and I saw it fly into the air. The next rounds landed in the same area, producing a series of violent explosions as the ammunition that was stacked near the enemy mortar blew up.

"Cease fire! Cease fire! Good shooting, Perk. You too, Kelly."

Lieutenant Lee had seen the display of mortar marksmanship. "Very good shooting for a second lieutenant," he said. I swear there was a faint smile on his face when he said that.

• • •

Returning to the bottom of the hill, we saw two bodies lying under ponchos in the snow beside the road. One of the corpses was Gunny Foster. Nobody knew who the other one was.

"He was a replacement," Corporal Bahr told me. "We picked him up just before we came out to take this hill. I didn't get his name yet."

Lee barked at his men to form the column to return to Koto-ri. Gunny Foster had helped him organize and whip the machine gun platoon into shape, and Lee thought the world of him. As did everyone in Baker-One-Seven.

I felt bad about the dead replacement, too. He never even got his name on Sergeant Richard's roster.

• • •

When we again reached the accommodations of Koto-ri, I squeezed into a tent with Hank Kiser. It was crowded with Marines we didn't know, sleeping in their bags on the deck. Hank was feverish and sick, and he kept getting up to vomit and empty his bowels behind the tent. The men in the tent, who were stepped on every time Hank made a dash for it, growled at him to stay the hell out of there and quit stinking up the area.

"You people knock it off!" I shouted at those who complained about my buddy. For effect I snapped the bolt of my carbine. The protesters buried their heads in their sleeping bags and grumbled to themselves. Nobody wanted to mess with a wild-eyed, scruffy-faced second lieutenant holding a loaded weapon.

CHAPTER EIGHTEEN

Someone came into the tent early the next morning to get us out of our sleeping bags. There must have been fifteen of us sprawled on the deck, and during the night our breath had formed a thick coat of frost on the inside of the canvas. Hank Kiser shivered like a soaked dog.

"You OK, buddy?" I asked.

"Yeah." He coughed, a deep, hacking cough, and went about squaring away his blanket roll and pack. He moved slowly, not at all Hank's way of doing things, and his hands shook.

"You look like hell, Hank."

He glanced up at me. "You wouldn't pass inspection yourself, pal," he said. Neither of us had put soap to our faces for a long time.

The night before I had taken out my photos and looked at them with the aid of a flashlight. I must have fallen off to sleep while looking at them, for they were scattered throughout the bag. I gathered them together and studied them one final time before tucking them into the webbing of my helmet. The one on top, the last one I saw, was Dorothy in her white bathing suit on the beach at Camp Lejeune.

• • •

The cold was a shock, an icy blast that hit us when we came out of the tent. After the night in shelter it was worse than if we had stayed outside. Hank gasped when it hit him. I stomped my feet and pounded my arms against my sides. Our frozen breath blew into our faces and quickly coated our beards with white ice. The windblown snow was so thick we could hardly see where we were going.

It was the worst cold I had ever felt.

Joe Kurcaba was waiting for us when we came to the company assembly area. Hank was slouched over, and he was having trouble putting one foot in front of the other.

"Christ, you look bad, Hank," said our company commander.

"I'll be OK," Hank said weakly. "I just need to move around a little."

"We got a tough one today, Hank. You don't look like you can make it."

"I told you. I'll be OK!"

Kurcaba turned to me. "What do you think, Joe?"

"He had the runs and puked all night," I answered.

Joe gave Hank a long, careful look. "Sorry, Hank. The shape you're in, you can't take care of your men. You go back to sick bay."

"The hell I will!" Hank exploded. "I brought my platoon this far. I'm not about to . . ."

"Turn yourself in to sick bay," Joe interrupted.

Tears ran down Hank's face. They froze on his cheeks. "That an order, Joe?"

"That's an order, Lieutenant Kiser," said our company commander.

Hank stared at him for a moment. Then he said, "Aye, aye, Sir!" He turned and wobbled away from us.

"Sorry, Hank," Joe Kurcaba called after Hank Kiser.

Kurcaba told me to take over Kiser's platoon. There were only a dozen men left in it, out of the original forty-two—plus all the replacements who had come and gone. Chew Een Lee's platoon, and Woody Taylor's, were also reduced to squad size.

I told Kelly to take over the mortar section. "Just bring one gun along, Kelly. Won't be able to see anything to shoot at today, anyway."

"What do you mean? I'm not going with you?"

"No. You take the mortars."

"Naw. You need me to stay with you."

"Take the mortars, Kelly."

We stared at each other, standing in the cold with the wind blowing snow around us. Kelly's face was coated white with ice, like mine.

"You take the mortars, Kelly. That's it."

He shook his head. "Listen, Joe. Listen to me." Rank was forgotten. We were brothers. "Who do you think kept you alive all this time, Joe? All the stuff we've been through. You ain't going to last a day without me!"

"Maybe you're right, Kelly." I put my head down. If there were tears in my eyes I didn't want him to see them. "But you take the mortars. Like I told you. Now do it!"

Kelly turned and stomped away, back along the icy road. He muttered as he went, "Goddamn second lieutenants."

We had a hard time rounding up the company in the snow and dark. Staff Sergeant Richard was now acting gunnery sergeant as well as acting first sergeant. He sent out a detail to scour the tents in search of our people.

As we waited to form up, Joe Kurcaba gave his lieutenants the word. He didn't look much better than Hank did. Nor did Lee and Taylor and I. None of us could have passed a physical examination.

One-Seven, our battalion, and Two-Seven were to lead the break-out from Koto-ri. One-Seven was to take the high ground east of the road; Two-Seven, the west. Four miles south, on the MSR, the Chinese had blown out a bridge over a deep chasm. A battalion of the 1st Marines, coming from the south, would take the ground that commanded the other side of the gap. Then the engineers would put in a new bridge. Beyond that was a full Army division, the 3d, waiting to give us cover. After we crossed the bridge, the Army would take over the fighting.

All we needed to do was get through a few more divisions of Chinese soldiers.

● ● ●

Another young corpsman was sent to us. He was similar to the one who had been with us the day before: pink-cheeked, clean-shaven, clean clothes, and looking scared.

Sergeant Richard went over to him. "You just stick close to me, lad," our Old Corps NCO told the new doc. "Until you hear them yell 'Corpsman!' Then you get to work."

● ● ●

Able Company went out in front. The waiting Chinese immediately put down a sheet of fire—mortars, machine guns, burp guns, rifles. Able's casualties soon started to return. We huddled against blowing clouds of snow and prayed to God that Able wouldn't get so badly mauled that we would have to take their place.

Our prayers were not answered. Battalion ordered us to pass through Able and continue the attack. Although it was daylight, we could barely see where we were going.

The Chinese did not need to see us; there was only one way for us to get at them, straight along the road. They had our approach well marked and covered with their weapons. As soon as we went past Able, the Chinese mortars began to drop and their machine guns opened. The tracers were weird streaks of orange that flew at us out of the blinding snow clouds. Our new corpsman was quickly put to work.

Joe Kurcaba spread our diminished company off the road—Lee's platoon spread to the left and Taylor's platoon extended beyond Lee's. The Chinese were shooting down from a hill that flanked Woody, as well as from straight ahead. Joe didn't want to send anyone up that hill, fearing he would lose them in the heavy snow.

Our artillery and the big mortars were of no use to us; the Chinese were too close and we worried about taking friendly fire in the white-out. Kelly couldn't see targets for his remaining mortar, either. There was no support to help us push away the Chinese who blocked us. We had only rifles, BARs, grenades, and bayonets.

We put a machine gun into action, aiming roughly in the direction of the tracers. The gun soon jammed up with the cold, and I crawled over to see if I could get it going again.

The gun was manned only by a replacement, new to us that day. The regular gunner had been killed minutes before, and the new man hunched in the deep snow, trembling with cold and fear.

I pounded the gun's breech with the butt of my carbine. Gunny Foster had made that trick work in past firefights; it now worked for me, too. The gun fired.

It fired only a few short bursts. Moments after I moved away, a mortar shell exploded behind me and the replacement gunner was dead. He was another one whose name we never learned and who would never appear on Sergeant Richard's muster role.

We were getting nowhere. Joe Kurcaba was standing alongside the road, behind Lee's platoon, and he called me over to him. Bullets zinged and shrapnel whined around us, but Joe stood straight and I stood with him.

He had decided to risk a move up the hill on the left flank. "Move your platoon up there, Joe," he instructed me. "See if you can take those guns out. They're killing us." He spread out his map and traced the route that I was to follow.

Then he fell silent. A Chinese bullet had found its target, just below the rim of his helmet, in the center of his forehead. A small black hole appeared there. Joe Kurcaba's dead eyes stared at me for several seconds before he slumped slowly to the ground.

I caught him in my arms as he fell and held him for a moment. Then I lowered him gently into the snow. *Jesus, God! Joe Kurcaba. My friend. Joe, who had helped me so much, shown me so much. Who had gone to bat for me with Captain Wilcox. Who had been my big brother. Joe Kurcaba, whom I loved.*

Taking the map from his mittened hands, I went forward to give it to Chew Een Lee and to inform him that he was the new company commander. On the way over I got on my walkie-talkie to tell battalion that Kurcaba was KIA. Their CP was close behind us and the walkie-talkie worked.

Through the murk I spotted Lee's pink vest. He was walking the line behind his men who were prone in the snow, covering fifty yards of front. Lupacchini, with the BAR, was with him; I felt alone without Kelly. The Chinese fire was passing overhead, high. The enemy couldn't see us, either.

"Kurcaba's dead," I told Lee. "Caught one through the head."

"Damn!" was all Lee said in response.

"You're the new skipper," I added, giving him the map. "Joe told me to go up the hill on Woody's flank. See if I can get around those guns and take them out. You still want me to do that?"

"We must do something," Lee said. "They're killing us from up there."

"That's what Joe said."

"Yes. See what you can do. Is your radio working?"

"Yeah. I just talked to battalion on it."

"OK. Let me know the situation when you are ready to attack. If we can get artillery, I don't want you to run into friendly fire."

"Aye, aye, Skipper!" I said. First Lieutenant Lee gave me an ironic little smile at that.

I gathered my small platoon and told them our mission. They had done this sort of thing many times before, and they seemed glad to get moving. The cold had them frozen through.

I didn't see Woody Taylor when we crossed behind his line. I told one of his men to let him know what we were doing.

The path up the hill was wooded, so the Chinese were unable to see us as we climbed. It was quiet all the way to the top; nobody fired at us. The exertion of the climb warmed us.

The snow cleared when we reached the top. I tried to get Lee on my radio, but all I got was a burst of static.

To my right, in a line of brush, I could hear the Chinese who were firing down on the main body of the company, perhaps a hundred yards away. We would have to cross an open stretch of ground before reaching that brush. A perfect target for my sixties, but there was no way to call them in.

Gene Morrisroe, the machine gunner, was with us. His machine gun had given up, too, and now he was fighting with a rifle.

"Morrisroe!"

"Yes, Sir!"

"Take a man with you across that field. Get to the other side and signal to me if it's clear for us to cross. We'll give you cover from here."

"Aye, aye, Sir."

I nodded at another rifleman. "You go with Morrisroe."

"Aye, aye, Sir."

The two of them went, crouched low, across the open field. We kept our eyes on the brush and held our weapons at the ready.

The point men made it to the other side undetected. Morrisroe stood and waved us on. "Let's go," I ordered the men who were with me. "Spread out and follow me."

Someone called from behind us. "Sir! Lieutenant Owen!" It was Woody Taylor's runner. He was breathing hard from the effort he had made to catch up with us.

"Sir! Lieutenant Taylor wants you back down with the company. Lieutenant Lee's been hit and Lieutenant Taylor wants you. On the double, he says."

Damn it to hell! I might have been able to roll the Chinese from the flank and take out the guns that were holding back the company. I tried to get Woody on my walkie-talkie. I got more static.

I waved for Morrisroe to rejoin us and then my tiny platoon slipped and slid back down the hill. As they came behind me, the men cursed and complained about second lieutenants making up their minds.

Woody Taylor waited for us at the base of the slope. He was senior to me in rank, and with Lee down, he was our new company commander.

He said that battalion had sent a pair of tanks, and their fire power would cover a frontal assault up the hill. The snow had thinned and visibility improved. We could catch glimpses of the enemy firing down on us from the crest of a long, low ridge that began to rise fifty yards from the road. The Chinese had concealed themselves amidst the boulders, and their white uniforms made them difficult to see. The dim outline of a bunker, where a machine gun was concealed, could be seen beneath the crest. The fire was sporadic now; the Chinese knew we were coming close and they waited for clear targets.

Taylor ordered me to meet the tanks at the road on our right flank. "Tell them to hit the ridgeline with their machine guns," he told me. "When we're squared away to jump off, I'll give you the signal. Then have them fire the cannons. We'll move out on that."

"Aye, aye, Woody," I responded and took off for the waiting tanks.

I crossed behind the scant line of our men that Woody had set up, Baker-One-Seven's remaining effectives. There were a few new men, people whose names I didn't know. The old salts, Marines who had been with us since Camp Pendleton, had faces that were dirt-pitted and coated with ice. Moloy and Kowalski and the big BAR-man, Keister; Kovar and Garcia; Corporal Hogan with Treadwell, Lineberry, and Burbridge, the only fire team that had lasted from the beginning; Bahr, Adcock, and Cartledge; Kott, who had been Lee's runner; and Sergeant Richard. All lay flat in the snow, weapons before them. They spooned at fruit rations and drank the diluted alcohol from their canteens.

Bifulk and Perkins from the mortars were there, now fighting side by side as riflemen. I knelt beside them for a moment. "How are you holding out?" I asked.

Perkins was no longer the baby-faced teenager; he had the grizzled, combat-wise look that comes to a man who has faced the enemy many times. "We'll do OK, Lieutenant," he said. "Hope we get this fight over with, so we can go and get warm."

"Yeah, Joe," added Bifulk. And he said, for the hundredth time, "It's colder than hell."

Lupacchini arose when I went by him. "Hey, Lieutenant Owen, you take over from Mister Lee, eh?" he asked with his thick Italian accent.

"Yeah. I'm going to see if we can get us moving again, Lupacchini."

"Goddamn Chinks. All over the place up there." He pointed his BAR toward the hill. "They get Mister Lee bad."

"Were you with him?"

"Yeah. Right in the face they get him. Blood in his eyes, couldn't see nothing. Me and Corporal Hogan, we get him to some corpsmen over by the road. Damn good officer, that Mister Lee.

"Yeah, he was. You did a good thing, getting him to the docs."

"Hey, Mister Owen? Now I stay with you, OK?"

"Yeah, Lupacchini, OK. You stay with me."

The two tanks squatted off the road, waiting for orders. Except for the sound of their engines, they were still. Small drifts of snow formed against the treads, and Chinese bullets spattered their hulls. I went to the aft end of the first tank, to its phone. The warmth of the exhaust hit my face, a soothing warmth. In spite of the fumes, I leaned against the grille while I held the phone and spoke with the tank commander.

"Put your thirties up below the ridge. Gook machine gun at ten o'clock. Then on my command, hit them with the cannons. We'll jump off on that."

A tinny voice came from the tank. "Hear you. Loud and clear." The .30–caliber twin machine guns of both tanks began their jack-hammer pounding. I watched the red tracers stabbing up the snow-covered hill toward the dug-in Chinese gun that we could now see dimly.

Along with the tanks' machine guns several mortar rounds hit the ridgeline, near the enemy gun. With the improved visibility, Kelly was at work with our lone mortar.

I ignored the tank's recoil vibrations that shook my body, and the Chinese bullets that rattled off the hull, and I leaned over the warm grille. Lupacchini had gone prone in the snow beside the road. I motioned him over to share the warmth with me.

The dark shape of Woody Taylor appeared down our line, and he waved his arm forward. I gave the order to the tank to fire the jump-off signal.

"Fire your cannons and move forward at ten o'clock. I'll stay on the hook. Open fire!" I would move behind the tank with the phone in my hand to direct its advance.

The cracking explosions of both tanks' cannons came seconds later. The lead tank rocked with its own concussion, then lumbered forward, turning toward the incline. Lupacchini and I went behind it. The meager line of Baker-One-Seven arose from the snow and advanced with us.

The Chinese responded with the fury of every gun they had. Their machine gun and its tracers laced the air around us; mortars exploded and bullets clanged against the tank.

I could see the Chinese machine gun below the ridgeline. It was almost straight ahead. "Put your thirties at twelve o'clock," I told the tank commander. There was no response; the phone had gone dead.

The tank veered sharply to the right. Lupacchini and I were suddenly exposed to the Chinese fire that had been directed at the tank. Bullets spurted the snow around us and whined close to our heads.

We scrambled to the left, joining the line of advancing Marines. In teams of twos and threes they hit the deck and fired up the hill while other teams bounded forward. Lupacchini was with me, as was Morrisroe.

Kelly's mortar pounded the ridgeline, now a hundred yards above us. On the other flank of the attack I heard Woody shouting for his men to move forward with him. Chinese voices shrilled down at us, "M'line bastard die!" and "Sha! Sha!" The Marines answered with rebel yells and their own cries of fury.

Our line moved up the hill.

Twenty-five yards above me two Chinese soldiers appeared from behind a large boulder. One had a rifle, the other a burp gun. As I swung my carbine toward them, I heard a grunt from Lupacchini. His BAR fired straight into the air, and he fell forward in the snow. He did not move and I knew he was dead, the best BAR-man we had.

Goddamn! You've lost Lupacchini!

I couldn't get my weapon on the two Chinese above me fast enough. The one with the rifle put a round into my left shoulder that spun me around. Its impact generated a shock, like a powerful jolt of electricity, that went through my entire body.

Damn! How could I be hit? After all this, how could I get hit?

I saw the burp gunner trigger a burst at me. The snout of his weapon flashed, and I could not lift my feet above the knee-deep snow to get out of the path of his bullets.

Two slugs tore into my right arm. Two more of the electric jolts and my carbine flung itself from my grasp. I saw it rise into the air as I fell into the snow.

This cannot be happening!

I tried to raise my head and reach to retrieve my carbine. *Get the bastards!*

My arms wouldn't move. I could not raise myself.

"Joe's down!" someone shouted. Bifulk's voice.

"Get the bastards!" I heard myself yelling. "Get the bastards!"

I screamed in pain and overwhelming anger, and my Marines rushed past me and up the hill, leaving Lupacchini and me in the snow. "Get the bastards!" I yelled again and again. It was all I could think to do.

• • •

Even before I fell, Gene Morrisroe had his M-1 on the Chinese rifleman and dropped him. Somebody else got the burp gunner, maybe Perkins or Bifulk who were close by. Morrisroe stopped at the Chinese position and saw that the rifleman had been preparing to put a fresh clip of ammo into his Japanese rifle. The bullet that hit me was the last one in his previous load. Morrisroe took the fresh clip from the dead Chinese and kept it as a souvenir of the fight.

Dick Bahr saw me fall and continued to move his squad up the hill. The Chinese machine gun that had caused us so much difficulty was within grenade range. He lobbed one and followed its explosion. Another Marine grenade landed only feet above him. It was too far to reach and toss away. Bahr buried his head in his arms and awaited the explosion.

The grenade sputtered—a dud. Bahr leaped up and charged the gun that had gone silent, perhaps from the grenade he had thrown earlier.

Tom Lineberry, spraying automatic fire with his BAR, followed Bahr. Both of them went over the edge of the barricade that shielded the machine gun. The Chinese gunners were stunned or frozen, the two Marines didn't care which. They blasted at the Chinese and jumped into the hole. Bahr turned the gun around to fire on other enemy soldiers who were withdrawing rapidly. Lineberry continued the pursuit.

Conrad Kowalski moved up past Bahr at the captured machine gun. When he reached the ridge, he rose up to sight on a retreating enemy soldier. A burst from a burp gun caught him. Conrad Kowalski was Baker-One-Seven's last KIA in the Chosin Reservoir campaign.

• • •

The young corpsman who had been assigned to us for the day's battle heard my screams. Although enemy fire still flayed the hill, he ran clumsily through the snow to reach my side. I was flat on my back and he crouched beside me.

"OK, Lieutenant." He gasped for air with the exertion of the run, laden with his aid kit and cold weather gear. His breath made puffs of white steam, and his smooth-shaven face was red with the twenty-five-below-zero cold.

With bullets zinging around him, the new corpsman cut away my parka. The bullet through the shoulder had nicked my lung and blood gushed from my mouth and down the front of my parka, covering his bare hands.

"Give me some morphine," I told the kid. The pain was terrible.

"I . . . I can't, Sir. I'm sorry." He shook with the cold and his own fear. Bullets stung the air and raised little fountains of snow a few feet away.

"Give me some goddamn morphine," I yelled, spraying my blood on him.

"Sir, the morphine is frozen. I can't give it to you."

"What the hell's wrong with you? Carry the goddamn stuff in your mouth. Don't you boots know that?"

"Yes, Sir. I'm sorry, Sir!" He put the syrette in his mouth and continued to cut away at my clothing. "Just try to be still, Sir."

Even with the pain and the rage I realized that no one had told the new doc how to take care of casualties in below-zero weather. I gritted my teeth and tried to shut up.

I didn't feel the jab when he shoved the syrette into my flesh, but I soon felt a wave of warmth come over me. The pain flowed away and the noise of the fighting above us receded.

"You're a good lad," I told the corpsman. I felt his hands doing something. "You'll be a good Marine."

"Yes, Sir." He sounded far away.

Before I drifted off I remembered the photos in my helmet. "My pictures," I said. "That's my wife and kids. Don't let the gooks get them."

"I won't, Sir," said the corpsman who had risked his life to save mine, and whose name I never knew.

• • •

When they reached the top and the Chinese were cleared away, Bifulk and Perkins looked down the hill and saw me still lying in the snow. They came back and slid me carefully onto my poncho. Then they dragged me down to the road, before rejoining the company and continuing the fight. Later, somebody else brought down the bodies of Lupacchini and Kowalski and laid them beside me.

I regained consciousness once and my feet were terribly cold. I remembered to wriggle my toes against the frostbite.

• • •

Woody Taylor was the only officer left with the company. He led the troops to the crest of the hill, fighting as a rifleman himself. The Chinese were on the run, and battalion ordered Baker-One-Seven to keep after them. The troops were frozen and exhausted, but Woody pushed them on. Late in the day they reached their objective. With their small number they set a tight perimeter on the high ground overlooking the gap in the road that the engineers would bridge next day.

• • •

Kelly lost contact with the company when they went up the hill where Lupacchini, Kowalski, and I had been hit. He had used all of his ammo covering the assault, so he picked up the mortar and carried it down the road, following the tanks that led the advance.

The ditches on both sides of the road were filled with the dead and wounded waiting to be picked up by the meat wagons. Kelly almost passed by me; my blood-smeared face was all that showed from under the poncho that Bifulk and Perkins had laid over me. My feet stuck out from the end, though, and he recognized me from the length of my body.

"Jesus! That you, Joe?" Kelly dropped the mortar and knelt beside me. "You alive? Jesus!"

No response. I was still out from the morphine, and blood dribbled from my mouth, from the nicked lung.

"Goddamnit, Joe! I told you you'd get it without me, didn't I?" my runner whispered at me, but I didn't hear him.

An ambulance was parked fifty yards away. Its engine was running and two corpsmen sat inside, getting warm before resuming their grisly work of picking up mangled men and transporting them to the aid station. Kelly ran to it.

"I got a wounded lieutenant who needs to be taken back. On the double." Kelly told the corpsmen.

"There's a whole bunch of wounded people we got to take back," one of the corpsmen said. "We'll get to him as soon as we get warmed up here."

Kelly took the carbine from his shoulder and snapped the bolt. His face was red with the cold and his beard was matted with ice. "You people are warm enough already. My lieutenant's in a ditch down the road. Follow me."

The corpsmen looked into the face of a man whose sanity was not to be relied upon, and at the carbine that he had poked into their warm ambulance. They followed Kelly to the ditch and loaded me aboard and took me to the aid station.

I was one of the last casualties flown out of Koto-ri the next day. I remembered very little of what happened until I regained consciousness in a clean, warm Navy hospital in Japan.

• • •

Woody Taylor put the weary company on fifty percent watch against the enemy assault that he knew would come in the dark. It was the coldest night that the men had yet endured, a reported thirty degrees below zero. The wind howled at them from every direction.

All through the unbearably cold hours until dawn, Taylor and Sergeant Richard moved from man to man to assure that no one froze to death. A detail of South Korean soldiers who had been attached to the Army arrived to bolster the perimeter, but most of them filtered away during the night.

Several times the Marines heard the enemy moving around their lines in the darkness, but no attack came. Woody put out patrols early in the morning, before light. Within a hundred yards of the line they found dozens of Chinese soldiers whose feet and hands were frozen to ice. The extreme cold had been on our side, holding back the enemy attack.

• • •

While Baker and the other companies of the 7th Marines protected the high ground, the division's engineers worked under enemy sniper fire to bridge the chasm that separated the north and south columns.

When their work was completed, General Smith ordered all the units of the 1st Marine Division across the bridge.

The division column carried the wounded who had not been flown out, and most of the dead. They brought their equipment, vehicles, tanks, and the big guns; there would be little left behind for the surviving Chinese to scavenge. After they had crossed the bridge, the Marines were protected by the Army's 3d Division.

• • •

Corporal Kelly made his own way, carrying the mortar and hoping to join up with the company when it came back to the road. He never found it again, but he stayed on the road, heading south with the column as it filled with men, vehicles, and equipment headed for the bridge.

Kelly had begun to limp badly and he thought that frostbite had claimed him at last. After hobbling along for a long time, he could go no farther. He sat down in the ditch beside the road. When he removed the shoe-pac, he noticed a hole in its leather top. Then he saw that he had taken a bullet in his lower leg. With the boot off, the leg began to swell and the wound throbbed fiercely.

He stood up and used his carbine for support until he could hitch a ride on the fender of a passing truck. On the other side of the bridge was an aid station and Kelly turned himself in. He left the mortar on the truck.

• • •

Woody Taylor brought the remnants of the company down from the hills, marched them across the bridge, and into the shelter of the town of Chinhung-ni: their battle ended there. Sergeant Richard took roll call. His final count was twenty-seven men.

• • •

The 1st Marine Division went by train and truck from Chinhung-ni to Hungnam where they boarded ships that carried them to South Korea. There they replenished their ranks and went out to fight new Chinese armies. The ten Chinese divisions that had fought us up and down the frozen mountains around the Chosin Reservoir were permanently out of action. They never fought again. The 1st Marine Division fought for two and a half years more, until the Korean War ended in a truce. Neither side could declare victory.

EPILOGUE

Lieutenant Colonel Davis and Platoon Sergeant Van Winkle were both awarded the Medal of Honor for their actions in the Chosin Reservoir campaign. Lieutenants Kiser, Kurcaba, and Lee were awarded the Navy Cross.

Lieutenant Colonel Davis rose to the rank of four-star general. When he retired he was Assistant Commandant of the Marine Corps.

Captain Wilcox recovered from his wounds and returned to duty. He retired from the Marine Corps after twenty years' service with the rank of major.

Lieutenant Graeber recovered from his wounds and returned to duty. He retired from the Marine Corps after twenty-five years' service with the rank of lieutenant colonel.

Lieutenant Lee recovered from his wounds and returned to duty. He retired from the Marine Corps after twenty years' service with the rank of major.

Lieutenant Taylor was wounded in May 1951, still fighting with Baker-One-Seven. He recovered from his wounds and accepted a regular commission. He retired from the Marine Corps after thirty years' service with the rank of colonel.

Lieutenant Kiser was the only officer who served with Baker-One-Seven in 1950 who was not wounded in Korea. He retired from the Marine Corps after thirty years' service with the rank of colonel. Someone gave the pictures that I had carried in my helmet to Hank. Several years later he returned them to me.

Father Griffin recovered only partially from his wounds, but he stayed on duty with the Navy. He retired after thirty years' service with the rank of captain.

Platoon Sergeant Van Winkle recovered from his wounds and elected to stay in the Marine Corps as a regular. He was commissioned as a second lieutenant and, after thirty years' service, he retired with the rank of colonel.

Staff Sergeant Richard retired from the Marine Corps after thirty years' service with the rank of master gunnery sergeant.

Sergeant Winget was disability-retired from the Marine Corps with the rank of platoon sergeant.

Corporal Burris recovered from his wounds and elected to remain in the Marine Corps as a regular. He retired after twenty-four years' service as a master sergeant.

Corporal Kelly recovered from his wounds and was assigned to Parris Island as a drill instructor. At the completion of his hitch he left the Marine Corps as a sergeant. He became a locomotive engineer on the Illinois-Central Railroad.

Corpsman Davis recovered from his wounds and remained in the Navy. He was commissioned and became a specialist in hospital administration. He retired from the Navy after thirty years' service with the rank of lieutenant commander.

Pfc. Rendon was disability-retired from the Marine Corps with the rank of private first class.

Pfc. Galtere left the Marine Corps at the completion of his hitch as a private first class. He became a crop-duster pilot, then skipper of a tramp steamer along the Central American coast. He was then ordained as a Methodist minister and became a missionary, serving in South Africa.

Pfc. Gallapo recovered from his wounds and left the Marine Corps. He became a fireman and retired from the Chicago Fire Department as a chief.

Pfc. Perkins was promoted to corporal in 1951 while still with Baker-One-Seven in Korea. After he completed a thirteen-month combat tour, he was assigned to train new second lieutenants at Quantico on the use of the sixty-mortars. On his first day at Quantico, a spit-and-polish base, he met a captain on the street. Perkins had a row and a half of combat ribbons on his uniform; the captain wore none. Up until then, almost all of Merwin Perkins's time in the Corps had been spent in combat. He was only faintly aware of the protocols of military courtesy. Corporal Perkins passed the captain without rendering a salute. The captain stopped Perkins, demanding why he had not saluted. Perkins looked at the captain's uniform, empty of ribbons, and said, "Sir, I thought you were supposed to salute me!"

• • •

My wounds were treated in U.S. naval hospitals for seventeen months, until May 1952. I was unable to regain full use of my right arm, and I was disability-retired from the Marine Corps as a first lieutenant. Dorothy and I had four more children. Mike became a neurosurgeon and Dinny is a writer.

Epilogue

ABOUT THE AUTHOR

Joseph R. Owen was an active duty Marine during 1943–1946 and 1948–1952, when he received a medical discharge. He is now retired from his own marketing company and makes his home in Skaneateles, New York, and Naples, Florida. He and his wife, Dorothy, have six children and fourteen grandchildren. He has written articles and stories that have appeared in the *Marine Corps Gazette* and *Leatherneck. Colder Than Hell* is his first book.